P9-BZV-034

Global Television

Global Television

edited by

Cynthia Schneider and Brian Wallis

Wedge Press, New York

The MIT Press, Cambridge, Massachusetts and London

Staff editors for this issue
Maud Lavin, Phil Mariani, Cynthia Schneider, Brian Wallis

Photo Research
Hilton Als, Wayne Rothman, Leslie Sharpe

Design
Bethany Johns

Production
Cathy Clarke

Typesetting
EyeType, New York; set in Bembo and Helvetica Bold Extended

Special thanks to
Judith Barry, Martha Gever, Annie Goldson, Todd Haynes, Nancy Markota, Media Network, Mark Rakatansky, Wayne Rothman, Leslie Sharpe, Carol Squiers, Patty White, Women Make Movies

Reproduction Credits   We gratefully acknowledge the sources and permission to reprint for the following previously published articles: Armand Mattelart, Michèle Mattelart, and Xavier Delcourt, "International Image Markets," from *International Image Markets,* trans. David Buxton (London: Comedia Publishing Co., 1984); Richard Collins, "Wall-to-Wall *Dallas,*" *Screen* 27, no. 3/4 (May-August 1986): 66-77; Tapio Varis, "Trends in International Television Flow," *International Political Science Review* 7, no. 3 (July 1986): 235-249; Francis N. Wete, "The New World Information Order and the U.S. Press," excerpted from "The U.S., Its Press, and the New World Information Order," Freedom of Information Center Report No. 488 (Columbia: University of Missouri, 1984); "Going Global," transcript of a *MacNeil/Lehrer Newshour* report, broadcast September 29, 1987; Paul Virilio, "The Third Window," originally published as "La Troisième Fenêtre: Entretien avec Paul Virilio," *Cahiers du Cinema,* no. 322 (April 1981): 35-40; Julianne Burton and Julia LeSage, "Broadcast Feminism in Brazil," excerpted from the forthcoming *Documentary Strategies: Focusing on Latin America,* edited by Julianne Burton (University of Pittsburgh Press, 1989); Timothy Landers, "Bodies and Anti-Bodies: A Crisis in Representation," *The Independent* 11, no. 1 (January-February 1988): 18-24. We thank the authors, editors, and publishers.

This publication constitutes issue no. 9/10 of *wedge*.
This special issue of *wedge* was made possible in part through a generous grant from the New York State Council on the Arts, Media Program.

Wedge Press, 141 Perry Street, New York, NY 10014
The MIT Press, Massachusetts Institute of Technology, Cambridge, MA 02142
Copyright © 1988 Wedge Press and Massachusetts Institute of Technology
All rights reserved. No part of this book may be reproduced in any form by any electronic or mechanical means (including photocopying, recording, or information storage and retrieval) without permission in writing from the publisher and authors.
Library of Congress Catalogue Card Number: 83-640994   ISBN 0-262-69123-X

Cover photo: Tony Kelly, Chicago/Evanston; from Zenith Annual Report, 1982.

Contents

III. Representation and Resistance

Introduction

Cynthia Schneider and Brian Wallis

When broadcast television was first introduced at the 1939 World's Fair, the implicit promise was that the new technology would somehow bring the nations of the world closer together. Whether broadcasting the Golden Gate Bridge to New York or the King's Coronation to Washington, the message was clear: television could unite the world. However, parallel developments (such as constraints on the evolution of interactive television despite its early technological possibility) made clear how the terms of television's ownership and social function were being set, and how these would determine the role of television on a global scale.

Today, particularly with the introduction of new technologies and the expansion of existing ones, to assert that television is global is to utter a commonplace. To speak of "global television" however is quite another thing. Global television refers not only to the international dissemination of television images, but also to the radical restructuring of television as a geopolitical concept. For television has created a space of its own through a unique merger of entertainment and information technologies. Allied with home computers, satellites, and conventional communications systems, television introduces more than just new signs and representations, it also establishes an important new political formation: a class structure based not on wealth, but on access to information.

The social, historical, and economic processes at work in the production and reception of television, as well as the structural changes that merged previously separate cultural industries (film, television, publishing, surveillance information) require attention as we examine the implications of global television. Already in the 1960s, before Guy Debord's baptism of the "society of the spectacle," leftist critics were beginning to analyze television as a social and political issue. The writings of Raymond Williams, Herbert Gans, and Herbert Schiller, for instance, critiqued television as a weapon of cultural imperialism, in contradistinction to

Marshall McLuhan's more phenomenological concern with the identification of the individual viewer with the television set and its "cool" definition. The theory of cultural imperialism argued that the United States, far and away the leading producer and exporter of television programming in the 1960s, was imposing its values on the rest of the world. Through its vast and seductive influence, and as a microcosm of a larger political redistribution, television was propaganda, urging conformity to American beliefs and values at the expense of local languages, traditions, and cultures. On a larger level, this threat to cultural identity was seen as a threat to national identity.

More recently, the question of cultural sovereignty has been further exacerbated by the economic growth of cultural information industries and their role in global politics. Television transmission knows no boundaries, and in a free market television programming circulates like any other commodity. This is both a boon and a threat to the maintenance of national cultures, national identification, and national purpose. Thus when the issue of cultural imperialism resurfaced in the 1980s, particularly around the phenomenal success of the nighttime soap opera *Dallas* (in 1983, French minister of culture Jack Lang labeled *Dallas* a "symbol of cultural imperialism"), many countries sought immediate remedies: restrictions on American television imports and enhancement of national (or nationalistic) production. A common defense against "wall-to-wall *Dallas*" has been the production of stereotypically nationalistic versions of the show, such as France's *Châteauvallon*, Canada's *Vanderburg*, and the Netherlands' *Herrenstraat 10*.

Ironically, then, the movement toward global formations often has had the opposite effect. In some cases, this has encouraged the nationalization of television industries (as in France), the broadening of the state's televisual capacities (as in Israel), or the valorization of television as a principle cultural form (as in Germany). Indeed, at the very moment when television distribution is most versatile, local and national producers have become most assertive. One might argue that today television is more aggressively provincial than ever before. Each country seeks to maintain and exploit a local audience.

Although our heading "Nationalism and Imperialism" seems to assert antithetical propositions, many of the articles in this section actually encourage the reader to reformulate his or her own assumptions about this classic dichotomy in relation to the structures that effect international communications. Neither "globalism" nor American cultural imperialism is monolithic, and, as the studies of Richard Collins and Tapio Varis show, traffic flows in television distribution are never unidirectional.

In this anthology, we have not attempted to "scan the globe": notably absent from this volume are analyses of the implications of programming structures in the Eastern Bloc, Asia, and parts of the Third World. Recognizing these significant exclusions among others, this volume is nevertheless a step towards opening a self-critical, cross-continental dialogue about global television. It is a collection that focuses on hegemonic culture, the television that is dominating global traffic, and specific responses and critiques engendered by it.

It would be misleading to suggest that the dramatic changes in television culture in the past decade have been due only to technological changes. In "Expanding Technologies," therefore, we mean to analyze the shifts in the ideologies of technological expansion, particularly as they alter the geopolitical climate and thereby affect patterns of everyday life. In this sense, advertising provides a pertinent example of how television has put the concept of globalism into practice. Saatchi & Saatchi, now the world's largest advertising agency, has been particularly vocal about its support for the concept of global advertising. In 1985, as part of a major policy shift, Saatchi & Saatchi used the identical advertisement (a prize-winning, ninety-second spot for British Air entitled *Manhattan Landing*) in forty-six different countries with a voiceover in thirty-four languages. This approach countered the reigning philosophy of advertising (i.e., that products are sold to specific target audiences), but conformed to international money flows and to the apparently broad market for television. After all, *Dallas* was universally popular, why not British Air? As advertising executive Jay Chiat notes in his conversation with Carol Squiers, however, the concept of global advertising was ultimately not very successful. Local audiences, especially local television audiences, still have specific needs, specific customs, and specific expectations. Josh Elbaum, a television program distributor, emphasizes the binding nature of these local preferences.

Interestingly, then, one response to global television advertising was nonacceptance. Nonacceptance is the television audience's principal form of criticism. But there are limits to the subversiveness of just turning off the set as a protest, since certain levels of nonacceptance are built into the structure of the industry. However, the point is that criticism of television is not simply a question of being for or against the medium; no one today would take seriously arguments for the elimination of television. Rather, we must recognize that criticism is a function of participation in television viewing. The very notion of participation contradicts an earlier touchstone of critical opposition to television: that television pacified or "doped" the audience. Now it seems clear that the opposite is true: television is fully participatory. We practice mundane forms of participation daily, ranging from taping programs to joking about content. While interactive television has largely faded into novelty, its original participatory purposes have returned quite literally in the conjunctions of the home computer, the video game, the VCR, and cable switching. These new packagings of television components have yielded not only a new control of representations and their combinations, but also, as Paul Virilio points out, new architectural spaces, psychological relations, and temporal sequences (one can "control" time). Alternative groups (such as Peter Fend's Ocean Earth) have even entered into the seemingly closed circuit of satellite surveillance, and, in a radical reuse of the original data, analyzed it and provided source material for mainstream television news. But degrees of participation in television production and reception are far from balanced.

In this context, even seemingly outmoded, "avant-gardist" alternatives take on new relevance. In the early 1970s, two strategies for intervention in television seemed possible: alternative production (as in the "guerrilla television" of groups like Ant Farm and the Raindance Collective) and cable (particularly in terms of community access). Initially, both of these alternatives were quite idealistic, even utopian. In reality, they had little impact against a tightly controlled industry capable of either assimilating difference, quashing competition, or deregulating cable systems. Today, who "speaks" through television is made clear by the gross economic inequities of television's institutions and the unequal access to the means of communication. To cite a recent example of attempts to limit public access, in *Preferred Communications Inc. v. City of Los Angeles, California* (1985), cable companies argued, on First Amendment grounds, that their freedom of speech was denied by local laws that insisted on the availability of public access channels to and wiring of poor neighborhoods as well as rich ones. One potential ramification of this argument is that public access—which is to say public expression—would be excluded entirely. Significantly (though not surprisingly), today such arguments are being made more rigorously than ever. Even public television is not exempt from state/corporate censorship; in the limited realms of alternative programming, politically provocative programs (such as Koff and Mwinyipembe's *Blacks Britannica)* are highly restricted, many not even reaching the airwaves. And yet alternative television continues to be produced in the U.S. and in other cultural contexts. This work continues to signal openings for participation, criticism, and access.

If in the 1970s, access to production and distribution was the demand, today access entails criticism of the adequacy of media representations. "Representation and Resistance" includes articles critiquing existing programming, as well as those describing the production of alternatives. The spectator/consumer, implied both economically by marketing strategies and ideologically by the history of television criticism, is female. This section also continues the feminist examination of the relation of women in their diversity to the social fact of television and to mass cultural texts. In writing on television, feminists have reappropriated certain representations, shifting critical attention to issues of consumption and pleasure, exemplified in the work of McGee and Sharpe and of Ien Ang on the "feminine" genre by excellence, the soap opera. The independent production of the Lilith Video Collective in Brazil shows that women have also begun to appropriate the means of self-representation.

Mainstream television's regulation by and congruence with state interest should not be underestimated. Current U.S. network broadcasting strategies of "inclusionism" cannot be viewed simply as the product of corporate interests' perception and acknowledgment of changes in the social fabric. Indeed, as the essays of Maud Lavin, David Goldberg, and Michele Wallace establish in different ways, such programming strategies are all the more insidious in their failure to address their own biases and allegiances, masking continued prejudice under the guise of "tolerance." Timothy Landers identifies these preconceptions in the context of his discussion of AIDS, noting that "Commercial media representations in general are informed by a variation on the normal/abnormal paradigm. . . . The Body—white, middle-class, and heterosexual—is constructed in contrast to the Other, the Anti-Body (frequently *absent* from representation)—blacks, gay men, lesbians, workers, foreigners, in short, the whole range of groups that threaten straight, white, middle-class values."

This volume argues that television criticism has an important role to play in the formulation of an alternate discourse that seeks to identify and disrupt cultural and political misrepresentations. While "global advertising" points up the capitalist agenda of globalism, the concept also has currency on the left: "global village," "global feminism." *Global Television*, to some degree, explores this conceptual tension: globalism threatens the obliteration of difference while depending upon it. In giving space to local strategies of intervention, to criticism of the medium and of televisual texts, to differences, the volume perhaps critiques its title and goes on to pose the question of how effective opposition to "global" hegemony can be conceptualized and undertaken.

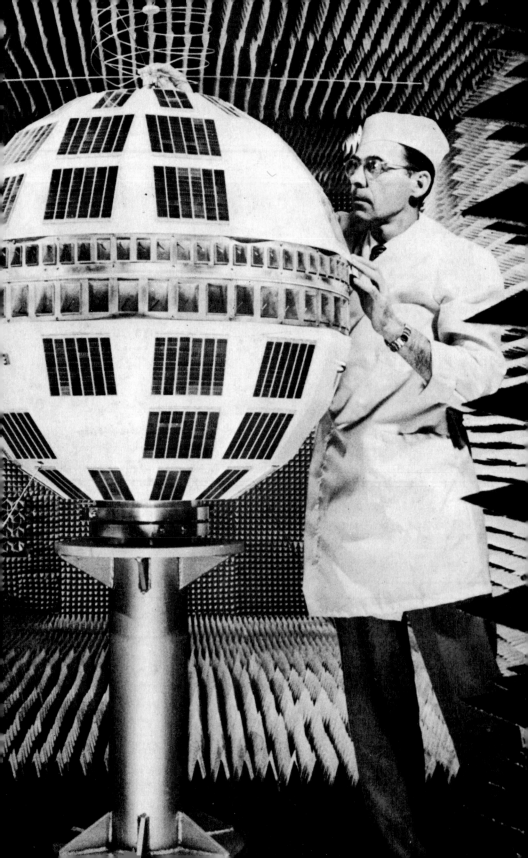

International Image Markets

Armand Mattelart, Xavier Delcourt,
and Michèle Mattelart

T he increasing commercialization of the cultural sector and the parallel
development of the new technologies of communication have projected culture into the heart of industrial and political structures. For the
majority of European countries, this situation is radically new. The relationship between culture and industry is gradually being added to a debate
formerly centered on that between culture and the state, an extension which
has produced a rupture with existing definitions of "culture."

In countries where the networks of mass-cultural production and distribution were immediately integrated into a market philosophy, an accel-
eration of the commercialization process is less likely to be experienced as a
radical rupture. In this respect, the influence of national conditions in the
formation of a theoretical framework appears to be a main element, though
generally underestimated (not to mention totally neglected). These national
conditions have been marked in Europe by the historical importance of the
state in the political and economic management of society, but also by
political movements and social organizations for which cultural demands
were primarily formulated in terms of access to the privileges of "high
culture." The way in which, up until the 1970s, the audiovisual media were
treated in France is particularly illustrative: the relationship between culture
and the state monopolized everyone's attention, leading to a blockage in the
industrial or commercial dimension of mass-cultural production. Theories
of the state, developed at the time by radical critics, particularly in France,
only confirmed this fragmented vision of a cultural apparatus confined to
the ideological and political sphere.

In Europe, until the second half of the 1970s, radio-television systems
were almost entirely under the thumb of the public authorities. To allow
broadcasting to face the laws of the market could only, it was thought,
constitute a diversion from the spirit of public service. Even when doors

opened for the private sector—as in Great Britain with the independent channel ITV, or in France and Italy with the introduction of advertising as a determining element in the financing of public enterprises—these openings remained subject to a strict framework of regulation and control.

From the end of the 1970s, however, the public service has been showing evident signs of crisis, destabilized and weakened by political, financial, and technological factors. First, the spiral of inflation, combined with cuts in public spending, is eroding the financial base on which public television has traditionally rested. Second, faced with an almost saturated market for television sets, the combination of license fee income and authorized advertising resources is no longer sufficient to absorb the increase in production costs and investment demand. Third, the expansion of the audiovisual market through both the new communications technologies and the additional TV channels has meant the arrival in strength of the private sector. This expansion has also exposed the way in which the public service finds it difficult to satisfy the demand of users whose fragmented interests conflict with a public monopoly's mass audience profile. At the same time, the crisis within the public radio-television monopoly is itself encouraging governments to relax direct state control in favor of private initiatives.

On top of these national factors, the state of the world economy has had important repercussions in the communications field. The accent on productivity and accelerated realization of surplus value is transforming both work organization and production processes. The most significant areas are those of publishing and the press—confronted with the introduction of computers and telematics—and the audiovisual media—forced to implement an increasingly industrialized production. The growing penetration of international products into national communications markets testifies to the progress of internationalization in publishing, advertising, marketing, and audiovisual production.

In this development of new markets, both cable and satellites are crucial factors. The enormous initial investment involved, and the sheer length of time needed for them to reach profitability, has stimulated new alliances between the state, the financial sector, and private industry. The state, taking charge of providing the technological infrastructure, has thereby given the go-ahead to the development of markets and the manufacture of hardware like terminals. The financial crisis affecting public resources has therefore led to new ways of getting consumers to participate in the financing of this infrastructure. Ultimately, profitability is tending to supplant the media's traditional function of preserving the *res publica,* and in the process is transforming profoundly the rules of democracy.

Information, communications, and culture are increasingly to be found at the center of international debates, and have formed the basis of multiple confrontations. Since 1973, through organizations like UNESCO or the Non-Aligned Movement, Third World countries have repeatedly denounced the unequal international flow of news—produced and distributed as it is by a limited number of press agencies belonging to the developed nations. The demand for a "new world information and communications order" subsequently gave rise to a series of meetings and conferences. These meetings led up to the General Conference of UNESCO in Belgrade in 1980, where the MacBride Report on the problems of communications was approved.[1] Since that time, meetings of the nonaligned countries have continued to draw up a balance sheet of progress, noting for instance that new forms of alliance between the countries of the South have emerged, principally through the creation of national news agencies and regional networks of these agencies.

Initially centered on combating the imbalance of news flows, this debate on communications has progressively widened its scope under the pressure of nonaligned countries. The declaration on computers and development adopted during the meeting in New Delhi (1983) testifies to this. International organizations of an essentially technical nature have also begun to feel the political effects of an increasingly global questioning of the geopolitical distribution of power in the field of information. One example is the debate within the International Union of Telecommunications on the allocation of frequencies, an allocation which the ten biggest broadcasting countries (controlling 90 percent of the available wavebands) thought had been resolved once and for all.

Around the issues thrown up in each phase of these debates, alliances are made and unmade. But an analysis of these splits shows that they cannot simply be reduced to the sinister East-West conflict hawked by the news agencies and media of the industrialized countries. For the Third World, this interpretation both denies its autonomy and expropriates problems it has itself formulated. And by brushing aside the imposition of an East-West mold on these debates, we are also silently acknowledging one of their principal lessons: the political emergence on the international scene of a new force with its own interests. As a Peruvian researcher pointed out in 1982: "It is only very recently, and partially, that the Soviet Union and the other socialist countries have come around to supporting efforts for the construction of a new international communications order. Furthermore, the observations of Sergei Losev, a member of the MacBride Commission, made clear more than once the coolness and reservations of the Soviet Union in the face of Third World demands."[2]

This collision between national interests and so-called natural political alliances emerged very early in various areas of the communications field. As early as 1974, the debate over the necessity of regulating satellite teledetection activities showed that the higher interests of military alliances were insufficient in themselves to ensure cohesion among the Western bloc states. These satellites, monopolized by the United States, had accumulated from the beginning of the 1970s gigantic stocks of information on the soil and subsoil of all the continents. At the height of the energy crisis, some countries feared that multinational firms could thus discover deposits or diagnose agricultural problems, and use this information against them by causing, for example, price fluctuations. The United States refused all controls in the name of "freedom of space," a thesis it had already proposed during the 1972 discussions over direct broadcasting satellites—and found itself alone against the votes of 102 countries. Argentina and Brazil, whose political regimes were very different at the time, put forward the suggested rule of "prior consent to teledetection by satellite." The Soviet Union and France, directly threatened in their own projects to develop this technology, joined forces to propose a middle way: that the information obtained by teledetection cannot be made public without the express consent of the state concerned.

These fluctuations of alliance, disconcerting for those wishing to reduce debates on communications to a simple episode of superpower confrontation, clearly show that by overthrowing the ground rules, the Third World has confirmed its eruption onto the political scene.

Recognition of this new phase in the political and cultural emancipation of the Third World should not, however, allow us to pass over the tensions within this movement. For are we really talking about a new information order or simply a new sharing out of the established order? The "Third World" consensus explodes as soon as we come to the central problems of a genuinely alternative form of communication. Who will produce this information? What subject matter will emerge from this transformation? What are the means of communication best adapted to these producers and to this content? Roberto Savio, founder of Inter-American Press Service, an agency created in the wake of the international discussions on com-

The Video-Tape Center of the Shanghai Spare-Time Engineering University, December 1982.

munications, drew the lessons from ten years' experience: "The real problem," he wrote in June 1982, "should not be posed in terms of quantitative transfers of informational capacities from North to South. Rather it should be in terms of creating new flows of information with contents, personnel, priorities, and needs which are absent from current flows. Following this logic, it is not specifically in the North/South context that the various groups making up the social fabric—unions, academic institutions, cooperatives, associations, and communities—must be situated in order to produce information that existing channels do not supply. The problem is therefore qualitative and not quantitative."[3]

This emphasis on quantity, which allowed certain Third World governments to pass over embarrassing questions of power within society, has so far limited the construction of a "new order" to the provision of financial aid, technical assistance, and professional training. And it is precisely this flaw which has enabled authorities in the West to reduce the idealism and generosity of the debate's initiators to a simple manipulation of institutions, remote-controlled by the Soviet Union, Disconcerted by the growth of Third World demands, which have expanded from the distribution of news to the control of communications technologies, they finally rallied in 1981 by decreeing an embargo on further negotiations.

The Declaration of Talloires, published May 18, 1981, at the close of a meeting organized by the World Press Freedom Committee, remains the most striking document of this counterattack by "newspapers, magazines, free radio and television stations of the West and elsewhere," uniting for the first time against the "campaign by the Soviet Union and some Third World countries seeking to give UNESCO the power to model the future development of the media."[4] Analyzing the meaning of this realignment of forces, the Peruvian researcher Rafael Roncagliolo wrote in June 1982:

The time when communications bosses acted in relatively dispersed fashion through organizations like the Inter-American Press Association and the International Press Institute has now disappeared. Today, we are seeing the formation of a big transnational bloc with a strategy whose principal objective—paraphrasing the terms of the Talloires Declaration—is to "no longer authorize discussions and activities which relate to propositions unacceptable to the West." Their complementary objective is to take over certain suggestions for a new world information and communications order whilst abandoning democratization in favor of "cooperation with the Third World, aiming to help it renew its production and training resources." The qualitative problem of the role of communications in the construction of democracy is thus transformed into a quantitative problem which boils down to an increased dependence through technology and professional and ideological training.[5]

One cannot resist on behalf of somebody else. The very idea of resistance implies an aggression felt in the very heart. Yet persuaded of the durability—even the superiority—of their culture, many in the industrialized countries have criticized the Third World for excessively politicizing the debate on the new world information and communications order, for having been caught up in the game of sorcerer's apprentice ideologues. But to challenge the choice of battlefield and the use of words, without relating them to the conditions of their selection, is surely to prevent oneself from identifying the historical origin of resistance, to understand the language it speaks and therefore to communicate.

Each form of resistance has its own language. In an age of crisis in politics, the France of the 1970s placed its confidence in the language of the economy. And it was precisely through the economy that it received the first signal of alarm. "In post-industrial economies," wrote the President of the Inter-Ministerial Commission on Transborder Data Flows in 1980, "where the processing of information today represents between 40 and 50 percent of its added value, it is natural that international information exchange plays a central role . . . The current development of transborder flows establishes and amplifies the *dominance that multinational systems are achieving over individual countries.* Certainly the nation state remains vigorous. But it runs the risk of being steadily drained of its strength."⁶

To make the shift from this alarm call to the development of a national debate, however, required a change in the political majority in France. "Power over communications is being concentrated in every country," declared President Mitterand during the Versailles summit of June 1982. "A handful of firms are expropriating all the networks necessary for electronic transmission. By controlling them, they influence in turn the traditional media: the cinema, the press, and television. Most of the new activities in which the majority of firms are engaged (production, storage, information processing) presuppose extremely heavy investment, which again leads to high concentration . . . More generally, the distribution of information developed and controlled by a few dominant countries could mean for others the loss of their history or even their sovereignty, thus calling into question their freedom to think and decide."⁷

At the same time, the world conference in Mexico City on cultural policies *(Mondiacult '82)* confirmed that the countries of the North, more sensitive to the imbalance of world trade because of their own recently-acquired vulnerability, had finally discovered the links between the economy and culture that the South had perceived as early as 1973.

This "discovery" established the failure of the so-called cultural democratization policies and marked the limits of a conception of development based on the introduction of planning tools in the cultural sector:

The past fifteen years have seen the emergence of three parallel phenomena: (a) a two, five, or ten-fold increase, according to the country, of public spending on culture; (b) despite increased spending, stagnation in the use made by the public of cultural institutions; and (c) a twenty, hundred, or thousand-fold increase in public contact with artistic works as a result of industrial cultural products . . . The conclusion that inevitably springs from this observation is that far more is being done to democratize and decentralize culture with the industrial products available on the market than with the "products" subsidized by public authorities.⁸

Culture and economy: the same struggle. It is useless to avert one's gaze and pretend nothing has changed: the facts are there and cannot be denied.

Cultural and artistic creation—several delegates have argued so from the beginning—is today victim of a system of multinational financial domination against which we must organize ourselves . . . Is it our destiny to become the vassals of an immense empire of profit? We hope that this conference will be an occasion for peoples, through their governments, to call for genuine cultural resistance, a real crusade against this domination, against—let us call a spade a spade—this financial and intellectual imperialism.[9]

For those familiar with international issues, such a declaration by French Minister of Culture Jack Lang speaking in Mexico City was a nonevent. However, hearing these words from an official representative of a large industrial country *was* an event, amply shown by the international and national divisions created by his intervention. Apart from the "total exasperation" registered by the United States, the speech from Lang, "well received by the Eastern bloc and Third World countries," caused a split within the Western camp.[10] "Thus if Finland, Denmark, and Norway, at least in private, and Italy in public appreciated the speech, others were more circumspect, notably Holland, Spain, and West Germany, whose delegate was reportedly 'shocked by' this chauvinist discourse."[11] "It was not only an 'incident' that broke out at the Mexico conference, but a new episode in the North-South dispute."[12]

Ignoring Lang's conjunction between economics and culture, comment in the French media focused instead on "American cultural imperialism" (although the United States had not been named once in the speech) and turned it into a battle of value judgments and assumptions. Lang was accused of having launched "a war of berets, bourrées, and Breton bagpipes"[13] against Dashiell Hammett, Chester Himes, William Irish, Orson Welles, Meredith Monk, Richard Foreman, Jackson Pollock, Andy Warhol, Merce Cunningham, etc. "The worst Broadway revue will always outclass the pathetic spectacle of folkloric dances in clogs," wrote one of the most violent critics.[14]

This outburst of "national masochism"[15] seemed to mark the emergence in France of an intelligentsia which, in order to denigrate its culture of origin, used the same contemptuous tone and derisory examples as many ruling-class elites in the Third World had done as they waited for previously despised popular cultural forms like reggae and salsa to return home on the wings of transnational corporations before celebrating their "birth." And yet this emergence is itself very much a French phenomenon. In its ability to consider culture either in its material or historical context, it anchors itself in the French tradition of antagonism between the "cultural" and the "technical." As *Technology, Culture, and Communication* noted:

Why is there such fierce resistance to the linking of culture and technology? Why is there a tendency to dissociate the two, that is to perceive the former through the exclusive outlets of literature and aesthetics—therefore as essentially prestigious—

Earth stations on Stanley Peninsula link Hong Kong with the world by satellite over the Indian and Pacific oceans.

and the latter as a product of utilitarianism? Why is there this difficulty in reconciling culture with its own materiality and historical conditions of production? Why have intellectuals so long been reticent not only in analyzing the apparatuses of cultural massification but above all in critically posing, other than in terms of sheer indifference or elitism, the problem of their own relations with the media?[16]

Of course, one does not have only the culture of one's personal taste and aesthetic leanings but also that of one's social class and professional interests. And admitting this enables us to see that there exists a dynamic link between knowledge and ignorance, between what one chooses to learn and what one cannot ignore. Paradoxically, the loudest demands for "cosmopolitanism" are accompanied in France by a localism that borders on illiteracy.

The debate over "American cultural imperialism" came at just the right time to remind us that within the "Latin" countries, everyone doesn't speak the same language: "While waiting for further episodes of *Dallas,* Moroccan television is showing another series, *The Conquest of the West.* In French! This is a double insult to the Arab World via Paris."[17] As the Moroccan writer Tahar Ben Jelloun recalled, the paths of cultural subjugation follow the twists and turns of the colonial heritage. But this is not all, as the vice-president of the American delegation at *Mondiacult '82* underlined: "When Mr. Lang affirms 'culture and economy: the same struggle,' he ought to remember that multinationals flourish in France as well as in the

United States, that France exports its culture like the United States and like many other countries."[18]

A minefield? Much more so than these declarations would lead us to believe. For the denunciation of an evil "other" is never exempt from a certain holier-than-thou attitude to be found at the heart of the notion of cultural identity.[19] In the area of the audiovisual media, there are at least four ways in which cultural identity serves as a screen to reality, a way of not thinking in terms of an alternative.

Example One: Exclusive recourse to simple protectionist measures like the quota system on imported films. Although somewhat justified by the "defense of national territory," this policy has many adverse effects, not least that it establishes a geographical division between the here and the elsewhere. While it limits foreign influence, it proposes no other alternative than the limit itself. For the quota solution to be effective, it must at least be accompanied by the necessary complement of a production policy. A government that adopts the quota solutions seems to be doing a lot when it has done essentially nothing.

Example Two: The defense of cultural identity as a mask for greater profits to sectional interests—public servants, technicians, executives, artistic personnel, etc., all solidly installed in their ivory towers. When the defense of cultural identity becomes confused with the defense of a fixed past, it runs the risk of filling a strictly conservative role. It finds itself reduced to a role of complacency, reduced, in fact, to an asphyxiating localism.

Example Three: Cultural identity reduced to a national label stuck on what is essentially a transnational copy. A large number of television series, for example, have fallen into this trap. Admittedly the stories may be based on the national past, or real historical situations, but the general narrative style is still that of the big television empires. In the process, cultural identity becomes picturesque folklore.

Example Four: Cultural identity as the standard-bearer for an alternative cultural imperialism. This happens, for example, when a country presents itself as a champion of linguistic community and simply treats the latter as a market unified by common language, rather than taking account of its underlying diversity. The history of "Latinity" is a prime example of this tendency. As Guy Martinière explains:

The concept of Latin America, created in France under Napoleon III, was born on the eve of the military—and scientific—expedition to Mexico. The Latin definition of the political, cultural, and economic influence of the France of Napoleon III in

*relation to the America formerly colonized by Spain and Portugal responded admira-
bly to the* grand dessein *of the Emperor . . . France, heir to the European Catholic
dynasty, carried in America and in the world the torch of the* Latin races—*that is the
French, the Italians, the Spanish, and the Portuguese—in order to check the "rise of
the Protestant nations and the Anglo-Saxon race" while avoiding a European
decline. Already at the time, in the face of this French "cultural" initiative, reaction
was not slow in coming: the notion of "Hispanity" quickly appeared in Spain in
response to this Latinity.*[20]

By approaching the issue of communications in the Third World from
the point of view of dependency on the North, one often overlooks
the specific nature of each country's system. Because of this, the evidence
of a growing presence of Brazilian production in Italy, or even Mexican
production in the United States, comes to most people as a confusing
surprise. This confusion can only be dispersed by looking at the relationship in each country between culture, the state, and industry. Such an
analysis would enable us to understand why, at a time when many Third
World countries have yet to select their system of television, others are
already in the forefront of the transnational technological system; this explains the presence in Brazil and Mexico of international multimedia groups
at levels of ownership concentration scarcely paralleled in Western Europe.

Rede Globo, the largest Brazilian television network (opened in 1965),
is owned by the Globo organization. This includes the newspaper *O Globo*
(founded in 1925 and one of the biggest in the country); the Globo radio
system (inaugurated in 1944 and composed of seventeen stations on the
AM and FM bands); a publishing firm, La Rio Grafica Editora; the Globo
audiovisual recording company (SIGLA); the electronics industry Telcom;
a show-business promotion firm (VASGLO); the Global art gallery; and
last but not least, the Globo television network, which owns five broadcasting stations, thirty-six affiliated stations, and hundreds of retransmission
stations.

TV Globo's production level is such that imports make up no more
than two mass-audience programs out of ten. In 1978, Rede Globo created
the Roberto Marinho Cultural Foundation to work, according to its own
description, "alongside Brazilian communities in the search for solutions to
problems of common welfare." Today, Rede Globo accounts for 70 percent of advertising expenditure in the Brazilian media: in 1979, $760 million
was spent on advertising on Brazilian television. This compares to $950

million in Great Britain, where the GNP was almost twice as big and the consumer market three times as large.

In Mexico, Televisa, a group set up in 1973, owns four television channels with sixty-one transmission stations covering almost the entire country. Out of a total of 55 million viewers, this network attained 41 million in 1979 or 7 million households. The forty-seven companies that make up Televisa cover all aspects of the cultural industries. Televisa also extends its ownership to five radio stations, including the biggest in the country; five publishing houses (books and magazines), with the largest print runs on the Mexican market; nine show-business firms, ranging from theaters to a football club, as well as pop singers and cinema chains; three film production firms, including one exclusively given over to cartoons; four record companies; a tourist agency, etc. Following the trend of Rede Globo, Televisa also owns a cultural foundation which bears its name. Its mission was clearly defined in one of the group's reports.

Televisa, always concerned with the distribution of culture, has created the foundation TELEVISA, a non-profit making association which brings together twelve of the most brilliant Mexican intellectuals and has the following aims: 1) to plan how television can approach secondary school teaching with programs like Introduction to University; *2) to recover archaeological remains from foreign countries and restore them to the national heritage; 3) to encourage talented young people by awarding scholarships; 4) to establish a film library with more than 50,000 half-hours of video-cassettes, owned by TELEVISA.*[21]

Televisa is also a patron of the arts through the Rufino Tamayo Museum, the newest in the Mexican capital; and finally, thanks to the above-mentioned film library, it also runs an institute of research and historical documentation.

The many arms of the Televisa empire probably make Mexico a unique case in the history of radio-television, with a degree of monopoly control by a single private conglomerate practically without equal in any capitalist country. Everything has happened as if the single political party structure which characterizes the Mexican regime has been transposed to the commercial television system.

Far from being simple appendices to a commercial empire, the cultural foundations of Televisa and Rede Globo are powerful means of penetration into the field of formal education, allowing these companies to enlarge considerably their social function. One can readily envisage their importance for the introduction of new technologies and as laboratories for new

How do you say sun?

Still from *Varela in Xingu*, 1985, video, 13 min. Varela, a satirical caricature of a TV correspondent, attends the inauguration of a new tribal chief on the Xingu Indian reserve in the Amazon jungle of Brazil. The Indians give their impressions of white society, while Varela pokes fun at the orgy of network news crews who have arrived to cover this "media event."

forms of cultural action. For these so-called philanthropic enterprises, an excellent means of tax avoidance for the companies are also important examples of the state delegating some of its responsibilities to private enterprise. By means of the *Telecurso, 2e Grau* (TV Course, 2nd degree) of the Roberto Marinho foundation or the university courses of the Televisa cultural foundation (six hours a day, over 7,500 programs broadcast since 1980), an original model of collaboration between the public and private sectors has been established.

Whether viewed in terms of the formation of multimedia groups or in terms of communications hardware production, "Third World" appears today as an increasingly meaningless term. A whole series of interchangeable terms (the South, developing countries, peripheral countries, etc.) no longer grasp the realities they supposedly refer to. Diplomatic language now makes a distinction between firstly, the oil-exporting countries (mostly members of OPEC); secondly, those oil-importing countries with a significant industrial base (described as the "newly industrializing countries"); and finally, those countries lacking in both energy and a sufficient industrial base, grouped under the term "less developed countries." This differentiation, however, does not affect in the slightest the reinforcing of the economic and financial power of the leading industrial countries. The five largest industrial economies—the United States, Japan, Federal Republic of Germany, France, and the United Kingdom—alone account for almost 40 percent of international trade.

This strengthening of the group of industrialized countries has been accompanied by important internal shifts: the relative decline of American international investment (from 60 percent of the world total in 1969 to 40 percent in 1980); the increased opening up of the United States to investment from other industrialized countries (the total amount of foreign capital in the U.S. increased from 10,000 to 66,000 million dollars between 1967 and 1980); the increase in the international investment position of West Germany and Japan (each now with 10 percent of the world total of direct investment); the decline of Great Britain (which fell from 20 percent to 14 percent of this total between 1960 and 1980); and the static position of France (5 percent of the world total in 1980). But the share of the industrialized countries among the whole of direct investment increased from 69 percent to 74 percent between 1967 and 1975.[22]

This redistribution within the industrialized "club," coupled with the relative weakening of American domination, has gone hand in hand with the emergence of two new technological front-runners: Japan and to a lesser extent, the Federal Republic of Germany. If we measure technological potential by the number of scientists and engineers working in research and development per one million inhabitants, there has been an increase of almost 50 percent over the last ten years in both these countries. By the end of the 1970s, there were 3,608 scientists and engineers for every million people in Japan, compared to 2,854 in the United States, 1,802 in West Germany, 1,419 in Great Britain, 1,327 in France, and 674 in Italy. These figures also enable us to measure the gap still separating the "industrialized countries" and the "newly industrializing countries": in South Korea, this proportion falls to 418 (despite having tripled in ten years); in Brazil, 208; in Mexico, 101. In the less developed countries, it falls still further: to 74 in the Ivory Coast and 20 in Niger.[23]

This imbalance of human potential is even more accentuated when we consider the share of each world region in electronics productions: in 1980, the United States accounted for 45 percent of turnover in this sector, Japan 11 percent, the whole of West Europe 28 percent, "the rest of the world" (excluding the Comecon countries and China) 16 percent.[24]

Does admittance to the relatively small club of "newly industrializing countries" (Brazil, Mexico, Singapore, Taiwan, South Korea, Hong Kong) necessarily mean the abandonment of organic, economic, political, and cultural links with their former partners in the statistical lists? Nothing could be more foolhardy than to approach international relations in terms of this narrow economism. In fact, the progressive mastering by Brazil of high technology sectors such as aeronautics and computers, and program industries like cinema and television, has been accompanied by a gradual redistribution among its export markets. In 1960 Brazilian exports to developing countries represented 9 percent of its total. In 1973, this had moved to 18.1 percent, and in 1977, to 24.1 percent. On the other hand, its exports to the "developed countries" fell from 84.8 percent in 1960 to 68.1 percent in 1977. As José David Amorim of the University of Brasilia emphasizes:

The tendency to greater trade with Third World countries can only increase with Brazilian industrial sophistication. As this occurs, competition with these countries diminishes and the complementary nature of the economies of the South is strengthened. The expansion of commercial exchanges with the Third World is also reflected in the diplomatic stance of Brazil. The record of 1,593 votes at the United Nations shows that in 47.4 percent of cases, Brazil supported the developing countries.[25]

This new type of South-South cooperation has been marked by the appearance of what have been somewhat quickly dubbed "the multinationals of the Third World." A recent study by the International Labour Organization (ILO) tried to identify the characteristics distinguishing them from transnationals created in the developed countries. According to this study, which analyzed companies in Argentina, Brazil, Hong Kong, India, Indonesia, Mauritius, Mexico, Pakistan, Peru, the Philippines, Sri Lanka, and Thailand, these multinationals are primarily distinguished by their supply of an alternative technology to that of the industrialized giants. Their "alternative" nature is found in their better adaptation of technologies to internal markets and greater labor intensity. By making greater use of a country's internal resources and local production methods, these companies respond better to national employment objectives.

Are "Third World multinationals" real alternatives to transnationals from the developed countries? To answer this, we must trace the limits of this new development. On the one hand, the technologies offered, essentially in the manufacturing sector, are generally only adaptations of technologies developed in the large industrialized countries. But they do not necessarily challenge the model of social growth that favors the formation of elites whose needs alone are taken into account—at the expense of an increasingly poorer majority.

In countries where the requirements of democracy really do influence technological policy, an "alternative communications strategy" doesn't look to factories—even those of the Third World—for a solution. Instead it looks to social experiments in the use of technologies. Thus, anxious not to import the dependent relationship attached to the audiovisual material it needed, Mozambique turned towards international alliances with groups which had a critical analysis in line with its own concerns. Nevertheless, although Mozambique is a rare example of a Third World country which has questioned the centralizing tendency of a national television system, its project has come up against the technical and scientific inequalities which plague "less developed countries": thus the political will to set up a horizontal, nonelitist communications system must confront, in these countries, a preliminary handicap—that of the historical lack of technical experience.

The appearance on the international scene of secondary peaks of economic and political domination blurs the previous map of the international power balance. However, the elevation of a few Third World countries to the rank of "newly industrialized country" has not led to a redistribution of financial power. For this industrialization has been carried out at the cost of a gigantic debt which reinforces financial concentration in the hands of a small number of the private banking sector. The majority of the debts of developing countries are to private banks: in 1981 commercial banks financed almost 60 percent of the total external debt of non-oil-exporting developing countries. The average interest rate on this debt has practically doubled between 1975 and the beginning of the 1980s, increasing from 5.5 percent to 10 percent; whereas its total size quadrupled between 1978 and 1983 through the rise in the value of the dollar (most debts being in dollars). In 1982, interest payments alone represented about two-thirds of the current debt of these countries. For countries with huge debts like Argentina, Mexico, and Brazil, the servicing of that debt (interest plus repayments) represents respectively 153 percent, 126 percent, and 117 percent of their export earnings.[26]

This phenomenon establishes the growing and perhaps irreversible integration of the economies of developing countries into the world economy. In 1983, these countries had to import massively to maintain the level of exports necessary for the partial payment of their debt and an industrialization process (imports of equipment, pesticides, and oil). Shifts in the exchange rate have worsened this situation, reducing the quantity of imports that a given quantity of exports can finance. At the same time, the surplus of the oil-exporting countries fell from $102 billion in 1980 to $12 billion in 1982.[27]

In the industrialized countries, the repercussions of the "globalizing" of the economy on communications systems are still essentially analyzed in terms of cultural and industrial dependence. For Third World countries caught in the spiral of deteriorating trade balances, the immediate requirements of sheer survival have emphasized dramatically the extent of the control of communications over consumption, particularly in the agro-food sector. By focusing solely on news sources, the debates within international organizations on the new information order have left this fundamental dimension in the shadows. And yet marketing and advertising are the backbone for any model of consumption; and their role is particularly striking in Latin America, where the extent of advertising mostly exceeds the accepted levels of tolerance in industrialized countries.

A comparison of advertising spending by media category throughout the world reveals that the press is still the largest, with 43 percent of advertising receipts in 96 countries (1976). Television came second with 21 percent and radio third with 7 percent. In Western Europe and North America, television received 14 percent and 20 percent of takings respectively. In Latin America, this figure climbs to 41 percent, although even this percentage is considerably exceeded by Mexico, where television accounts for 62 percent of advertising expenditure.[28] If we exclude government advertising, it is transnational agro-food firms which, in Mexico, spend the most on advertising. It is also in Mexico that the penetration of agro-food transnationals is the most advanced: 130 foreign enterprises own over 300 industrial establishments, 80 percent of these being of North American origin.[29] But, paradoxically, Mexico has to import over half of the basic foodstuffs needed by the population (e.g., wheat, beans, sorghum, corn).

Numerous studies confirm that the consumption model created by the transnational system demands, for anyone really to benefit from it, an income accessible to only 20 or 30 percent of the population. Thus the system of commercialization, the system of production, and the system of communications all play a complementary role within the transnational framework by promoting a model of social inequality. The main patterns to emerge from the installation of new technologies in countries like Brazil show that, far from democratizing access to cultural goods, they reinforce segregations and consolidate hierarchies.

The pilot experiment for videotex in Brazil, for example, carried out under the auspices of the French firm Matra, enables us to see how an "interactive" technology, which supposedly enables horizontal communication within a society, in fact accentuates the verticality of that society by simply updating its system of social and economic discrimination. Those chosen to benefit from the prospective videotex services were essentially recruited from the top of an already strongly concentrated financial and industrial system—a multimedia conglomerate, the banking sector, the public administration. The technological criteria for selection were thus automatically converted into criteria for social selection: to participate in this experiment, you had to have, at the very least, a telephone and a color television, and this in a country with seven telephones per 100 inhabitants and where less than 12 percent of households had color television.

An export strategy which thus reduces industrial cooperation to a simple system of market penetration can only be indifferent to the political, social, and cultural dimensions of the consumption model it promotes, whether in technology or food. In so doing, it pushes international relations into a neoliberal mold which, in celebrating the era of electronic democracy, proclaims in fact the end of legitimate politics, equating individual liberty with the liberalization of the market.

As the Chilean newspaper *El Mercurio*, remembered for its determining role in the overthrow of the constitutional government of Salvador Allende, trumpeted:

Instead of wasting its energies in the struggle to change structures as a means of social development, the great revolution of [the Pinochet] government is that each person can take private decisions, legitimately acquire what suits him and practically understand the dynamic value of property. Thus, poor people can buy equipment and material to enable them to live better. In this way they increase their comfort but, furthermore, they have access to a world not long ago closed to them: the world of information, advertising and light entertainment. . . .[30]

Banished from editorial offices, politics is today making its entry at the top through boards of directors. Whereas the French intelligentsia is now afraid to openly identify the increasing mechanisms of domination, transnational corporations have no hesitation in calling a spade a spade: despite resistance, they demand to take over the functions of the state for themselves, placing communications strategies at the center of this political demand.

In a speech to the Public Affairs Council in New York, a director of the European agro-food transnational Nestlé outlined the following argument:

The struggle in which we are engaged is of a political nature and on a political level, but it is not yet certain that the future will be one of economic, social, personal, and political liberty . . . Success in politics is not magical. Our enemies are not more intelligent than us and not supermen. And having begun a political reflection, we should give ourselves some political objectives . . . I feel it is essential that multina-

Still from *Chile's Forbidden Dream*, 1981, video/film, 13 min.

tional firms under attack create a united group of talented and experienced profession-
als and, when needed, occasional consultants who, isolated from the everyday public
relations of the firm, can concentrate their efforts on the political issues encountered
by multinationals. In the search for a receptive public and the elimination of a critical
attitude, multinational firms have an invaluable weapon at their disposal: marketing
and management personnel in the field.[31]

Thinking politically, as this "communications strategy" shows clearly, is
not only to equip oneself with tools but to think in terms of social alliances:

We must either reactivate our traditional professional associations, or look beyond
them for new allies among associations of peasants, workers, and owners of small
businesses, many of whom have been suspicious of multinational capitalism in the
past for good reasons. We must affirm the common interests of all institutions which
create wealth—large or small, private or governmental, national or multinational:
in short, we must affirm the pluralism and the diversity of the human condition, an
example of which is given by democracy as well as the free market of commerce and
ideas. Multinational capitalism must never appear as the dominating rival to local
interests or to national or tribal sentiments.[32]

It should not be too quickly forgotten that whereas the goal of democracy is the extension of freedoms and the multiplication of points of popular

decision-making, that of the market is based on the division of labor, power, knowledge, and wealth. Previously, firms saw themselves as the standard-bearers of an apoliticism which delegated all social functions to the invisible hand of the market. Today, the privatization process is pushing firms into a totally different relation with society, transforming them into pressure groups with new social responsibilities and political concerns.

The terrain of another international space is here marked out: it is not the supposedly "neutral" space of technological innovations but that of political will. The issue therefore extends well beyond international trading relations to encompass the very existence of democracy.

Notes

1. *Many Voices, One World: Towards a New, More Just, and More Efficient World Information and Communication Order*, final report of the International Commission for the Study of Communication Problems (MacBride Commission) (Paris: UNESCO; New York: Unipub, 1980).
2. Rafael Roncagliolo, "El 'Nomic': Communicación y poder," First International Forum on Communications and Power, Lima, June 1982, duplicated typescript, p. 8.
3. Roberto Savio, "Communicación y desarrollo en la decada de los 80," *IPS Newsletter* (Rome), no. 10 (December 1982): 40.
4. See Fernando Reyes Matta, "Información y desarrollo bajo la contraofensiva Reagan," *Comunicación y Cultura* (Mexico City) 7 (1981): 60.
5. Roncagliolo, "El 'Nomic,'" p. 16. In October 1983, the same organizations met for a second time at Talloires. There, the anti-UNESCO offensive retreated somewhat in the face of the resistance of news agency representatives and moderate Third World journalists. See Jacques Decornoy, "Qu'est ce que la liberté de communiquer?" *Le Monde,* October 8, 1983.
6. Alain Madec, *Le Flux transfrontières de données* (Paris: La documentation française, 1982), pp. 12-13, 15 (author's italics).
7. François Mitterand, "Technologie, emploi et croissance, rapport au sommet de Versailles," June 5, 1982.
8. Augustin Girard, "Cultural Industries: A Handicap or a New Opportunity for Cultural Development?" in *Cultural Industries: A Challenge for the Future of Culture* (Paris: UNESCO, 1982), p. 25.
9. Speech by Jack Lang, Mexico City, July 27, 1982 (typescript).
10. "Polémiques à Mexico," *Le Matin de Paris,* July 30, 1982.
11. Ibid.
12. "La conférence de l'UNESCO à Mexico," *Le Monde,* July 30, 1982.
13. Bernard-Henri Levy, "Anti-américanisme primair," *Le Matin de Paris,* August 3, 1982.
14. Guy Konopnicki, "A des années-lumières," *Le Monde,* August 7, 1982.
15. Guy Hennebelle, "Rêvons-nous de devenir portoricains," *Le Monde,* August 26, 1982.
16. Armand Mattelart, "Technology, Culture, and Communication: Research and Policy Priorities in France," *Journal of Communication* 33, no. 3 (Summer 1983): 60. See also Armand Mattelart and Y. Stourdzé, *Technology, Culture and Communication in France: A Report to the Minister of Research and Industry* (New York and Amsterdam, forthcoming).
17. See "Faut-il bruler les Américains?" *Le Nouvel Observateur,* August 7, 1982.
18. Polémiques à Mexico," *Le Matin de Paris,* July 30, 1982.
19. This argument is developed in Jean-Marie Piemme, "Identité culturelle et domination secondaire," contribution to the LAS commission, 1983 (duplicated transcript).
20. Guy Martinière, *Aspects de la coopération franco-brésilienne* (Grenoble: Presses Universitaires de Grenoble, 1982), pp. 27-29.
21. See Armand Mattelart and Hector Schmucler, *Communication and Information Technologies: Freedom of Choice for Latin America?* (Norwood, N.J.: Ablex, 1985).

22. Charles-Albert Michalet et al., *Nationalisation et internationalisation: stratégies des multinationales françaises dans la crise* (Paris: Maspero, 1983), p.43.

23. *Statistics on Science and Technology,* UNESCO, December 1982.

24. Statistics from the Ministry of Research and Industry, France.

25. José Salomao David Amorim, *Limites a união dos paises em desenvolvimento para establecimento da NOII: O caso da Brasil* (Lima: Foro Internacional de communicacão, June 12, 1982, typescript).

26. See "Endettement et chomage," *Vers un dévèloppement solidaire* (Lausanne), no. 66 (May 1983).

27. R. C. Lawrence, "L'endettement au coeur de la crise," *Le Monde Diplomatique,* June 1983, pp. 10-11.

28. Center on Transnational Corporations, *Transnational Corporations in Advertising* (New York: United Nations, 1979).

29. A. Montoya Martin del Campo, "Los determinantes nacionales y transnacionales de la informacion en Mexico," unpublished manuscript, Mexico City, 1980.

30. *El Mercurio,* May 2, 1982, cited by José Joaquin Brunner, "La vie quotidienne en régime autoritaire," *Amérique latine,* no. 12 (October-December 1982).

31. Rafael D. Pagan, Jr., president of the Nestlé Coordination Center for Nutrition, "Porter la lutte sur le terrain des détracteurs du capitalisme multinational," in *Vers un dévèloppement solidaire* (Lausanne), no. 66 (May 1983).

32. Ibid.

Telepictures:
An Interview with Josh Elbaum

Coco Fusco

M ost critical writing on television analyzes mass media as the primary
locus of information and social control in this country. The set
of power relations that define television, however, are not limited to local
production and the individual American consumer. For a long time, the
already saturated U.S. airwaves and a constant surplus production have
generated the need for targeting international markets. America's overwhelming technological advantage over most developing countries, together with aggressive sales strategies, have maintained U.S. hegemony in
global television sales and production for more than three decades (although Brazil's Globo is now the first Third World production company
to pose a substantial threat).

The current privatization of Western European television increases
U.S. sales potential, as new programming slots are opening before the
infrastructure for more local production is in place. Technological advances
in satellites, the introduction of cable in Western Europe, and the ever-
expanding home video market enable U.S. companies to capitalize even
more on television's high rate of return and near infinite recyclability.

Telepictures began as an independent distributor in 1981, at the onset
of the Reagan presidency and during a period of accelerated growth for
nonstudio-aligned film and television companies. Soon expanding to include production, it merged with Lorimar Pictures in 1986. Sales representative Josh Elbaum has left Telepictures since this interview took place, but
the phenomena he discusses, as well as his rhetoric's limits and silences,
remain current.

— C.F.

Can you describe Telepictures?

Telepictures started out as a distribution company for independent producers. For a percentage we will take a finished product and distribute it—we'll sell it, promote, service it, deliver the material. We'll do everything related to having the client station receive a single piece of information to telecast. The company started by doing that and did it very well, so well that it found itself in a good cash position. We also realized that a lot of the things that the independents were doing weren't that good. So Telepictures started producing on its own. The company eventually started its own production division, mostly miniseries. If you have a successful show that's being broadcast, what you're doing is selling five half-hours that go on every single week. And for the same energy that you might spend selling a TV movie that lasts two hours or a miniseries that will last seven hours, you can have a show that will last all year round. There's a lot of money in that in terms of station license fees, and a lot of money that can be made bartering with advertisers by giving up time for a commercial.

We sell to the domestic and foreign markets. We sell things that we make. We sell things that independent producers make. And since the salesman is the person who is out in the field speaking to broadcasters, we'll often read scripts and say, "Well, this reads well and it might do well in the United States, but it's not going to sell in Latin America." Or, "It will sell in Latin America and it won't sell in Asia." Or, "If you take this part out it will be acceptable in the Middle East." We're aware of the differences in moral values, things that can create problems, be they political or sexual.

What are the areas of sensitivity?

Well, sex is always a problem. If something is shown graphically, that's certainly a problem. There are certain nations that really don't care to emphasize the question of homosexuality, or the problems of AIDS or of premarital sex. It's pretty obvious which countries they are. There are often problems with politics. For example, Latin American countries don't like to show programs in which the story revolves around a dictator or an unpopular leader. Depending on whether a station is owned by the government—and many are throughout the world—they will simply censor it, they will reject it. It's funny—often Eastern European countries and governments like Duvalier's Haiti or Marcos's Philippines will agree on what can be shown and what can't be shown because there are issues that affect them both.

Josh Elbaum, International Sales Executive, at far right, then clockwise: Rosemary Mazzo, Contracts Administrator-International; Frances Reynolds, International Sales Executive; Michelle Kearney, Director–Latin American Sales; and Brooke Shields, star of the Telepictures movie *Wet Gold*.

Has the recent wave of "democratization" affected sales?

It has increased the variety of programs we can sell. There is a bit of nervousness in Latin America, especially in those countries with harsh governments, because most of the stations are privately owned and the last thing the station owner wants is for the government to close down the station.

Have you dealt with any countries where you felt there was very little state intervention in decision making?

For example in Norway, there's only one station and it's owned by the government. Freedom of expression, freedom of choice is a very sacred right there. If the chairman of a television station doesn't like what the buyer bought, it's simply too bad. They had a big controversy over either *Dallas, Falcon Crest,* or *Knots Landing.* Many members of Parliament thought that the program was trash, and did not want the station to broadcast it. The station defended itself by saying that there were hundreds of letters from Norwegian citizens and that they happened to like it. And those citizens didn't care that the Parliament members thought they should watch a show about Picasso, or the environment, or overpopulation. This was what they wanted to watch. In Norway, you can get away with that.

I should also say that at this point in time there is a revolution that is absolutely raging throughout Europe and it's being brought about because of cable and satellites. Soon there will be no such thing as the only show in town. Someone in Portugal with the emerging technology will be able to watch something being broadcast in Holland. He will be able to push the button on his television set and receive the program with electronic subtitles in Portuguese. And somebody else in Luxembourg or Turkey will have the same option.

What about Eastern Europe?

You'll have to have the technology and for that you need governmental approval. That's what's slowing down the revolution, but it's not slowing it down that much.

How does this technology increase profits?

Largely through what we call sequential marketing. We have a title—let's say, *Mr. Smith Goes to Washington,* or even better, *Rocky 2000.* The first thing we'll do is sell it to theaters. From there we sell it to the foreign equivalent of Home Box Office, or cable or satellite, where reception is more limited than public broadcast. And from there we sell it to home video and then to public television. Whereas five years ago, you'd only get the license fee from the public broadcast, now you'll be getting substantial increments.

In terms of the new technology, you can do one trip, speak to one company, and the show's on in thirty million houses. Before, you had to go to all of the outlets to make things available to those thirty million people. That's a lot of time, and a lot of money. The new technology gives an additional source to sell things to.

Telepictures Corporation logo

How does Telepictures figure in relation to other companies that sell programming abroad?

I want to mention that the primary reason why companies like this exist is that we offer foreign stations, particularly in the Third World, in underdeveloped countries, materials which if they were to make on their own would cost substantially more money. Local production is outrageously more expensive. For a country like Jamaica to be able to finance the production of ten hours of local programming is simply out of the question. That's the real reason we exist.

If the economic status of an underdeveloped country improved, would you be phased out?

It would take a long time.

Isn't there a strategy of keeping prices low for developing countries so that it will always be cheaper for them to buy than for them to make their own?

We cannot ask for ridiculous license fees in the Third World. One, because they simply can't afford to pay. They would simply say "No, thank you," and find another company that would give them a much more reasonable license fee. The stations agree to the license fees, which are the result of discussion. If, for example, you have *Miami Vice,* which costs a million dollars an hour to produce, we'd ask every single broadcaster from Britain to Haiti to chip in and give us a premium rate. If it's a low-budget production, we simply won't ask the outrageous fee. What we do is ask that they take packages.

What would the ratio of difference be between a developed and an underdeveloped country?

Bermuda is a good example. It's a very small island. If we offer them an extravagant miniseries and their license fee is generally $150 an hour we might say, "Look, everyone else in the world is going above budget and we expect the same from you, so why don't you give us $200 an hour?" But we might expect Britain to double their usual license, from let's say $10,000—which is too low a figure, by the way—to $20,000 an hour.

If you make that little money from Bermuda sales, why bother with them at all?

Because, number one, you want to make as much money as you can from sales. And if you forget about the Bermudas, Nigeria, etc. . . . add it up and it comes to a substantial amount of money.

You have negotiated some deals with the Soviet Union. What sort of programs are they interested in?

They have agreed to air a movie called *Arch of Triumph,* a remake of a postwar classic. It's a story about a refugee doctor living in France who falls in love with a Parisian lady. They also selected a program called *Lorne Greene's New Wilderness,* which is a nature series that focuses on a different animal every week.

What choices did you offer them?

Knowing their political sensitivities and constraints, we gave them a catalogue that took those sensitivities into account and said we wanted to initiate a relationship with Soviet TV because first of all there are a lot of viewers there. It's a source of pride to know that your show is being viewed by countless millions of people. And we also wanted to do it because we believe that in many ways international television can break down a lot of misunderstandings.

How did you set fees for the Soviets?

We don't have a precedent with the Soviet Union, so we really didn't know what to ask. We asked them for their offer, what they would be willing to pay. And we will consider it. We'll have to do some research. From my dealings with them, I believe they're very straightforward. No monkey business.

How do they evaluate the value of what you're offering them?

They probably simply have a cost per minute, as does the rest of Eastern Europe. I would assume they'd give a little more money for an American show, but I don't know for sure. They may just have a Western price.

In what sense does a love story set in Europe and a show about animals amount to cultural exchange?

Well, the movie wasn't written by a Soviet author. It wasn't portrayed by Soviets with their acting style. In the case of the animal show they may simply have chosen shows about animals that don't exist in the Soviet Union. They'll get a good idea of how Americans look at animals, what our relationship to animals is.

Did you have any idea of what they would be interested in before you showed them what was available?

No. They have very good poker faces. All you have to do is spend some

Title frame for *Newscope,* the daily news and information program developed by Telepictures as part of their syndicated video news service, N.I.W.S. (News Information Weekly Service).

time with broadcasters and then let them decide what they want. You simply can't shove something down their throat and then expect them to put some technology on and have an entire country watch.

What don't the Soviets want to watch?

We certainly knew that any sort of spy, cloak-and-dagger kind of adventure didn't really interest them. The Soviets, by the way, had a great deal of success with a spy show they made called *Tass Informs,* which is basically a Soviet version of *The Man From U.N.C.L.E.*

How much cultural understanding are you going to achieve when both sides are so selective about what is going to be shown?

It's something, which is better than nothing. On another level, the negotiations permit Soviet management to deal directly and personally with American management. It filters down. We in turn speak to the State Department and the Department of Commerce. Just to arrange with programming we probably talked to ten different organizations. We exchanged ideas, not so much about the programs, as about their concerns—their political concerns, economic concerns, management concerns, problems they have in running a television station. And they heard our concerns in terms of trying to do business with the Soviets, what our frustrations are in trying to deal with Surinam, or the business of the Hollywood jungle. So, it's more than just exchanging programs.

The Soviets are very interested in the technology and business of entertainment. That's not so much of a concern for them.

Although television is just as central to people's lives there as it is here.

It has an entirely different aim. It's purely educational and informational. There is entertainment, but it's 99.9 percent Soviet. Soviet television is unique.

What would a night of Soviet television be like?

I would imagine that there is a lot of news, probably one or two feature films, maybe a series. A French class, a Spanish class, or an English class.

What makes it unique?

It's unique because it's 99.9 percent Soviet. You might say, well, we're 99.9 percent American—however, the reasoning for that is different. We're not that concentrated on an American product because the broadcasters are protective of what we make here. That certainly is the case with the Soviet Union. Television is a tool. Television in this country is not so much a tool as it is a vehicle for entertainment or killing time, or whatever. Even though you do have your *60 Minutes,* and your *Firing Line.*

It is however the central source of information. You can say that it's geared toward entertainment, but in a way that entertainment is a kind of education.

No one has any pretension that the *Dukes of Hazard* or even *The Bill Cosby Show* are going to educate anybody.

Maybe not, but as in the case of the animal show, the shows present a way of looking at things, a model existence.

They do, but they are not conceptualized that way. They're not written that way. Whether someone gets that message is an entirely different issue. The Soviets plan to have a certain impact. The screenwriter who is picking out twenty different car chases for the *Dukes of Hazard* is not thinking about that at all.

What is he or she thinking about?

About getting the show on the air for several years and making a lot of money.

A scene from *A.D.*, a twelve-hour miniseries produced by Telepictures. Billed as a "blockbuster," it was shown on NBC-TV during Easter week, 1985.

What about your dealings with the Caribbean and Latin America?

They need a lot of movies, a lot of half-hour slots. Situation comedies, soap operas. It's just like the United States. They have a lot of air time to fill.

Generally what's popular in this country is popular in the Caribbean. There's a miniseries called *Sophisticated Gents* that was very successful. It's the story of four black men who went to high school together and didn't see each other for ten years. For obvious reasons, that was very popular. The movie we have about teenage suicide—*Surviving*—sure that's going to be popular. But there are fewer people in the Caribbean who can relate to it than to *Sophisticated Gents,* because first of all you just don't have affluent teenagers there with concerns about graduate school. I think Caribbean teenagers are concerned with something else. However, if it's a good story they'll watch it and they'll enjoy it. The hardest thing to sell in the Caribbean are music specials, because music is a very strong component of their own culture. Even a Bette Midler special with computer enhancement—you couldn't give it away there.

Could a developing country ever produce programming that would be considered feasible for exchange here?

Sure, there are several enterprising Caribbean businessmen who have identified pockets of Caribbean populations here. If they can't get time on a cable station, they will rent a theater and show a local production, regardless of whether it's a movie or news or dance. Because something from home is better than nothing from home. They're not going to attract non-Caribbeans, but the Caribbeans will show up.

What about dealing with the Middle East?

Well, there was a program that was such a hot potato that we had fun with it—*Death of a Princess,* the story of a Saudi Arabian princess who committed adultery and was beheaded. The Saudis went berserk and tried through public relations and outright pressure to stop the international broadcast. But it went on and was enormously successful. This was during the oil crisis.

What wouldn't you show there besides *Death of a Princess*?

You have to be careful about sex and women. And anything with religious content. *Anno Domini* wouldn't be popular there. Any movie that alludes to Judaism wouldn't even get to the point of being censored. It probably wouldn't be offered.

Can you describe a package that you might sell to several different markets in different countries?

Take a place like Surinam, or places like Malta, Israel, and Poland. I think they are all very different. The Lorne Greene program would play in all of them. *Thundercats,* an animation program for children produced with a child psychologist in which each episode supposedly teaches a different moral—that would play everywhere. Movies, you never know. If you can do a package—maybe two series, five specials, two documentaries—you've done well.

How would negotiations differ from place to place?

Surinam used to be a thriving, competitive market. It is not now. There are a lot of political frustrations, and there are certainly a lot of political considerations in dealing with them. Their price is somewhat set by the government, but they do have advertising. Malta—there's a set price. A movie costs X amount of dollars and that's it. The government has set the budget. The commercial money isn't that great. It's such a small market that my time is better spent elsewhere than haggling over $3.33 a minute. Israel is a combination of government and air time, but there's a flexibility. Poland—permanent price. It could be the best thing in the world or the worst. The idea there is to come up with a nice package.

What about something like *Falcon Crest*?

That program would only play in Malta.

Not Surinam?

I don't think they would be interested. I know they wouldn't. The government would probably say it's rubbish, find a nice North Korean feature, a socially important Third World movie.

Same response from Poland?

Pretty much, although at times there is some interest. Sometimes they'll put things like that on just to show the Poles what the West is so berserk about.

Have you ever offered material that you considered offensive, or that would be considered offensive to the buyer? Would this present a problem to you?

This is a business based on personal relationships. If you try to make a quick deal, you're not going to be in the business for very long. The next time you show up, the station manager will remember you. Fortunately, there's lead time. On the basis of their watching half a movie or my discussing it with them for ten minutes, they might say, "Sounds great," and we'll discuss a license fee. Then they watch the whole thing and come back and say there's one scene here or twenty minutes there that make it unacceptable. We'll say, "Fine," and edit it or offer them something else.

You'll change a program?

It probably says in the contract that you can't. A contract is a contract, so someone could probably go to court and sue. But you'd destroy your entire relationship, and this is an ongoing, long-term business. So you either cancel the contract or amend it and let them edit or offer them something else.

Would there be any reason to prevent you from doing business?

We'll sell anywhere and everywhere. South Africa is the most obvious example. If we said no to South Africa, where would it end? Sure, you do have Woody Allen, who says, "Listen, you have the right to distribute my film but not to South Africa." Personally, I think that is very honorable. I respect that. But I would foresee this as being a real bombshell. And I don't know who would make the decision not to sell, especially if it were a public corporation and you were trying to get a consensus among the stockholders.

Conflict and Consensus:
Television in Israel

Lisa C. Cohen

In Israel, private life and national identification are profoundly linked. This conjunction of interests, which is broadly played out in the country's political life, also informs the operation of Israeli television. Although TV is generally consumed in private, for example, viewing it is constructed as a collective experience. In addition, while television in many ways produces and is governed by the Israeli political consensus, it is also a site of conflict—and occasionally of opposition—in a society which thrives on conflict but rarely tolerates opposition.

In general, domains of life Americans regard as private are experienced in Israel as public, collective endeavors. The family, for example, is a national project; there is enormous pressure on Israeli women and men to get married and have children. While the family has traditionally been an important Jewish value, in Israel this concern is also tied to the desire to create a wholly Jewish nation-state on a piece of land already populated by "non-Jews." Israeli newspapers fill periodically with the latest reports of the Arab and Jewish birthrates, and the number of children each Jewish family should be encouraged to have forms the subject of Cabinet meetings and newspaper editorials. At the same time, spheres of public life that Americans tend to view with more distance, such as "national security," are personalized in Israel. Most Israelis have grown up with the idea that their nation is beleaguered and defenseless. This collective siege mentality, coupled with the country's small size and compulsory military service, means that Israelis experience national politics and policies as salient parts of their private lives.

A powerful communal ethos thus informs the military and the family, two central aspects of the social order in Israel. Men who don't serve in the army have a hard time getting good jobs, and women who fail to help foster "internal immigration"—as "natural" population increase is called—can find it difficult to feel at home in a society centered around child-rearing. In fact, the culture permits little space for deviation from any of its social standards. The response to such dissent is an example of the way the intimacy of the political and the politicization of the private work in Israel: those who criticize the status quo are regularly accused of being self-destructive traitors—a characterization which simultaneously invokes the rhetorics of psychology (the individual) and of state security (the collective).

Yet, the status quo in Israel is itself characterized by conflict. During my three extended visits, it was increasingly apparent that the country is maintained and renewed by contention as much as by common national values. In fact, partisan conflict between Jews—engagement with questions about "what is best for the Jews" and for Israel—is an important aspect of the collective life. But opposition beyond this level of "allowable" conflict continues to be overwhelmingly perceived as a threat to that life. Thus, challenges to the country's territorial and rhetorical assumptions— opposition to the state's occupation of the West Bank and the redesignation of that area according to its biblical place names, for example—clearly violate the political norm and are labeled disloyal. The conflicts which these challenges generate—including televised representations of them— have the potential to disrupt the country substantially and, as a result, the government manages them carefully.

In the twenty years that Israel Television (ITV), the national television service, has been in operation, television has displaced the theater, concerts, and movies as the favored form of entertainment in Israel. The popularity of the medium and the fact that local broadcasting has operated on a single channel (ITV) since its inception help make watching television a significant shared event. When they tune in, Israelis know that their friends and most of the rest of the country are also watching. As a result, the government sees TV as a tool to support the state, and has linked the station's administration to the Knesset (Israel's parliament) and to the Cabinet. In addition, the consensus that inhibits criticism of Israel's strong political and cultural norms also serves to consolidate the conditions of broadcasting. While in several cases Israelis have questioned the censorship of programming, few have challenged the fundamental need for such regulation.

But if television in Israel expresses and produces a certain amount of social coherence, it also produces, mediates, and represents conflicts in the culture. Television generates enough controversy—from arguments over programming choices to the station's frequent labor disputes—to make it regular front-page news. Whereas in the United States the television industry presents itself as an institution removed from partisan politics and able to include any viewpoint, in Israel the party affiliations of television administrators, reporters, and program hosts are common knowledge. Editorial disputes, in addition to being public, are openly partisan political struggles. Various members of the Cabinet and the Knesset, for example, regularly submit motions denouncing TV programs or employees to express their displeasure with the station's actions. Television also mediates conflict, both by representing it and by displacing Israelis' more immediate involvement in organized political life. Israelis who used to spend evenings at gatherings sponsored by their party, for example, now spend the time watching television. Most likely they are watching the evening news, the single most popular program in the country and one which depends on struggle and crisis for its subject matter.

Ironically, Israeli television's tendency to generate and represent conflict not only makes it more compelling to its viewers, but also strengthens the medium's power to create a sense of community in the society. Thus, the government and the military, which recognize and sometimes use television's ability to present images of conflict, often see its power to do so as a threat to the state and suppress or appropriate these images. Despite pervasive state control, on occasion employees of the station have effectively challenged their authority. The U.S. domination of the international television market and the facility with which TV signals cross political borders also undermine the possibility of a completely state-controlled television service in Israel. Television in Israel, then, is produced and consumed in the midst of efforts to regulate the medium, attempts to negotiate these restrictions, and technological conditions which allow television to exceed total regulation.

Israel was the last country in the Middle East to have its own television service. During the 1960s, TV became one more issue in the debate over the proper nature and function of the Jewish state. Though many Jewish Israelis were by then eager to have the option of watching TV in Hebrew, the government deferred authorizing the service for years, reluctant to assume the cost of a national station, yet unwilling to allow private owners and operators to establish one. The high cost of local production and the country's limited resources also meant that a majority of the programming would have to be imported, and many Israelis (including then-prime minister David Ben-Gurion) argued that sponsoring mindless or violent American entertainments was inimical to the values of the Jewish people.

Other groups objected to television because they believed it would disrupt the distribution of wealth in the country. Government economists contended that a national television industry would be an unwise investment of state money, especially since it was impossible to collaborate with other countries in the region already operating television stations. They also warned that encouraging people to buy TV sets—which in the late 1960s cost the equivalent of the average monthly salary—would endanger the economy. Cinema and theater owners lobbied against television because they anticipated a loss of business as a result of the competition, and newspaper publishers objected that their advertising sales would fall if the station were supported by commercial revenues.[1]

The most significant challenge to the government's intransigence was the fact that thousands of Palestinians living within Israel already owned televisions. The government estimated that prior to the 1967 war, there were approximately 22,000 television sets in the country, all but 3,400 owned by "non-Jews."[2] Viewers tuned in nightly to Jordanian, Lebanese, Egyptian, Saudi, Syrian, or Cypriot television broadcasts (often consisting primarily of British and American imports). The proximity of these countries to different parts of Israel and the particular atmospheric conditions in the Middle East (which trap the TV signal close to the earth and allow it to travel unusually long distances) made an uncontrollable range of programming available. Clearly it was problematic for Israel to leave the Palestinians living inside the green line—in most other ways cut off from the rest of the Arab world from 1948 to 1967—exposed to broadcasts from hostile neighbors. In addition, Israel recognized the importance of presenting to the residents of the territories it had occupied in the 1967 war its own version of Middle East history and current events. Finally, Jordan's plan to begin broadcasting television news in Hebrew convinced the Israeli government that failing to establish its own television industry would create a national security risk. By the end of the war, the Cabinet and the Knesset had decided that they could no longer forfeit their ability to control and benefit from television.

Israel Television began broadcasting in 1968 with the live coverage of a military parade celebrating the twentieth anniversary of the founding of the state.[3] Following this inaugural program, the station was briefly operated under the auspices of the prime minister's office. Since then, the

Interviewing the President of Israel

Israel Broadcasting Authority (IBA), a semi-governmental body which also oversees radio programming, has administered the station. The IBA, created to make broadcasting independent of the government, is nevertheless run by a board whose membership is apportioned according to party representation in the Knesset. The 1984 Coalition Agreement between the Labor and Likud parties allows for each to designate an equal number of delegates to the eleven-member board; a representative of the National Religious Party occupies the remaining position. Broadcasting Authority law calls for Israel Television to reflect "the life, struggle, creative effort and achievements of the State" and to strengthen ties with and deepen knowledge of "the Jewish heritage and its values."[4] The Cabinet appoints the director general of the Authority as well as the directors of radio and television, and the government can, "for compelling military reasons or under pressure of emergency conditions," void or restrict the IBA's powers.[5]

Current proposals for a second, commercial channel make it clear that the government's approach to regulating the medium has not changed much since TV was first incorporated into the Broadcasting Authority. Though a consortium of private companies would run the new station, the version of the authorizing legislation that is likely to pass stipulates that the companies would lease air time from a government-controlled

Second Channel Authority and would be responsible to the minister of communications. The Second Channel Authority would itself run the station until it chose the participating companies.

During the British Mandate in Palestine, the goals of the Jewish press and radio broadcasters were consonant with those of the leaders of the organized Jewish community there: all were committed to working for a Jewish state. Since the establishment of Israel in 1948, the press, radio, and television have continued to support the premium placed on military security for the state and to avoid issues that might threaten—or be perceived to threaten—Israel's existence. Indeed, television professionals in Israel are overwhelmingly from the same social and ethnic background (educated, middle class, of European descent) and subscribe to the same value system (that represented by the Labor movement, the party in power for most of Israel's history). Today, however, those values place television workers somewhat to the left of the center of Israeli public opinion. So while the government's claim that ITV is a hotbed of radicalism and resistance is clearly exaggerated, the station does occasionally produce shows that vividly depict and question the more brutal aspects of the "achievements of the State."

Israeli-produced television programming, which represents less than half of ITV's scheduled broadcasts, includes children's shows, documentaries, concerts, dance and theater performances, talk shows, specials on Jewish life, and the half-hour evening news program *Mabat*. Though much is made of the influence of Israel's minority Orthodox population on political and cultural life, most Israelis do not consider themselves religious, and television is clearly directed to that majority.[6] The scheduling and content of the station's "religious" programming indicate that even this genre is intended primarily for the secular majority, TV's regular customers.[7] Shows are often aired on the Sabbath or a holiday, when observant Jews wouldn't use a television, and they tend to address the significance of those holy days for people whose lives don't include ritual observance of Judaism.

Mabat is unquestionably the most important television program in the life of the country. Israelis are addicted to the news in any form, and 96 percent of the over 90 percent of Israeli households owning televisions watch *Mabat* every evening—more than any other regular broadcast. The program presents national news—stories on "national security, foreign affairs and economic development"—almost exclusively, and these topics are as compelling to Israeli viewers as local news is to most Americans.[8] *Mabat* broadcasts are frequently analyzed in the following day's newspapers, and this commentary is not relegated to the television section but is generally found in the first few pages of the paper. Everyone watches *Mabat,* therefore an appearance on this or one of the other interview and information shows ensures instant national celebrity.

Since employees of the station have tenure, they do not risk being fired when they produce a program or news segment that is likely to displease the government. They do risk never getting the material broadcast. Rafik Halabi, an Israeli-Arab employee of the station who covered the West Bank for *Mabat,* has described the suppression of some of his reporting from the occupied territories in his book *The West Bank Story.*[9] A well-known example of a film ITV produced but never showed depicts the return of a Palestinian family to the house in Jerusalem it had occupied before 1948, and the family's encounter with the present owners. Another program documents the Turkish genocide of Armenians in 1915; like many other references to that event, the program was suppressed both because of Israel's close ties with Turkey today and because of Israel's reluctance to divert attention from the mass murders of the Jews during World War II.

Programs that question elements of national history and contemporary politics are shown occasionally and always generate public debate. *Hirbet Hiz'ah,* a fictional account of the 1948 evacuation of a Palestinian village, was produced by Israel Television and broadcast in 1979. At that time, the film was widely denounced and labeled PLO propaganda (as was a more recent program on Israel's twenty-year occupation of the West Bank). Since the invasion of Lebanon in 1982, however, Israel and its supporters have been increasingly concerned about protecting the country's image as "the only democratic state in the Middle East," and *Hirbet Hiz'ah* is now displayed as proof that democracy thrives in Israel.[10] The movie, a docudrama, questioned the official version of how and why many Palestinians left their homes in 1948; the Israeli version holds that the Palestinians fled entirely of their own accord, urged on by Arab leaders. The strong and widespread negative response to the film's interpretation of historical events, however, restored and reaffirmed the official version as an essential national value. Subsequent self-congratulation for allowing *Hirbet Hiz'ah* to be aired merely assimilated the film's dissenting view into a conventional idealization of the state. In this context, *Hirbet Hiz'ah* and programs like it serve to rupture and rehabilitate the Zionist consensus.

The case of Mordechai Vanunu provides another example of the way Israel Television programming responds to issues that violate the political consensus; it also demonstrates how ITV reporters sometimes negotiate the formal controls that regulate television and buttress that consensus. Vanunu is a former technician at Israel's nuclear facility in the Negev Desert. In 1986 he revealed to the *Sunday Times* of London that Israel is capable of producing sophisticated nuclear weapons. Since then he has said that he spoke out in order to generate discussion of an issue that is taboo in Israel. As a result of his disclosures, Vanunu has been broadly condemned as a traitor in Israel, and the government—charging him with espionage, treason, and passing secrets—has held him in solitary confinement and is refusing to try him in public.

When Judy Zimmet, an American advocate and friend of Vanunu's, traveled to Israel to publicize his case, she appeared on the popular television show, *This Is the Time*. She told me that before the program was taped, she was pre-interviewed twice and warned against "glorifying" her friend.[11] It was Zimmet's impression that her interviewer and his producers were interested in promoting wider discussion of Vanunu's actions, and that these screenings were intended to reduce the chances that her segment of the program would be subject to military censorship. The host's strategy, during the version of the interview that was finally taped and broadcast, was to carefully avoid focusing his questions on the case and instead to ask Zimmet "soft" questions about her childhood, personal life, and feelings about Israel. This done, the host directed her at the end of the interview to speak briefly about her view of Vanunu's disclosures and of the outcome of his case. Devoting this sort of diluted attention to a controversial topic is one way employees of the station maneuver within the constraints of what can and cannot be said on Israeli TV. On other occasions frustrated television workers have expressed their dissent by disabling the station for limited amounts of time. Rafik Halabi writes that once when the director-general of the Broadcasting Authority refused to run a report Halabi had prepared, his colleagues at the station voted unanimously to protest that decision by blacking out the screen for the length of time the story would have run.[12]

Israel Television's reliance on imported programming, and the effects of regional geography on television reception in Israel further interfere with the government's ability to control what is seen on Israeli television sets. About 60 percent of what is broadcast under ITV's name is imported, largely from the United States and England. Jews and Arabs in Israel also

A.P. wirephoto, December 22, 1986: "Former nuclear technician Mordechai Vanunu, accused of revealing Israel's atomic secrets presses his hand to the windows of a police van on his way to a Jerusalem court Sunday. The message he wrote on his hand reads: 'Vanunu was hijacked from Rome, ITL., 30.9.86 21.00, BA504.' The 30.9 refers to Sept. 30, 1986. 21.00 apparently referred to a 9 PM flight of British Airways from London to Rome. Israeli military censor has barred the publication of pictures or contents of Vanunu's message until Monday."

tune their sets to other regional television stations, which are similarly dependent on exports from American commercial television. In the Israeli context, the worldwide distribution of U.S. cultural commodities such as television programming reflects more than the imposition of one culture on another. Israel once looked to Europe for its cultural and political models, as well as for financial support, but it now identifies with the United States and, in turn, is seen in this country as the U.S.'s ideological twin. Israel is also substantially dependent on U.S. funding. It now receives approximately $3 billion in annual subsidies from the American government, in addition to numerous private contributions. The proliferation of U.S.-made television programs on Israeli TV is not simply a product of the United States' cultural imperialism, but also another element of the symbiotic "special relationship" between Israel and the U.S. One way television figures in this relationship, according to an Israeli observer, is that watching U.S.-made programming on some level prepares the growing number of Israelis who move to the United States for life in this country.[13]

Jordan TV is the most watched of the regional stations available to viewers in Israel and the West Bank. Israeli and Jordanian television compete with and appropriate from one another in much the same way that they maneuver for control of the West Bank. The stations pirate from each other's news programs items unavailable in their own countries due to political and military restrictions on broadcasting. In Israel, newspapers regularly carry program listings for one or both of Jordan's stations, sometimes accompanying them with the admonition "unofficial," and Israeli television reviewers often comment on Jordanian programs in their columns. Several years ago, when Israelis were glued to *Dallas,* Jordan TV also broadcast the series, strategically timing it to coincide with *Mabat.* Viewers in both countries, as well as residents of the West Bank, were thus able to watch two weekly episodes of the popular program. Israelis who started following *Dallas* on local television soon found they could accelerate their gratification by changing the channel, since Jordan's broadcast of the series had begun several months earlier than Israel's. In southern Lebanon, Pat Robertson's Christian Broadcasting Network (CBN) operates a subsidiary station, known as Middle East TV, which provides another source of U.S. programming for Israeli viewers.[14] No matter what station the offerings from American commercial television are shown on, they are enormously popular and their predominance further solidifies the country's partnership with the United States.

Television has clearly become a force that both creates and affirms the sense of intimate political community which is so striking in Israel. But it is equally clear that Israeli television can also occasionally provide those who watch it with views—opinions, and glances at scenes—which deviate from the Zionist consensus. Certainly the effects of geography and an economy which makes the station dependent on imported programming complicate the government's efforts to manage TV in Israel. But even more threatening are the oppositional strategies of some producers and reporters, including their use of television's ability to "objectively" reproduce scenes of conflict. The "view" of the demolition of a Palestinian home I saw on the news in Israel in 1984 was one such scene. This sort of broadcast can expose the political and military controls that help to maintain the Israeli political consensus, and hints at television's largely contained power to challenge.

Notes

1. For more on the organization and early history of Israel television see: Dina Goren and Rozann Rothman, "Government-News Media Relations in Israel," in *Government and the News Media: Comparative Dimensions,* ed. Dan Nimmo and Michael Mansfield (Waco, Texas: Baylor University Press, 1982); Timothy Green, *The Universal Eye* (New York: Stein and Day, 1971), pp. 191-203; and Judith Elizur and Elihu Katz, "The Media and the Israeli Elections of 1977," in *Israel at the Polls: The Knesset Elections of 1977,* ed. Howard R. Penniman (Washington, D.C.: American Enterprise Institute for Public Policy Research, 1979).

2. Central Bureau of Statistics, *Statistical Abstract of Israel* (Jerusalem: The Government Press, 1969).

3. One sort of Israeli television had, in fact, begun in 1966. Instructional Television, as the service is called, was originally designed to overcome the shortage of teachers for Israel's new immigrant population from Northern Africa. It was, as one report early in the debate put it, to be used in classrooms in "new areas inhabited by immigrants from backward regions" *(New York Times,* November 22, 1962; this and other newspaper and magazine articles documenting the history of Israeli television are available at the New York Public Library, Lincoln Center branch, Performing Arts Research Center). The educational format had also been blocked for years, by the same constituencies that lobbied against general programming, on the grounds that it was bound to lead to expanded, and inevitably less salubrious, offerings. Instructional Television now broadcasts in the morning and afternoon on the same channel Israel Television uses in the evening.

4. *The Broadcasting Law,* Section 3 (Jerusalem: Israel Broadcasting Authority, 1970), pp. 2-3.

5. Ibid., Section 47, p. 23.

6. In Israel state enforcement of religious observance is governed by the Status Quo Agreement, a compromise between Orthodox and secular political leaders which holds that all "infractions" of Jewish religious law current during the British Mandate would be allowed to continue in Israel. Radio had broadcast on the Sabbath before 1948 and thus was permitted to continue to do so following the establishment of the state. Television's conformity to the agreement was initially debated, since the medium had not yet been introduced when the bill was signed. Today ITV runs seven days a week. The station's Arabic language programs are shown for a couple of hours each night, and those in Hebrew follow them from approximately 8:00 p.m. to midnight.

7. Viewers are literally "customers," since programming is primarily supported not by corporate sponsors but by the annual fee charged to all television owners. A smaller fraction of the budget is supplied by program sponsorship (until 1984 Israel Television was completely noncommercial); public service announcements; the Foreign Ministry; and the semi-governmental funding organization, the Jewish Agency.

8. *Israel Broadcasting Authority* (Jerusalem: IBA Spokesman's Office, c. 1986), p. 24.

9. Rafik Halabi, *The West Bank Story* (New York: Harcourt Brace Jovanovich, 1985), p. 132.

10. Ella Shohat, in "The Return of the Repressed: The Palestinian Wave in the Recent Israeli Cinema," *Cineaste* 15, no. 3 (1987): 10-17, makes this important point about a new genre of Israeli filmmaking. She argues that "the very exhibition of an Israeli film on a Palestinian issue certifies, as it were, the reality of democracy and reassures the liberal conscience of both producers and the receivers of the images."

11. Judy Zimmet, telephone interview, April 1987.

12. Halabi, *West Bank Story,* p. 132.

13. Benjamin Beit-Hallahmi, interview in August 1987, New York City.

14. According to network spokesperson Berton Miller, Manager, Media Relations, Christian Broadcasting Network (interview, March 1987), 70 percent of Middle East TV's schedules consists of "wholesome, family-oriented entertainment" (American sit-coms and sports). About one-quarter is "inspirational programming," including an international edition of *The 700 Club,* and the rest consists of nightly news programs in English and Arabic. Israeli newspapers also include this station's schedule on their television pages. CBN assumed control of the station in April 1982, with the cooperation of what the spokesperson called "the apparent government in the region," or the leaders of Israel's proxy in the area, the South Lebanon Army. The South Lebanon and Israeli armies have provided security for the station, and Israeli customs has facilitated its receipt of broadcasting equipment (see "TV Diversity Grows in Israel," *New York Times,* April 4, 1984). Israel has also taken advantage of the parent network's willingness to promote the state. In early 1987, the Ministry of Tourism sponsored a ten-day visit to Israel by *The 700 Club.* CBN traveled around the country taping a week of programs on Israeli culture and on the country's significance for American Christians.

The Internationalization of French Television

Jill Forbes

The HBO production of *Le Sang des Autres* (1984) might serve as a paradigm of the internationalization of French television. The film was adapted from Simone de Beauvoir's second novel, published in 1945. Like most of her novels, *Le Sang des Autres* eschews a clear narrative drive, concentrating instead on the discussion of philosophical issues through the exemplary stances taken by the communist printworker, Jean, and his lover, Hélène. Although the film is set in Paris during the Occupation and has a French director, Claude Chabrol, it is designed as much for North American as for European viewers, with the principal roles played by American actors. It is, in fact, an English-speaking film in which interpersonal relations, the way individuals address each other, their gestures, their posture, and even the way they make love, are almost tangibly North American. The focus of the narrative has also changed: from the dramatization of moral and political issues—where a choice has to be made between immediate interests and long-term responsibilities—to what the scriptwriter described as a portrayal of how a woman "learns to survive in a man's world."

If the novel is viewed as pure commodity, the film might be regarded as a successful exploitation of an intellectual property, but it strikes any viewer with a knowledge of the text or a familiarity with French history as pure travesty—or, what's worse, theft. However, such a reaction is difficult to justify when any contemporary reading of the novel is bound to be a complex of intertextual constructions that render notions of authenticity in adaptation highly problematic. Occupied France is particularly fertile soil for such constructions: it has a history on film to which both the French and the American industries have contributed with works such as John Frankenheimer's *The Train* and François Truffaut's astonishingly successful *Le Dernier Métro*. In the same way, to a generation of readers in France as well as in the English-speaking world, Simone de Beauvoir, Jean-Paul Sartre, and existentialism are a virtual synecdoche of France. Some of these constructs were wittily and lucidly taken apart in Edgardo Cozarinsky's brilliant film, *Le Guerre d'un Seul Homme*—itself a contributor, of course, to the intertextual web—of which the filmmaker wrote: "Rather than illustrate the truth defined in advance, I wanted to study the play of lies (because I knew there would be lies!), reproduce on a small scale the contradictions and blind spots of an epoch without ever assuming the voice of History but rather recreating the difficulty of seeing clearly the way in which people live in any period."[1] It hardly seems necessary to labor the point that cultural identity and cultural authenticity are incapable of definition outside a historical and ideological framework and that this is particularly the case in film and television, which thrive on adaptation. Therefore, in the international market in cultural commodities, a national perspective might seem difficult to sustain or even to justify.

However self-evident these truths may be, they have not informed French policy towards film and television, which continues to evince some fascinating contradictions. Media policy in France is intimately bound up with cultural policy in general, and for the past thirty years—that is, since television first began to penetrate France—cultural policy has been strongly influenced by foreign policy. As is well known, cultural policy under André Malraux, the Fifth Republic's first minister of culture, was an arm of Gaullism and was used to underline the fact that France represented a "Third Way," a set of values different from either of the superpowers. Under Malraux's direction, culture was conceived as an agent of prestige and reputation, an ideological weapon and an export, sometimes providing justification and sometimes providing camouflage for foreign and industrial relations. The ambiguities of France's relations with NATO were translated almost wholesale into an ambiguous cultural rapport with the United States—a combination of fascination and repugnance, admiration and condemnation—in which the role of culture was to articulate an ideological opposition to what was in reality France's foreign policy, namely support for the West and the Atlantic Alliance.[2] The advent of a Socialist government in 1981 did nothing to alter this state of affairs. In a series of speeches in 1982 and 1983, Jack Lang, the Socialist minister of culture, set out a program of international cultural relations, emphasizing in particular the "European dimension" and the "North-South dimension." The European dimension was inspired by a period when France was both ideologically and politically preeminent: "We are building

Jack Lang, French Minister of Culture, who called *Dallas* "the definition of cultural imperialism."

a movement which affirms the European conscience that was so strong in the eighteenth century."[3] As for the North-South dimension, this was set out in a speech to the UNESCO Conference in Mexico City in July 1982:

Culture is certainly universal but we are careful not to reduce everything to the same level . . . Today we are aware that there is no single world culture . . . The first cultural right is that of people to take their own decisions . . . All our countries accept too passively a certain invasion of or submission to images produced elsewhere and to standardized and stereotyped music, which inevitably wear away national cultures and transmit a uniform lifestyle which it is attempted to impose on the planet as a whole. Basically, this is an attempt to interfere in the internal affairs of such states. Is our fate really to become the serfs of the huge empire of profit?[4]

Thus cultural self-determination is seen as an inalienable right which international empires are attempting to destroy. Lang's discourse is shot through with cold-war paranoia with, on the one side, Stalin's "engineers of the soul" and, on the other side, the American project of "winning hearts and minds." This configuration is posited as a military and economic order with cultural consequences to which European, and more particularly the French, response should be to establish a countervailing cultural order.

For postwar French governments, therefore, both film and television have had a key role to play, not simply in maintaining a national identity but in establishing a sufficiently firm international identity for economic survival to be assured. This highly ambiguous role was neatly summarized in Sean MacBride's remark to the effect that "France is the only country which has realized how important moral and cultural values are at a time of crisis, but she is also . . . the third largest arms exporter in the world."[5]

Unfortunately, French filmmakers and film critics were not so strongly persuaded of the benefits of a national cultural identity. Immediately after the end of the Second World War, the Hollywood studios set about negotiating the conditions under which American films were to be imported into European countries. The agreement signed in 1946 on behalf of France by the former prime minister, Léon Blum, recognized no limit to the import of American films "out of gratitude to the Americans." For many, this was the cultural equivalent of Marshall Aid, since in France Hollywood cinema was frequently regarded as the Trojan Horse of American imperialism.[6] But this was not the attitude of younger French filmmakers who, on the contrary, were enthusiastic admirers. Both the *politique des auteurs* developed by the *Cahiers du cinéma* critics in the 1950s and the practices of the Nouvelle Vague filmmakers in the 1960s testified to their profound admiration for American cinema. Godard, Truffaut, Rivette, Chabrol *(lui-même),* and their contemporaries did not necessarily want to make films that were imitations of classical Hollywood cinema, nor did they always subscribe to their mentor André Bazin's claims that the very *mise-en-scène* of Hollywood cinema was democratic.[7] The source of their admiration lay in what they perceived as cultural authenticity and centrality.

If one recalls Truffaut's celebrated attack on the *tradition de qualité* which supposedly characterized the French cinema of the early 1950s, it was that French cinema was inauthentic: it was not dominated by writers with a personal statement to make, but by adapters whose task was the *mise-en-scène* of existing literary successes. By contrast, the Nouvelle Vague, "defined in part by a new relation between fiction and reality . . . talk about things we know about . . . we attempt to look at France."[8] What the Nouvelle Vague directors admired in Hollywood cinema and attempted to emulate in their own films—so far from being new or avant-garde—was a kind of classicism: "To quote Fénelon," wrote Godard, "I seek 'a sublime so familiar that everybody might be tempted to think he could have achieved it without effort.' "[9] The cinema they admired

Catherine Deneuve in *Le dernier Métro* (François Truffaut, 1980).

combined economy with elegance and was not ashamed of the simplicity which derived from universal pretensions and a moral approach to narrative, a cinema which took both itself and the human predicament seriously and which had a confidence uncomplicated by the self-doubt of modernism. As Godard again wrote: "We should not forget that the facility of transatlantic filmmakers echoes that once found in France in the delightful but unfortunate eighteenth century."[10]

The fact that both Lang and Godard invoke the eighteenth century when talking about the media is instructive. The *grand siècle* of French neoclassicism was also the century of France's imperial power when she ruled the world politically, militarily, and ideologically. The twentieth century represents the equivalent for American imperialists whose cultural expression is quintessentially the cinema. Therefore (or so the argument runs), were France to discover an "authentic" media voice, it would have a weapon with which to challenge American imperialism. Such a voice is clearly not to be found, however, in American producers' adaptations of American material such as *Le Sang des Autres*. In terms of French cultural policy, the media *are* American; the point, however, is to render them French.

There was a period when this appeared to have been achieved to a certain degree in the cinema of the Nouvelle Vague, but to a much greater extent in television, where an interesting symbiosis may be observed between television and Gaullism. It would appear that the majority of new recruits, in the pioneering days of French television, "had suffered under the Occupation or had fought it." Morally speaking, at least, these people were companions of the Resistance since "they were very close to the Liberation period and their elation inspired them to explore the cultural riches of the country which had been repressed for the preceding four years."[11] They had a notion of public service similar to that of Jules Ferry's schoolteachers, so that under the guidance of its first directors, Jean d'Arcy and Albert Ollivier, French television took on the mission to educate, to inform, and to take culture to the people.

Such evangelical certainty had its impact on television production. Television's originality and much of its attraction was based on the live broadcast, and this was the foundation of a school of documentary which set out to explore France and the world. More importantly, perhaps, "a close look at fiction on television in the early 1960s reveals that we had great nineteenth century television . . . Most of the directors had literary training and television simply threw itself into the nineteenth century."[12] This was the great period for television adaptations of Balzac, Stendhal, Flaubert, Hugo, and the rest, largely because, as Stellio Lorenzi explained, "The nineteenth century was a century of hope, of belief in progress, in man." France, said Michel Mitrani, "is a country with a heritage and she is nostalgic for the period of power when that heritage was produced."[13]

The early days of French television fiction were thus animated by a mission and a sense of purpose that led graduates fresh from IDHEC to queue up for jobs. The Buttes Chaumont studios were opened in 1956 to provide working conditions and production norms similar to those which obtained in the cinema. The studios created a sufficient homogeneity of subject matter and *mise-en-scène* in their fictional output to justify calling it a school. Until the advent of the Nouvelle Vague, the Buttes Chaumont School sustained a perfect fit between fiction and viewing public which bespoke a political and ideological consensus, a shared view of the national identity and the role of the media in it. This consensus has not existed since the 1960s, but has remained a nostalgic aspiration for politicians and filmmakers alike.

By 1974, however, any attempt to recapture a position or preeminence for France had effectively been abandoned; the question now became how best to manage a subordinate role. In foreign policy this implied a rethinking of the Atlantic relationship which Giscard d'Estaing undertook

Macha Meril in the title role in *Colette*, a four-part dramatization of the life of the famed French writer featured on Channel Thirteen's "Vive la France!" series, which "presented to metropolitan audiences the best of French culture and cinema."

immediately upon his election as president in that year. In cultural policy, it meant the attempt to establish structures which would enable some vestiges of national specificity to be retained.

In 1974, French television underwent a far-reaching reform. The old ORTF was broken up into seven separate companies, ostensibly in order to introduce some competition between the three television channels. However, the long-term effect of this reform was to drive a wedge between production and distribution and to remove vertical integration within television companies. One of the seven new companies—the successor to the Buttes Chaumont studios—was the Société Française de Production (SFP), from which the television channels were supposed to commission productions. The reform was a failure in that the SFP proved inadequate to the task of production (it was too expensive, too inflexible, and lacking in innovation). As a result, the channels began producing again as well as entering into an increasing number of co-productions. But the question that must be raised, even though it cannot be answered, is the extent to which the SFP's failure was ideological. This, after all, was the studio which throughout the 1950s and early 1960s had the task of presenting the French nation to itself and it is arguable that the real difficulty with the SFP was not union restrictive practices or inadequate accountancy procedures, as critics implied, but a loss of moral nerve. Thereafter, with all television channels increasingly dependent on co-financing and co-production agreements to fill their schedules, the arguments in favor of privatization became overwhelming. Public service broadcasting, which had always been upheld as the guarantor of quality, had become manifestly incapable of producing quality programs by the end of the 1970s.

After their election in 1981, the Socialists duly set about implementing private or nonpublic service television, with a fourth pay-TV channel, Canal Plus, followed by a fifth and a sixth. Of these, only the Fifth Channel was likely to prove a stimulus to indigenous production, since Canal Plus relied on films, series, sports, and increasingly, pornography to sell its wares, almost all of which were imported, while the Sixth Channel, the "music channel," scheduled only pop promos, video clips, and the like. Even if the production houses for such programs were identifiably French, the genres were not. In fact, quite the reverse—and this was precisely the source of their appeal. The government's clear intention was to enable some production and advertising revenue to be retained domestically and to abandon program content to determination by market forces. The Fifth Channel was the only potential new outlet for French production, but the existing quotas for foreign material were deliberately reduced in order to enable it to screen more imported material. In other words, after 1981, government policy with respect to television did nothing to prevent increased imports of mainly American material, although this position contrasted with Jack Lang's stated concern that France "accepts too passively a certain invasion of and submission to images produced elsewhere." Indeed, government policy did much to encourage the importation of foreign material. More than that, however, by introducing a pay-TV channel and a music channel, it aggressively attempted to restructure television so as to accommodate international genres. The Socialist government gave positive encouragement to television in France to lose its national identity. On the one hand, therefore, the French television channels looked increasingly to co-financing as a means of survival and increasingly entered into agreements with HBO and the like, when constrained by lack of resources and production facilities in the second half of the 1970s. On the other hand, the intimate association between public service broadcasting and national television was exploded by pressure from outside and inside (the threat of satellite broadcasts from surrounding countries and the need to invest in cable technology domestically). Just as important, though less tangible, was a moral and ideological evolution brought about by the end of Gaullism. Television for the first two decades of the postwar period was an important factor in national reconstruction in many European countries. As soon as this ceased to be politically necessary, the case for national television collapsed. What is interesting about France is how relatively early this was realized by policy makers and enacted in government legislation, for French television ceased to be national as long ago as 1974.

Notes

1. Quoted in Jill Forbes (ed.), *INA: French for Innovation* (London: British Film Institute, 1984), p. 26.
2. Cf. Jill Forbes, "Cultural Policy: The Soul of Man Under Socialism," in *Mitterand's France,* ed. Sonia Mazey and Michael Newman (London: Croom Helm, 1987), pp. 131-165.
3. Ibid., p. 143.
4. Ibid., p. 162.
5. Ibid., p. 143.
6. Cf. Luc Boltanski, "America, America. Le Plan Marshall et l'importation du 'Management' en France," in *Actes de la Recherche en Sciences Sociales* 38 (May 1981): 19-41.
7. "Le profondeur du champ de William Wyler se veut libérale et démocratique comme la conscience du spectateur américain et les héros du film," *Cahiers du Cinéma* (February 1948): 70.
8. Cf. Jill Forbes, "French Film Culture and British Cinema," in *Imagining France,* ed. C. Crossley and I. Hall (London: Macmillan, 1987), p. 165.
9. Ibid., p. 164.
10. Ibid., p. 164.
11. Forbes, *INA: French for Innovation,* p. 7.
12. Ibid.
13. Ibid., p. 8.

(Not) Coming to Terms With *Dallas*

Ien Ang

Since the early eighties, the prime-time soap opera *Dallas* has been one of the most popular products of American television throughout the world. Currently, more than a hundred countries regularly broadcast *Dallas* on their national networks. Yet, immersed in their own overwhelmingly nationalist television, Americans are generally unaware that since millions of people abroad watch American TV shows day after day, American media hegemony has a very real impact on the texture and substance of foreign cultural experiences. In Holland, for example, the country I come from, when television began to offer American shows in the sixties, *Bonanza* and *The Brady Bunch* were among the first. In the late sixties, *Peyton Place* was very popular on Dutch TV, so popular in fact that when the show was canceled there were loud protests from every segment of the audience. In the seventies, a proliferation of generic theme shows, particularly police dramas such as *Cannon, Starsky and Hutch,* and *Police Woman,* were imported from the U.S. But in spite of this steady diet of American television, it was not until the arrival of *Dallas* in 1981 that an American TV show became such a phenomenal popular success. By the spring of 1982, when the popularity of *Dallas* was at its peak in Holland, more than half of the country's population watched the series every week. The popular press was flooded with stories about Larry Hagman, Victoria Principal, and the rest of the *Dallas* stars; there were JR look-alike contests, bars named after Southfork Ranch, and other promotional spinoffs. There was no doubt that *Dallas* had, in some way, managed to capture the popular imagination. But for this reason, *Dallas* also became the object of great debate among the arbiters of official culture.

Although *Dallas* has been quite a phenomenon in America itself, and will undoubtedly go down in American television history as the beginning of a new and forceful TV genre (i.e., the glamorous prime-time soap opera), in Western Europe the introduction of *Dallas* in the early eighties had a more dramatic and far-reaching cultural impact.[1] In this article, I would like to unravel some of the elements of the specific *ideological context* in which *Dallas* was received in Western Europe, drawing especially from the Dutch experience. To do this, we need to recognize that although the popularity of the show may be almost global (with some telling exceptions, such as Japan and Brazil), its meaning and significance is not the same in every culture. It is the nature of its articulation in the specific cultural context of contemporary Europe that has made *Dallas* so controversial.

Dallas was already extremely popular in America and England when it was launched in Holland. Fueled by this awareness, its introduction was by no means an "innocent" event; on the contrary, it was accompanied by an extraordinary amount of publicity, speculation, and rumor. As a consequence, a "moral panic" was created around the show, even before the first episode was shown. One magazine caption screamed, "Help, *Dallas* is coming!" This set the tone for the way in which the show was culturally positioned in serious public discourse. *Dallas* signified *danger,* a threat to the national community, especially because critics expected (and feared) that the show would "overwhelm" and "conquer" large sections of the audience. The "Americanness" of the program—denoting both the substance and form of the show as well as its commercial production context—was one of the key terms through which concern was articulated.

The predominance and enormous popularity of American television remains a very controversial issue in Europe. Shows like *Dallas* are not exactly the type of program that politicians and broadcasters have in mind when they speak about what is ideal for television. Since the fifties, television's ideal mission has been generally conceived as pedagogical. Most critics assert that television should be a "window on the world" for the mass audience, meaning that it should broaden mass understanding of society, elevate taste, and generally enhance people's awareness of their duties as national citizens. Although the European public-service networks have always offered a large number of entertainment programs, the programs that are generally perceived as providing television with status and legitimacy are current-affairs programs. But these "quality" programs have never been as popular as some domestic entertainment shows—and American television shows. The popularity of American entertainment is particularly irritating to official cultural guardians. The former chairman of the Dutch Broadcasting Foundation says disdainfully: "The Dutch networks of course don't exist primarily to broadcast *Dallas*. No one can

Tina Louise, guest star on *Dallas*.

maintain that these American series are of a high standard as regards content. They are at most cleverly made."[2]

It is not so strange, then, that *Dallas* has caused sleepless nights for many European broadcasting officials. The conventional model of European television, organized according to a state-controlled, national public service policy, is in crisis. The advent of new commercial channels, the introduction of satellite and cable broadcasting, the popularity of American programming, and the restructuring of television viewing habits have combined to drive the existing institutions into desperate, defensive positions. Thus, the commercialization of European television—and by extension, American media imperialism—is frequently cited as a metaphor for the ever-intensifying decline of classical European culture (a particularly precipitous decline now that Europe has lost its economic and political hegemony in international affairs and finds itself sandwiched between the two superpowers). And when it comes to debates over the future of European culture, television occupies a central role, with American television—in particular, *Dallas*—representing the values to be avoided. As Michèlle Mattelart has observed, *Dallas* "has become the perfect hate symbol, the cultural poverty . . . against which one struggles."[3]

So, *Dallas* is not just another popular TV show. In official public discourse, it symbolizes cultural erosion, a menace to European standards and values, a threat to popular consciousness and public well-being. The former French minister of culture, Jack Lang, proclaimed *Dallas* the "symbol of cultural imperialism." In several countries the show has even been an issue in parliament. In West Germany, for example, a Social Democrat speaking in the *Bundestag* dismissed *Dallas* as a drama populated by "plastic people from another world," which would be dangerous for a mass audience because it would reinforce hatred, jealousy, and selfishness. Here, *Dallas* was denounced as a glorification of capitalism, but in Denmark one member of parliament argued that *Dallas* was communist propaganda, an evil agitation against the values of family life. Meanwhile, in England, "wall-to-wall *Dallas*" became a common expression used to suggest a nightmarish future of television overtaken by commercialism. Apprehension, aversion, and contempt were the dominant tendencies in the official European public responses to *Dallas*. Underlying these responses was a fundamental judgment: *Dallas* lacks quality.

Yet, this negative judgment is not simply a lofty but basically well-intentioned and dignified reaction to an unwelcome development. If *Dallas* is rejected because of its supposedly "low quality," more then pure aesthetics is at stake. For, as Andreas Huyssen has observed, "to reduce all cultural criticism to the problem of quality is a symptom of the anxiety of contamination."[4] Lurking behind what Huyssen has called "the Great Divide" (i.e., the kind of discourse which insists on the categorical distinction between high art and mass culture) is a deeper fear of contamination: the fundamentally *political* concern over the defilement and, eventually, the elimination of European cultural identity.

This cultural contamination is all the more threatening because it involves a sort of "conspiracy" between external and internal forces. The intrusion of American mass culture into European domains is one thing, but it is even more disconcerting to European aesthetes that the "unruly masses" obviously fall for it—with a vengeance.[5] In spite of all the criticisms and official denunciations, millions of viewers continue to watch *Dallas* week after week. Clearly, these people *enjoy* watching *Dallas,* for them the show serves as an object of pleasure. The "official" discursive positioning of *Dallas* as "bad object" is thus in flagrant contradiction to the practical pleasures it offers its viewers. This dialectic is characteristic of its European reception. As a consequence, in Europe, watching *Dallas* is not an innocent cultural practice, but one that is heavily charged with ideological meanings in that it takes place within the context of this

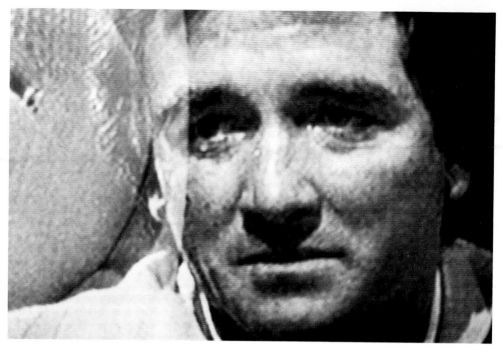

Patrick Duffy as Bobby Ewing on *Dallas*.

ongoing public debate. Of course, everyone can freely choose to watch *Dallas* or not, but socially speaking, the meaning of watching *Dallas* proves to be tightly bound up with the way the show, as a popular American TV product, is positioned in the larger cultural field.

The cultural discourse which defines *Dallas* is not limited to the boardrooms of policy makers or to the minds of high culture-oriented critics. It also makes its authority felt in a much wider social environment, among the strata of the general television-viewing population. This is evident when we analyze how ordinary viewers who hate *Dallas* tend to account for their dislike. Their sense of anger and indignation reflects an official cultural antipathy toward mass-culture forms. Their rejection of *Dallas* tends to be accompanied by a total moral, political, and aesthetic denunciation of the show.[6]

My opinion of Dallas? *Well, I'd be glad to give it to you: WORTHLESS RUBBISH. I find it a typical American program, simple and commercial, role-affirming, deceitful. The thing so many American programs revolve around is money and sensation . . . The stories themselves are mostly not very important. You never have to think for a moment, they think for you.*

Apparently, those who dismiss shows like *Dallas* can be so judgmental and can express their opinion in such a seemingly self-assured way because they are widely encouraged by the aesthetic norms and valuations established by an official discourse that privileges high culture. This discourse not only delivers the terms and justifications for a rational repudiation of the show, but also tends to induce a feeling of superiority in those who hate *Dallas*. Those who oppose the show often ridicule those who consider themselves *Dallas* fans. Yet, as a result, the opponents often seem to feel frustratingly isolated, part of an enlightened minority surrounded by a horde of passive cultural dopes.

I don't understand . . . why so many people watch it, as there are lots of people who find it a serious matter if they have to miss a week. At school you really notice it; when you turn up on Wednesday morning, it's "Did you see Dallas, *wasn't it fabulous?" Now and then I get really annoyed, because I find it just a waste of time watching it . . . Then you hear them saying that they had tears in their eyes when something happened to someone in the film, and I just can't understand it.*

The debate over the merits of high culture versus mass culture then, is not limited to the official circles of politics and culture. It also creates a real tension among "ordinary people," an everyday rift between those who loathe *Dallas* and the show's fans. Since the accepted position—that affirmed by national cultures—is to reject *Dallas,* opponents can assume a comfortable position of legitimacy. For the *Dallas* fans, however, the position that dismisses mass culture constitutes a massive assault on their personal "taste," their pleasure. Fans respond in two different ways to this assault. They may react in a cheerfully defensive manner, as did the viewer who remarked, "When I say I like watching *Dallas,* I often get odd reactions. But I also like eating at McDonalds and like poetry a lot, things that get just as strange a reaction." More often, however, viewers are uncomfortable with their own attachment to the show, since rationally they tend to *agree* with the cultural norms that discriminate high art from low. Their responses are often rather self-demeaning and contradictory. One viewer observed:

I myself enjoy Dallas *and the tears roll down when something tragic happens in it . . . In my circle too people react dismissively to it, they find it a typical commercial program far beneath their standards. I find you can't just relax with a program like this, although you have to keep your eye on the kind of influence such a program can have, it is role-confirming, class-confirming, etc. And it's useful too if you think what kind of cheap sentiment really does get to you.*

Victoria Principal as Pam on *Dallas*.

In other words, even though she enjoys watching *Dallas,* this viewer does not take issue with the official judgment that it is an inferior and potentially damaging form of culture. To her, enjoying *Dallas* is somehow "wrong," even though her "experience" may tell her differently.

Here, the effects of the public or "official" condemnation of popular culture appears in its most dramatic and detrimental form. The privileging of "good" television produces a sort of ideological closure; its authority makes it difficult if not impossible for *Dallas* fans to construct an autonomous *positive* discourse about what the show means to them. In other words, what this "discourse of the Great Divide" produces is a silence as to the very real pleasures that people experience from watching *Dallas.* It entails a downright rejection of that pleasure, it cannot understand it except in a negative way. It is "cultural absolutism."

I do not want to defend *Dallas* without any qualifications. Nor is it my intention to pursue a mere reversal of the high art/popular culture debate and advance a ruthless populist stance in which anything goes that is popular with "the masses." What is desperately needed, however, is to break the discursive closure, to deconstruct its assumptions and presumptions and to develop an alternative discourse in which the pleasures of commercial American television are at least taken seriously *as* pleasurable. By denying the legitimacy of this appeal, European broadcasters have failed to comprehend the success of American television, and large parts of the viewing audience have lacked the terms to account for their experiences of pleasure or displeasure, enjoyment or boredom. What the discourse of the Great Divide makes impossible, in short, is the development of alternative, intellectually sophisticated discourses which can come to terms with *Dallas* and its look-alikes in a manner that is sensitive to both its pleasures and its discontents, that remains constantly open to the *different* ways in which people can view a single television show.

One discursive strategy for addressing *Dallas* has flourished and seems to ameliorate superficial high art/popular culture distinction: irony. Watching *Dallas* ironically means that the show is celebrated precisely because it is such a "bad" show. Here, pleasure in *Dallas* takes on a parodic twist; the adoption of a willfully superior and euphoric attitude towards the show creates a very comfortable form of pleasure. A regular viewer recounted:

Dallas, *God, don't talk to me about it. I'm just hooked on it! But you wouldn't believe the number of people who say to me, "I thought you were against capitalism." I am, but* Dallas *is just so tremendously exaggerated, it has nothing to do with capitalists anymore. It's just sheer artistry to make up such nonsense.*

Another viewer confessed in similar terms:

As you may notice, I watch a lot, and (you may find this a bit big-headed) I find it amusing precisely because it's so ghastly (if you know what I mean). If, for example, I had had to play Miss Ellie's role, when her breast is amputated, I would really kill myself laughing, with that slobbering Jock hanging over me, full of good intentions.

How can we make sense of this ironic viewing attitude? Formally speaking, we could evaluate this twisty fondness as a symbolic "declaration of independence" from the power of the show, as a way of maintaining or constructing a certain critical distance towards its representations. However, the ideological significance and implications of this ironical attitude depend on the larger cultural context into which popular television is inserted. Therefore, although the stance of ironical distance may function as a liberating *moment* of critical disengagement from the seduction strategies of commercial culture, given the dominance of the discourse of the Great Divide it merely tends to reinforce existing cultural hierarchies in which cultural elitism and paternalism are still a dominant force. There

Larry Hagman as J.R. on *Dallas.*

the popularity of shows like *Dallas* is basically viewed with suspicion because it indicates that the mass audience does not behave according to the standards of taste and cultural values set by the European cultural elite. Irony is a response that produces a "resolution" for this antagonism: it is a means to devalue something while at the same time enjoying it from a disdainful position. A very conservative position indeed.

Notes

1. Textually speaking, the *Dallas* Europeans get to see is somewhat different from the *Dallas* Americans watch. First of all, no ads are inserted between parts of an episode. *Dallas* is shown as one long TV movie of fifty minutes. Secondly, of course, there is the problem of language. In Holland, all American shows are subtitled, but in Germany, France, or Spain they are dubbed so that the viewers in those countries get to hear the characters speak German, French, or Spanish.
2. Eric Jurgens, in *De Volkskrant,* November 14, 1981.
3. In Armand Mattelart, Xavier Delcourt, and Michèlle Mattelart, *International Image Markets* (London: Comedia Publishing Group, 1984), p. 90.
4. Andreas Huyssen, *After the Great Divide* (Bloomington: Indiana University Press, 1986), p. ix.
5. For a history of the conflicted reception of American mass culture in Britain after World War II, see Dick Hebdige, "Towards a Cartography of Taste, 1935-1964," in *Popular Culture: Past and Present,* ed. Bernard Waites, Tony Bennett, and Graham Martin (London: Croom Helm, 1982), pp. 194-218.
6. Reactions to *Dallas* were acquired through an ad placed in a popular woman's magazine in the Netherlands. People were asked to write letters to the author about what they think about the show. For a more extensive account of the responses I received, and other issues discussed here, see Ien Ang, *Watching Dallas: Soap Opera and the Melodramatic Imagination* (London and New York: Methuen, Inc., 1985).

Wall-to-Wall *Dallas*:
The U.S.-U.K. Trade in Television

Richard Collins

M edia analysis is in danger of repeating the behavior of the Bourbons: learning nothing and forgetting everything. Slowly and laboriously, simple behaviorist stimulus and response models of effects and audience research are being driven from the field by more nuanced and mediated models of the consumption and effects of the mass media. A variety of studies, including Stuart Hall's "Encoding and Decoding"[1] and Dave Morley's *The Nationwide Audience*[2] have asserted the differentiality of audience understandings and actions. Yet this understanding of the specificity of microcosmic responses to television programs is rarely replicated when the macrocosmic impact of programming is considered. Studies of world information flows assert confidently that imperialistic relationships exist, that cultural imperialism is rampant, and that everywhere the media are American.[3] However, much evidence suggests that the same differential found at the microlevel of consumption is found at the macrolevel, though there has been little reconsideration of the media imperialism thesis other than the 1980 studies by Lee[4] and Ravault.[5]

In Europe the alarm at the impact of American television programming (for which *Dallas* has become a codeword) has continued, becoming sufficiently fashionable to have assumed the dimensions of moral panic. "Wall-to-wall *Dallas*" is by now the accepted shorthand of critics anticipating the effects of the general introduction of pay cable television to the UK (Chris Dunkley even used that as the title for his recent book[6]) and a French government minister warned that Luxembourg's broadcast satellite was "attacking our artistic and cultural integrity."[7] Indeed, the dreaded *Dallas* was chosen by the Commission of the European Communities to exemplify the perils of non-European television:

There is already a certain uniformity in the range of films screened on television in the Community. Programmes such as Dallas *are carried by almost every television channel in the member states. The creation of a common market for television production is thus one essential step if the dominance of the big American media corporations is to be counterbalanced.*[8]

National broadcasting authorities have recently attempted to regain audiences lost to *Dallas* by reworking it in a national idiom—e.g., France's *Chateauvallon,* Canada's *Vanderburg,* and the Netherlands' *Herrenstraat 10.* These initiatives are in turn perceived as imitative amplifications of U.S. imperialism and distinctive symptoms of the decline of authentic national cultural production. But the impact of *Dallas,* and of U.S. television in general, is far from unambiguous.

The trade in television programming between the U.S. and the U.K is not one of unequal exchange from which only the United States benefits. The factors that have sustained U.S. dominance in the world trade in audiovisual media—whether films for theatrical exhibition or programming for television—may be changing and new opportunities may be arising for foreign producers to exploit the comparative advantages in the U.S. domestic market that have hitherto been the prerogative of American producers. Twenty years ago the American automobile industry's command of its domestic market was considered unassailable. It was unimaginable that Americans would drive anything other than six-seated V8s. Now Chrysler has gone to the wall and come back again and the bottom end of the U.S. automobile market is dominated by Toyota, Nissan, and Subaru, the top by BMW and Mercedes-Benz. There are grounds for believing that U.S. television programming may experience similar import penetration.

Information is a tradeable product like vehicles, fish, coal, and chemicals. Just as nation-states see the terms of trade and import/export ratios in coal and fish as legitimate national interests, so do they in information products. Given that comparative advantage in the production of tradeable productions resides at different times with different producers, there is no particular economic reason why a nation-state should seek autarchy in the production of information goods any more than Switzerland should seek to be self-sufficient in seafish, Britain in bananas, or Egypt in forest products. In the production of other commodities an international division of labor takes place, why not with information goods?

The evidence of history is that for the kind of information product represented by *Dallas* (high-budget soap opera/family melodrama narrative fiction), the U.S. has long been the overwhelmingly dominant producer.

By 1925 a third of all foreign revenue came from the United Kingdom alone, where American films captured 95% of the market. In the same period, 77% of the features shown in France came from the United States, as did about 66% in Italy.[9]

In 1925, Guback adds, 235 million feet of motion pictures were exported and 7 million feet imported by the United States. This American dominance in the world market for audiovisual information goods has been consolidated subsequently by successive innovations in technology and product and by raising the costs of production and therefore barriers to the entry of competitors to the market (the star system, sound, color, wide-screen, 3D, epic scale, special effects, and so on). In most European countries, a national-film production industry survives only through state subsidy and import quotas. The U.S. industry has very successfully exploited its major comparative advantage, the large size of its (rather chauvinistic) domestic market. Gordon[10] shows the relative size of the U.S. and EEC film markets in 1972:

1972 Box Office Grosses in Millions of Dollars	
US	1300
Italy	364
France	202
West Germany	186
Britain	154
Belgium	33
Netherlands	29
Denmark	23
EEC	991

The large size of the U.S. domestic market, its resistance to penetration by foreign products, and the evolution of large firms capable of accommodating both great demand and considerable market capriciousness (of ten films, one may make very high profits, six may lose greater or lesser amounts, three may break even; thus long-term success will only be available to large-scale producers) has given the U.S. film and production industry very substantial advantages in the international audiovisual information goods markets. Many of these characteristics have been replicated in the television programming market. Varis[11] has shown the United States' importation of foreign television programming to be exceptionally low (between 1 percent and 2 percent imports). The U.S. market for television programming in 1980 was $2.8 billion.[12] This sum is enormous in comparison with the size of the U.K programming market—£937 million in 1982.[13] The U.S. market was divided in these proportions: the networks, 63 percent; syndication and barter (i.e., the independents), 23 percent; PBS, 4 percent; Pay TV, 9 percent. The U.K. market was simply divided: ITV, 69 percent, and BBC, 31 percent.

However, the dominance of U.S. producers in European markets is considerably less marked when the television distribution and exhibition system is considered—particularly when compared with that which exists for film. Film distribution in Europe was, and is, dominated by U.S. companies; in television (with some recent exceptions, notably Italy), distribution and exhibition is the monopoly of a state agency or is closely regulated by the state. The film exhibition sector in Europe expanded beyond the capacity of domestic producers and a conflict of interests developed between the domestic exhibition sector, enjoying a kind of comprador relationship with U.S. producers and distributors, and the domestic production sector. Exhibitors in Britain had to be compelled by quota legislation to exhibit British films—their economic interests were in general better served by exhibiting imported material made with higher budgets and featuring international stars, and sold to exhibitors at low cost. In 1982, in a belated recognition that the British film production industry was producing too few films for the exhibition sector to fulfill its 15 percent British quota, the quota was reduced to zero percent by the national government.

In contrast to the long-accepted dominance of the United States in the film business, British television has been more resistant to U.S. penetration. In 1981, television transmission of non-British/non-EEC programming was, for commercial television, limited to 14 percent. In October 1984 this quota was raised by 1.5 percent to permit more programming from the Commonwealth. No formal restrictions exist for the BBC which has in general limited itself to the 14 percent prescribed by the statute for commercial television. However, there are signs that the BBC's financial difficulties are leading to its transmission of increasing quantities of foreign programming. In 1982 (BRU 1983), 31 percent of the Corporation's prime-time television came from overseas, 26 percent from the U.S. Seventeen percent of BBC1 programming that year was of non-BBC origin, 22 percent of BBC2 programming was of non-BBC origin (although these percentages may, of course, have included British or EEC material originated "out of house"). The balance of trade in television programs between the U.K. and North America (statistics that

"For God, for Country, and for Texas."

disaggregate Canada and the U.S. are unavailable), over the last five years for which information is available, has turned against the U.K. However, a longer term indexical analysis modifies this conclusion by demonstrating that there is considerable variation in the trading relationships between the U.K. and North America:

Balance of Trade in Television Programs between UK and North America:

£m	1977	1978	1979	1980	1981	1982	1983	1984	1985	1986
	+11	+5	+3	+12	+2	-1	0	-13[14]	+28	+12

During the period 1977–84, U.K. exporters maintained the largest proportion of their sales to North America. (The North American component of overall television program sales was 56 percent both in 1977 and 1984 and varied between 43 and 61 percent overall.) But U.K. importers increased the proportion of overall purchases from North America (the North American component of overall television program imports varied between 43 percent in 1977 and 71 percent in 1984).

Essentially British television distribution/exhibition capacity has been rationed by the national government. The protected and rationed domestic distribution/exhibition sector has permitted the production of high budget, high production values, quality programming in the U.K. Revenues from the sale of audiences to advertisers or from the sale of broadcast receiving licenses are deployed to supply programs to a market that is both guaranteed 84.5 percent of broadcast hours (for U.K./EEC programs) and limited (four channels). Control of the distribution/exhibition sector is tight and has permitted the growth of a production sector in Britain where the quality and quantity of domestically produced programs strengthens the bargaining position of British broadcasters in their negotiations for the purchase of foreign programming and whose own products can successfully be sold in international markets.

At a level of economic analysis, then, it is an open question whether the public interest in the U.K. has been best served by the film industry regime; supplying the British entertainment/information goods market with cheaply purchased, high-budget, quality products imported largely from the U.S.; or by the television industry regime, denying entry to 86 percent of the British entertainment/information goods market to foreign productions. Either way, it is clear that with information goods other criteria than purely economic ones obtain. One of my purposes has been to show that some form of economic analysis and policy has to be formulated if questions of communication sovereignty and cultural imperialism are to be addressed sensibly. But the arguments about a New World Information Order, free flows versus balanced flows, etc., show that many interests see more than economics at stake in the production and consumption of information goods.

Concern about the effects of mass communications has been persistent since the beginning of the mass media era—whether that is dated from Gutenberg's or Marconi's time. However, in the decades since World War II, the focus has shifted from concern for individuals and under-represented or vulnerable groups within a particular nation-state to concern with and for the nation itself. The threat to communications sovereignty latent since the beginning of the twentieth century and slowly actualized in North America (Canadian subordination to U.S. broadcasting remains the classic, even though earliest, instance) has with the triple impact of new distribution technologies, new ideologies of deregulation, and the accelerating demand for quantities of high-budget but low-cost software, become a matter of general concern. In Western Europe, national governments have lost confidence in their ability to maintain communications sovereignty previously buttressed by national newspaper and publishing industries and state control of broadcasting. Italy's experience is typical: following the Tele-Biella judgment, the national broadcasting monopoly's

Dallas: A Lorimar Production.

access to the Italian people eroded, principally in favor of unregulated private broadcasters distributing largely U.S. programming. Moreover, the critique of the loss of communications sovereignty customarily runs in harness with a qualitative judgment that the new order and its product are inferior to the old. The concept of cultural imperialism is dependent on both quantitative and qualitative judgments. The conditions of quantitative subordination are economic and organizational, the conditions of qualitative subordination are cultural and aesthetic.

It is an enduring European trope to hold up a mirror to U.S. chauvinism. In the U.K., critical concern focuses on the proliferation of U.S.-style hamburger outlets, not on the proliferation of Turkish, Greek, and Lebanese kebab houses, or French, Italian, Indian, and Chinese restaurants. At the same time, the productivity of U.S. cultural influences in Europe are very quickly forgotten—e.g., the appropriation of its practices by modernist artists (e.g., Brecht and Grosz), or the impact of Hollywood cinema on the postwar European cinema (the Nouvelle Vague, the New German Cinema, or Italian filmmakers like Sergio Leone or, as has recently been claimed, Gianni Amelio).

The shift in film and television production from an artisanal mode of production, where products are strongly marked by an authorial signature, whether that of director or scriptwriter, to series production, in which it hardly makes sense to ask who is the author of *Dallas* or *Coronation Street,* is customarily deplored as a particularly insidious form of cultural imperialism. Yet this seems to me no more cultural imperialism than the adoption in Britain of the electrical engineering manufacturing techniques of Halske and Siemens, Pascalian mathematics, or the astronomical theories of Copernicus and Galileo. U.S. television series production techniques have dominated television in Britain since the 1960s, co-existing with (some would claim making possible) British television's substantial dominance of the U.K. audience ratings. It is this format that broadcast media have uniquely made possible and conjured into existence.

Radio and television's creation of an audience consuming a "flow" of programming at a rate of four hours of broadcasting per day makes possible (and demands) temporally extensive continuous fictions in a way that neither the newspapers nor the cinema did. Cultural forms like *Coronation Street* and *Dr. Who* have endured in the U.K. for more than twenty years. What literary or dramatic precedents are there for narratives that exist without closure for such duration? It is this shift in program form, as well as the demand from audiences for choice *and* high-budget productions, that has created an international marketplace for products like *Dallas,* although U.S. producers are not the only players.

One condition of consistent success in the international market is the production of a product appealing to international tastes and with a national content confined to the internationally current stereotypes of individual national histories and formations. Thus British television presents to the world a costumed image of Britain as a rigidly, but harmoniously hierarchized, class society: *Brideshead Revisited, The Six Wives of Henry VIII, Upstairs, Downstairs;* Japan, the shogun and samurai pasts; Italy, *The Borgias. Dallas, Dynasty, Hotel,* and *Flamingo Road* represent the United States to international television viewers in contemporary melodrama in which the values of capitalist business and the family are presented both positively and negatively. But so popular are serial melodramas generally on British TV, that in May 1983, *Dallas* came only eleventh in the fifty highest audiences of the month, beaten by sundry episodes of the ITV serials *Coronation Street* and *Crossroads.* (Of the fifty, twenty-four were watching domestic melodramas, of which twenty-two were British and two of U.S. origin.)

Nonetheless, screening American programming is an attractive option for British broadcasters. By doing so, programs with high production budgets acquired at low cost will tend to attract and retain audiences at a

Southfork Ranch, the principal setting on *Dallas*.

lower cost per thousand viewers than will domestically produced material. To establish relative production and acquisition costs of the programming is extremely difficult. The industry is a remarkably secretive one and both sellers and buyers are reluctant to reveal the costs of transactions. To these difficulties should be added those of fluctuating sterling/dollar rates and significant and rapid changes in production costs. (Grieve, Horner cite a 60 percent rise in cost per episode of *Lou Grant* between 1977 and 1981.[15]) Both factors mean that the figures that follow should be treated with some caution. However, they are figures around which there is significant convergence from a variety of sources, industry journals, consultants' reports, or my interviews (mostly off the record) with industry sources.

In 1983, *Variety*[16] estimated the U.K. costs per hour of TV programming as follows: ITV £40,000; BBC £30,000; Channel Four £25,000; bought in U.S. programs £2,000. In the next month, the same paper[17] estimated the production fee per episode of U.S. TV series as follows: *Dynasty,* $850,000; *Hotel,* $700,000; *Dallas,* $850,000; *Falcon Crest,* $750,000; *Knots Landing,* $650,000; *St. Elsewhere,* $750,000 (i.e., for an hour of product). A year earlier *TV World*[18] estimated the following world prices for U.S. sales of a half-hour TV series: Belgium $1000-1500; France $8500-10,000; Italy $4000-4200; Netherlands $1900-2000; Spain $1400-1900; U.K. $9000-10,000; West Germany $8500-18,000.

However, *Broadcasting* points out that half hours are

considerably cheaper . . . less than 50% of what it costs . . . to license a full hour episode. . . . The reasons half hours are considerably less expensive . . . than full hours are numerous but heading the list is that video tape is used. . . . Another factor that contributes to the less expensive half hour show is that they are usually produced on permanent sets in studios and do not require the elaborate location shooting and special effects often required by full hour dramas.[19]

The *TV World* figures for exhibition prices are likely to be less reliable than *Variety's* for production prices, but even as ballpark estimates it can be seen that for, say, an episode of *Dynasty* costing $850,000, a TV channel in the U.K. paid about $20,000, and the Netherlands $4000.

In 1985, *Variety* reported that the BBC had been acquiring *Dallas* for $43,000 per episode and that unprecedented competition between the BBC and the British commercial company Thames led the BBC to bid $47,500 per episode and for the rival—and successful—bidder to secure the series for $60,000 per episode. *Variety* noted that "this may be a record for a series import in the British market."[20] Programing costs per thousand viewers for the BBC showing *Dallas* in a May 1983 screening attracting 12.7 million viewers at a cost per episode estimated at $43,000 would then have been $3.39. If we calculate the cost per thousand of the highest rated British program transmitted by the BBC in May 1983, *That's Life*—screened to 12.6 million viewers at *Variety's* figure of £30,000 or $47,000 per hour—it will have a cost per thousand viewers that is higher than the cost of *Dallas*, i.e., $3.70 per thousand. The economic benefits of showing *Dallas* hardly need underlining.

With a more successful U.S. program than *Dallas* benefits are even higher. In 1984, the *Financial Times* estimated the cost to the BBC of the eight-hour U.S. miniseries *The Thorn Birds* as £600,000. The last episode's screening attracted an audience of 15.75 million viewers (then the BBC's biggest audience for more than two years, though still well below peak audiences for *Coronation Street,* a serial that has run on ITV for twenty-five years). The *Financial Times* hypothesized the costs of the BBC originating *The Thorn Birds* at a minimum of £2 million.[21] However, if we believe those commentators who suggest that the BBC's screening of *The Thorn Birds* was the provocation that led the government to establish the Peacock Committee to review BBC funding, the costs of *The Thorn Birds* may have been very high indeed.

British TV is required to exhibit 84.5 percent British/EEC productions and has developed a successful production strategy for British and international markets. Thames Television produces 950 hours of programming annually at a cost of £30,000,000,[22] i.e., at an average cost per hour of approximately £31,600, of which an unspecified number of hours produced revenues from foreign sales of £18,000,000 (of which £9 million were U.S. sales and £2.5 million Australian). The *Sunday Times*[23] estimates revenues from U.S. sales of $20,000 per hour for British producers, i.e., there are grounds for belief that British producers are able to sell an hour of television into the U.S. market at about the same price that U.S. producers sell an hour of television into the British market. I have been unable to confirm this supposition since U.S. commercial stations and distributors have been unwilling to reveal the acquisition costs to U.S. television stations of British programming (e.g., of *The Benny Hill Show,* cited as yielding "the biggest grosses of any overseas production in the USA"[24]). Nor are audience ratings in the public domain in the United States. However, interviews with a senior executive in Mobil Oil (the sponsor of *Masterpiece Theatre* on PBS) and senior figures in PBS and the Corporation for Public Broadcasting have enabled me to establish acquisition costs of programming for *Masterpiece Theatre* and ratings for representative screenings.

Masterpiece Theater acquires its programs principally from the U.K. and to a lesser extent from other Anglophone producers such as Ireland and Australia. A June 1983 screening (chosen as close as possible to the May 1983 screening of *Dallas* already discussed) of an episode of the BBC drama *Sons and Lovers* achieved a share of 4.2 percent of the U.S. national audience (reached by 273 PBS stations offering *Masterpiece Theatre)* or 3.5 million households, each of which is estimated to have a prime-time viewing population of 1.7 people. Therefore, 5,950,000 Americans watched an episode of *Sons and Lovers* (after at least three previous episodes had been transmitted and an audience for the series built). If we assume an acquisition cost of $100,000 per hour for *Sons and Lovers* (at the low end of $100,000/$200,000 per hour range of acquisition costs cited for *Masterpiece Theatre*), we find a cost per thousand viewers of $16.80. Compared to the BBC's cost per thousand viewers of $3.39 for *Dallas, Masterpiece Theatre's* British programming in the U.S. looks expensive. Though the cost of acquisition by Mobil is, of course, less than the cost of production of a comparable *ab initio.*

The strength of the U.S. market and its resistance to colonization by foreign information goods is the foundation of the success of U.S.

producers in world markets. But there are interesting signs that the comparative advantage long enjoyed by U.S. audiovisual media producers may be ending. The major strength of the U.S. producers has been their ability to recoup their production costs—even costs of $850,000 per hour—from U.S. sales. This ability is in turn dependent on customers'—U.S. television stations'—ability to pay such sums for programming. This ability is in turn conditional on the existence of a small number of exhibition channels—the networks—and their ability to command the lion's share of TV advertising revenues and recycle them (after taking profits and network costs) to producers. But now it seems that the dominance of the networks is waning. Independent broadcasters are increasingly challenging the networks and are—within the limits of FCC regulation—constituting themselves through common ownership and syndication of programming as challengers to the networks. Grieve, Horner[25] projects a trend in which the U.S. network share continues to decline:

Percentage Share of Viewing	1975	1981	1986	1991
Network Stations	84	75	67	56
Independent & Public	16	22	22	23
Pay Services		2	7	13
Non Pay Cable Services		1	3	7

If the attrition of the networks' share of audiences and revenues continues to be faster than growth in aggregate revenues then the revenue pool will be shared more evenly among a greater number of broadcasters with each commanding less resources than do the biggest current ones. The ability to pay for the production costs of an episode of, say, *Dallas* at an acquisition cost of $750,000-800,000 for an initial screening and $65,000-70,000 for a second screening[26] will decline. But the ability of a greater number to pay intermediate prices for programming will rise. In this new regime, where very high-cost programming may no longer be afforded and in which demand and ability to pay for low to mid-cost programming increases, there may well be increased opportunities for sale to the U.S. by foreign producers. Increase in U.S. distribution capacity (through licensing of new terrestrial broadcasters and satellite and cable-delivered pay television) and redistribution of advertising revenue among broadcasters are likely to diminish the comparative advantage of a strong home market resistant to foreign products long enjoyed by the U.S. film and TV producers. But there are also counter indications to this scenario: the merger of one network, ABC, with one of the principle independent

Julie Goodyear as Bet Lynch with Roy Barraclough as Alec Gilroy in *Coronation Street*, Britain's longest-running prime-time drama serial. Consistently among the top-ten-rated shows, it is the story of everyday life in a small English working-class community.

groups, Capital Cities Communications,[27] to form the largest broadcasting group in the U.S. suggests that other resolutions of this conflict are possible.

Studying the trade in TV programming between the U.S. and the U.K. shows that the media imperialism thesis is by no means clearly demonstrated. U.K. producers are able to sell to the U.S. markets on considerably better terms than U.S. producers are able to sell to the U.K. The volume of trade between the U.S. and U.K. in TV programming now favors the U.S. but there are grounds for supposing that that balance may in the future become less unfavorable to the U.K. This does not disprove the general thesis that media imperialism is practiced by the United States, but it does suggest that the thesis demands more thorough demonstration than it customarily receives. The tasks for advocates of the thesis are not only to demonstrate (as I suspect could be done) that the U.S.-U.K. trade is an exceptional one and may best be regarded—as does Tunstall[28]—as the U.K. acting as a kind of cadet to the U.S. in the imperialism game. Other tasks include showing that an adverse balance of trade in one sector, cultural goods, correlates with a general economic, political, or cultural subordination. As Ravault[29] points out, this is not easy to do. Countries such as West Germany and Japan or the Nordic countries have all combined economic prosperity and political and cultural independence with high levels of importation of cultural goods from the Anglophone block—notably the Unites States, the U.K., and Australia. It would further require demonstration that consumption of U.S. cultural goods produces the feared threat to cultural integrity and independence of consumers and a disadvantageous homogenization and "Americanization" of audiences. Liebes and Katz's work,[30] among others, suggests that different audiences produce highly differentiated readings of *Dallas*. These appropriations of *Dallas* may, of course, though different, be equally "bad" for audiences, but here, too, there are some grounds for skepticism. Since the 1950s, work of film theorists has established a convincing aesthetic and cultural case for Hollywood cinema of the 1940s, 1950s, and early 1960s. Contemporary feminist theory positively reappropriates the despised melodramas and women's weepies of the American cinema. If it can be done for Universal films, why not for Lorimar television?

A number of Québécois writers have testified to the positive influence of the U.S. mass media in breaking the grip of "La Grande Noirceur" in Quebec and the development of a modern secular society in Francophone North America. Gilles Carle's recollection of his childhood may stand as emblematic of this testimony that not all transborder data flows are baleful indices of the rest of the world's subordination as periphery to the dominant central metropole of the United States:

Our radio picked up Buffalo and Montreal, always together, never separate, so that the religious broadcasts always had a pleasant background of country and western music. . . . We seven children would thus recite our rosaries at a gallop, learning that in Quebec the most contradictory dreams are possible.[31]

Notes

A version of this article was published in *Screen* 27, no. 3/4 (May-August 1986): 66-77.

1. Stuart Hall, "Encoding/Decoding," in *Culture, Media, Language,* ed. Stuart Hall et al. (London: Hutchinson, 1980), pp. 128-139.
2. David Morley, *The Nationwide Audience: Structure and Decoding* (London: British Film Institute, 1980).
3. Herbert I. Schiller, *Mass Communications and American Empire* (Boston: Beacon Press, 1969); Anthony Smith, *The Geopolitics of Information* (New York: Oxford University Press, 1980); Jeremy Tunstall, *The Media Are American* (London: Constable, 1977); Tapio Varis, "The Global Traffic in Television," *Journal of Communication* 24, no. 1 (Winter 1974).
4. Chin-Chuan Lee, *Media Imperialism Reconsidered* (Beverly Hills: Sage Publications, 1980).
5. R. J. Ravault, "De l'exploitation des 'despotes culturels' par les téléspectateurs," in *Recherches québécoises sur la télévision,* ed. A. Mear (Montreal: Editions Albert St. Martin, 1980).
6. Chris Dunkley, *TV Today and Tomorrow: Wall to Wall Dallas* (Harmondsworth: Penguin, 1985).
7. *Financial Times,* May 31, 1984, p. 3.
8. Commission of the European Communities, *Television Without Frontiers* (Brussels, 1984), p. 47.
9. Thomas Guback, in *The American Film Industry,* ed. Tino Balio (Madison: University of Wisconsin Press, 1976), pp. 388-391.
10. David Gordon, in *The American Film Industry,* pp. 458-470.
11. Varis, "The Global Traffic in Television."
12. Grieve, Horner and Associates, *A Study of the United States Market for Television Programs* (Toronto, undated consultants' report, probably published in 1981), pp. 108-109.
13. Robin Scott, et al., *A Report from the Working Party on the New Technologies* (London: Broadcasting Research Unit, 1983).
14. *British Business,* September 16, 1983; October 5, 1984; August 30, 1985; September 9, 1985.
15. Grieve, Horner and Associates, p. 94.
16. *Variety,* September 14, 1983, p. 40.
17. Ibid., October 5, 1983, pp. 56, 57, 70, 71.
18. *TV World,* July 1982, p. 46.
19. *Broadcasting,* October 22, 1984, p. 70.
20. *Variety,* January 23, 1985, p. 1. (Thames later succumbed to BBC/IBA pressure to return the series to the BBC.)
21. *Financial Times,* February 1, 1984, p. 19.
22. *Variety,* April 27, 1983.
23. *Sunday Times,* February 5, 1984, p. 51.
24. *TV World,* October 1985, p. 52.
25. Grieve, Horner and Associates, p. 4.
26. *Broadcasting,* October 22, 1984, p. 70.
27. *Philadelphia Inquirer,* March 19, 1985, p. 1.
28. Tunstall, *The Media Are American.*
29. R. J. Ravault, "De l'exploitation des 'despotes culturels' . . ."
30. Elihu Katz and Tamar Liebes, "Mutual Aid in the Decoding of Dallas," in *Television in Transition,* ed. Phillip Drummond and Richard Paterson (London: British Film Institute, 1985).
31. James Leach, in *Take Two,* ed. Seth Feldman (Toronto: Irwin, 1984), p. 162.

New York skyline relayed to London by Telstar, shown by the BBC, July 28, 1962.

Trends in International
Television Flow

Tapio Varis

International life and world politics today are marked by two parallel tendencies that complement each other and to some degree overlap. One can be called the globalization of international problems, and the other regionalization. These processes are reflected in global and regional efforts towards integration and creation of common cultural consciousness. In these processes the ideological component in international relations seems to grow in importance as reflected, for example, in the competition of values in current international propaganda.

The impact of the new communication technology in particular has been debated both in the fields of basic information services (computers, data services, satellites, and so on) and in the production and dissemination of cultural information in cultural industries.[1] Direct broadcast satellites have been at the center of this debate.

The present debates have had different dimensions. At the global level, issues such as the transnational concentration of information production and dissemination, reflected in the debate on the new international order in the field of information, have been on the agenda. On the regional level, international cooperation and integration have been discussed among the poor countries as well as in areas such as Europe. Furthermore, the present international political climate has brought certain ideological elements to the debate.

In this article an empirical analysis is made of the amount and nature of the present international flow of television programs as part of these processes. The data are from a two-week period in 1983, and the results can be compared with respective figures from 1973 by the same author.[2] A few speculative future trends are also discussed.

Although international communication and world television can be discussed as a global problem now reaching an audience of more than one billion viewers, the transmitters and receivers worldwide are strongly concentrated in a few regional centers. To be more precise, almost half of the world television audience is in the United States and the Soviet Union. Among the ten largest television audiences, covering three-fourths of the world television audience, there is only one country from the developing world: Brazil *(Screen Digest,* 1983). Some researchers claim that because the basic global flow of television programming is among eight rich countries (United States, United Kingdom, Canada, Japan, Australia, Germany, France, and Brazil) which have most of the receivers and the largest audiences, one should concentrate on these to understand the flow.[3] To me, however, such an approach is too narrow and an attempt is made here to give a worldwide picture of the problem. The survey begins with an analysis of the two big television countries, the United States and the Soviet Union, which can be expected to be rather self-supportive in their programming. This is followed by a look at Western and Eastern Europe, where regional cooperation is rather advanced and efforts towards unification are strong. Finally, different regions of the developing world are reviewed briefly.

The basic information on the general amount of foreign versus domestically produced material in percentages, gathered from more than fifty countries, shows that the global average of imported programs is approximately one-third of the total time of programming. When compared to the 1973 figures, the 1983 situation is not radically different, although there are interesting regional developments. These details are not discussed in this article, which concentrates on the amount and sources of foreign programming in different countries as a share of total time of broadcasting. This analysis reveals the orientation and amount of foreign programming in various regions. Additional qualitative information is also available for each region and country. The present data are from traditional broadcast media and references to non-broadcast systems such as cable television are not systematically made.

The United States and the Soviet Union

Figure 1 illustrates imported programs as a share of the estimated total of U.S. television broadcast time and the distribution of the total import. Among all other nations of the world, the United States is a particular case in international television program flow because:

- there is a major domestic market for television programs in the United States without equal in any other country;

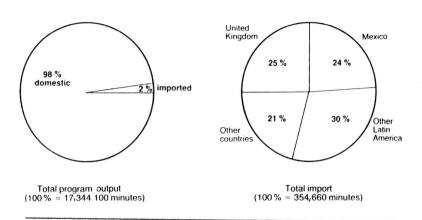

Figure 1. Imported television programs as share of estimated total U.S. television broadcast time, two-week period.

- the U.S. producers and companies are the largest program exporters in the world; and,
- in relation to total output, U.S. television networks import fewer foreign programs than any other country and one might claim that foreign programs are not shown at all in the United States.

As shown in Figure 1, imported programs account for approximately 2 percent of all programming in the United States. If commercials were included in the calculations, the figure would be even lower. Furthermore, the source of these imports are very narrow: two nations, Mexico and England, account for almost half of the time devoted to imports. Entertainment and culture are the dominant categories.

Comparable figures for the Soviet Union are given in Figure 2. Soviet television also has some characteristics that deserve special attention:

- Soviet television is multinational in character. In addition to the two all-union networks, 120 regional or local stations are in operation, broadcasting programs in most of the languages of peoples living in the country;
- the present data are from the two national networks broadcasting in Russian. Only programs that have been imported from outside the Soviet Union are classified here as foreign.

When compared to the 1973 study, the total share of imported programs has increased from 5 percent to 8 percent, and to 18 percent in prime time while that of U.S. television has remained about the same. According to

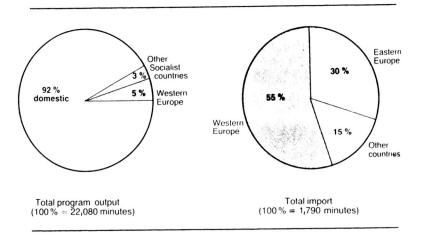

Total program output
(100% = 22,080 minutes)

Total import
(100% = 1,790 minutes)

Figure 2. Imported television programs as share of estimated total USSR television broadcast time, two-week period.

Figure 2, approximately one-third of the foreign programs originate in Eastern European socialist countries and more than two-thirds elsewhere, primarily in the Federal Republic of Germany, France, the United States, and so on. Imported programs appear mainly in entertainment, children's programs, and cultural programs. There are also co-productions with other countries.

Europe

Western Europe

Western Europe is here defined as the area of the European Broadcasting Union, which means that, for example, Yugoslavia is included in the aggregate total of Western Europe. Israel is not included in the present analysis, although there were data for Israel in 1973. Figure 3 summarizes the imported programs as a share of the estimated total Western European television broadcast time and total import. It should be emphasized that the cable systems of European countries are not included in these calculations, which most probably means that the present figures are too low with respect to imports rather than too high. There are some case studies from Italy, for example, which show that as much as 80 percent to 85 percent of the total broadcast time of the private stations consists of imported material, mainly from the United States.

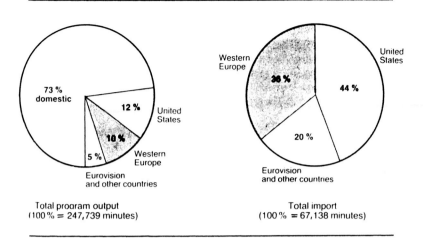

Figure 3. Imported television programs as share of estimated total Western European television broadcast time, two-week period.

Approximately one-third of Western European programs are imported (Figure 3). Here the category "import" refers to programs from other Western European countries and those from other regions. In Britain, for example, where the IBA strictly limits material from countries other than Britain, programs from other EEC countries are not classified as foreign. There are special rules for programs from other Commonwealth countries, too. In the present study, however, all imported programs are classified as foreign.

According to Figure 3, the bulk of imported programs in Western Europe originates in the United States. More than 10 percent of the total Western European broadcasting time is made up of American programs. Other major sources are the United Kingdom, the Federal Republic of Germany, and France. Of all the imported materials, American programs make up almost half (44 percent). When compared with the 1973 figures, the U.S. share has slightly decreased, although it may now be stronger in the private and cable systems not included in the present analysis. Eastern Europe, including the USSR, provides approximately 3 percent of Western European imported materials. They were shown in a few countries only, mainly in France, the Federal Republic of Germany, England, Finland, and the Basque television in Spain. There are no changes in imports from Eastern Europe when compared to the situation ten years earlier. In general, imported programs were mainly entertainment, but there are notable differences between individual European countries.

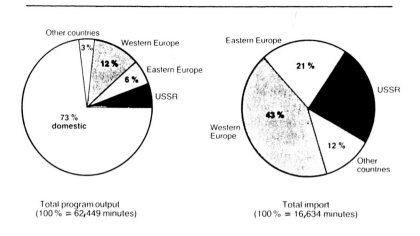

Figure 4. Imported television programs as share of estimated total Eastern European television broadcast time, two-week period.

Eastern Europe

The figures for the Eastern European region, excluding the Soviet Union, are presented in Figure 4. It seems that the share of imported programs in the Eastern European region has increased during the ten-year period with the exception of Bulgaria which, however, has been explained as being a statistical chance. The share of imported programs in Eastern Europe is approximately the same as in Western Europe, about one-third. The sources, however, seem to be more diversified. For example, the Soviet programs do not have as dominant a role in Eastern Europe as American programs have in Western Europe. Only 6 percent of Eastern European broadcasting time is made up of Soviet programs whereas, for example, 12 percent are from Western Europe and another 6 percent from other Eastern European countries.

Of the total imports, Soviet programs make up approximately one-quarter, whereas almost half originate in Western Europe. Imported programs appear in several categories, mainly in entertainment, children's programs, and cultural and educational programs.

Canada

The data for Canada are not included in figures for Western Europe, although Canada is taking part in the European process of security and cooperation. Neither are they included in the United States figures, although due to the geographical location of the country, the availability of American broadcasting is significant. Research data from the Montreal area, which is regarded as a representative area for most of the country, confirm that the United States accounts for the vast majority of imported programming, on private and public, French and English networks, except in the case of the educational network, Radio-Québec. Approximately 40 percent of the programs are imported and almost a third of the total output is made up of United States programming. As much as 70 percent of all imported programs originate in the United States, the rest coming mainly from France, the United Kingdom, Italy, and elsewhere. The movie and entertainment categories comprise the highest proportion of imports.

The Developing Countries

Latin America

Figure 5 summarizes the data for imported programs in Latin American countries. In general, the amount of imported programs varies from one-fourth (Cuba) to two-thirds (Ecuador) of the total time of programming. United States' programs have a dominating role in that region: more than a third of the total time is comprised of U.S. programs, forming as much as 77 percent of all of the imported material (Figure 5). The share of imported programs is higher during prime time than in the overall output.

When compared with the situation in 1973, it seems that the structure has remained much the same. For example, Mexico and Argentina imported, then as now, approximately three-fourths of their foreign programs from the United States. An interesting regional development, however, is the fact that programs from other Latin American countries make up a notable share of foreign programming: 6 percent of the total output and 12 percent of the imported materials. Programs from the socialist countries are transmitted only occasionally in countries like Mexico, but Cuban television statistically shows a unique diversity of sources: slightly more than one-fifth of imported programs from the

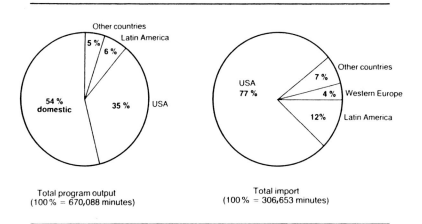

Total program output
(100 % = 670,088 minutes)

Total import
(100 % = 306,653 minutes)

Figure 5. Imported television programs as share of estimated total Latin American television broadcast time, two-week period.

Soviet Union and an equal quantity from the United States, 20 percent from the Western European countries, 13 percent from the German Democratic Republic, and approximately 20 percent from other countries.

In general, Latin American television is entertainment oriented, with approximately one-half of the total broadcasting time devoted to entertainment. Most of the imported programs appear in this program category.

Asia and the Pacific

The region of Asia and the Pacific includes countries that have great differences in the extent, nature, and history of broadcasting. Among the fourteen countries in this region, there are two fairly advanced television broadcasters, Australia and New Zealand, which are included here in the aggregate total of the region and, in consequence, introduce some error to the total as far as developing countries are concerned. Japan is not included in the present data. The amount and nature of data from this region permits only one figure to be presented in Figure 6, that of the share of foreign programs in the total program output.

Certain general aspects of television in this region must be taken into consideration before analyzing the data:

- in Asia, television has largely remained concentrated in urban areas, especially in countries like India, Malaysia, Pakistan, the Philippines, and Thailand;

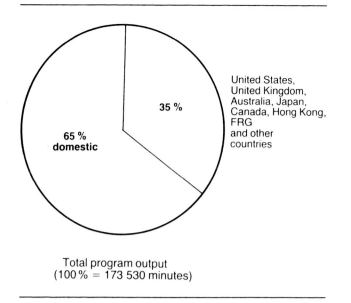

35 %

65 %
domestic

United States,
United Kingdom,
Australia, Japan,
Canada, Hong Kong,
FRG
and other
countries

Total program output
(100 % = 173 530 minutes)

Figure 6. Imported television programs as share of estimated total Asian and Pacific television broadcast time, two-week period.

- there are a limited number of transmitters, limited transmission time, and exorbitant costs for television receivers in some of the countries; and

- there are several languages, dialects, and cultures within many of the countries.

On the average, the Asian audience has access to about ten hours of television broadcasting every day. The lowest was approximately three hours (Vietnam) and the highest twenty hours (New Zealand). It could be concluded that the share of imported programs increases considerably with the increase of transmission hours. Television is primarily used for entertainment and information in that region because these two categories combined constitute approximately three-fourths of the total transmission time, and considerably more during prime time.

The number of imported programs is largest among the children's programs, followed by entertainment. Information, educational, cultural, and religious programs, however, are largely produced domestically. The situation varies from station to station and country to country. Comparisons with the 1973 situation are not always possible because new countries have since started television broadcasts in the region. The People's Republic of China had very few imported programs in 1973 (1 percent, mainly from Northern Korea, Albania, and Romania), but now shows 8 percent imported programs. These include educational material and information programs from the United Kingdom. The Philippines has seventy-

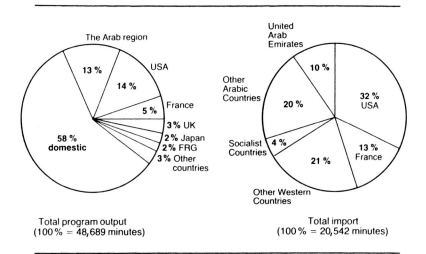

The Arab region

13 %

14 %

USA

France

5 %

3 % UK

2 % Japan

2 % FRG

3 % Other
countries

58 %
domestic

Total program output
(100 % = 48,689 minutes)

United
Arab
Emirates

Other
Arabic
Countries

10 %

20 %

32 %
USA

Socialist
Countries

4 %

21 %

13 %
France

Other Western
Countries

Total import
(100 % = 20,542 minutes)

Figure 7. Imported television programs as share of estimated total Arabic Region television broadcast time, two-week period.

two television stations throughout the country and, in 1973, imported two-thirds of its foreign programs from the United States and the rest mainly from the United Kingdom. In 1983, the U.S. share was close to 90 percent of the imported programs. Television in the Philippines is primarily an entertainment medium; 62 percent of the prime time and half of the total time is allotted to entertainment programs. The U.S. share has also been high in countries like the Republic of Korea, Hong Kong, or Malaysia. In Taiwan (which is not included in the figures but which I have studied separately) practically all foreign programs came from the United States in 1973.

It should be added that the Calcutta station in India is concentrating on domestic productions and imports very little, whereas the Delhi station has more foreign programming.

The Arab Region

Data from the Arab countries are summarized in Figure 7. Again, certain specific characteristics concerning television broadcasting in this region should be considered:

- although television activity began in the region in the 1950s, most of the stations started in the 1960s. Recently, exchanges between the Arab countries have been intensified by their own satellite systems; and

• the language of broadcasting plays a special importance in the region. There are classic Arab, local Arab dialect, and foreign languages.

The results of this study confirm that there is a clear tendency to use the classic Arab language in broadcasting. On average, slightly more than 40 percent of the programs are imported, including programs from other Arab countries. Compared to the 1973 figures, it seems that the share of imported material has decreased in the region. Foreign policy changes obviously influence foreign television programming. In Egypt, for example, almost one-fifth of the imported material was from the socialist countries in 1973; ten years later they are not visible in the statistics at all. U.S. programs are still dominant in most of the Arab countries, but their share has decreased from that of one-quarter of imported material in the People's Democratic Republic of Yemen in 1973 to 8 percent in 1983. As shown in Figure 7, American programs make up one-third of all of the imported programs in the region. In Syria, for example, U.S. programs make up 23 percent of imported programs, while Soviet television programs account for 17 percent. Compared with other regions of the world, the Arab countries import more from the socialist countries than Latin American, Asian, or African countries. Obviously, French imports dominate in several Arab countries, especially in Algeria, Tunis, and Lebanon. Imported programs dominate the categories of television plays and documentaries. Inter-Arab exchanges seem to have developed well.

Africa

Figure 8 summarizes the research findings for African countries. The specific aspects of African television include:
   • forty-six broadcasting organizations in sub-Saharan countries, but almost one-half of the television stations are in Nigeria. The Nigerian television stations broadcast a little over half of Africa's total;
   • as in other developing regions of the world, television sets are concentrated in urban areas; and, as elsewhere in the developing countries, the cost of a receiver is beyond the means of the average income earner.

Due to the dominating role of Nigeria, the present statistics were calculated first including, then excluding, Nigeria. When Nigeria is included, the share of imported programs is 36 percent; when it is excluded, the figure is 60 percent. U.S. programs make up about one-half of the imported material, one-fifth of the total output. Another major source is the United Kingdom. Programs from the socialist countries very rarely get time in

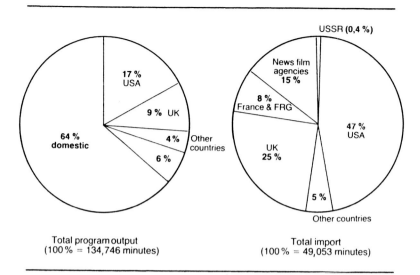

Figure 8. Imported television programs as share of estimated total African television broadcast time, two-week period.

African broadcasting. Instead, the international news film agencies and international organizations are a major source of program material in African countries. No inter-African television exchanges exist.

Although American and British programs dominate in English-speaking Africa, the French have a strong influence in francophone Africa. In Senegal, for example, 60 percent of imported programs originate in France and only 5 percent in the United States. Imported programs are mainly entertainment or information programs.

Conclusion

The trends discovered in the 1973 study seem to persist in 1983: one-way traffic from the big exporting countries to the rest of the world, and a dominance of entertainment material in the flow. However, there are also important regional developments in various parts of the world. World television continuously seems to be influenced strongly by the United States. This is especially true of the poorer regions of the world, but also of Western Europe. In Europe, however, the regional process of integration has strengthened arguments for improving inter- and intra-European exchanges and program production. This has been especially true in the plans for direct broadcast satellites, first in the Nordic area[4] and most recently in the European Community.[5] Consequently, serious discussions about quota systems for foreign programming have been activated in

Europe.[6] The problems of cultural identity, however, have been discussed more and earlier in countries like Canada that have been under strong foreign domination in the field of communication.

The European discussions have also included the East-West dimension. According to the present figures, there are only a few changes to the earlier finding that there are more Western programs in the East than vice versa. There seems to be a slight increase in the number of Eastern programs on West German television. The Eastern broadcasters, however, have slightly increased the share of Western programming. In assessing these exchange figures, one has to remember that there are a number of practical problems such as financing, and that not all of the problems are ideological or political.

In most Third World countries, television remains a medium found in urban centers and available to the relatively wealthy segment of the population. Furthermore, foreign programming almost exclusively originates in the major Western countries and tends to have a dominant role. Recent conflicts like that between Iran and the United States have aroused some Western concern in international television circles about the Third World "becoming more skilled" in international communication.[7] New conflicts in the Third World only confirm the importance of international communication.

Notes

1. Thomas Guback and Tapio Varis, *Transnational Communication and Cultural Industries,* Reports and Papers on Mass Communication, no. 92 (Paris: UNESCO, 1982).

2. See Tapio Varis, *International Flow of Television Programmes,* Reports and Papers on Mass Communication, no. 100 (Paris: UNESCO, 1985). For partial reports by the same author, see "The International Flow of Television Programs," *Journal of Communication* 34, no. 1 (Winter 1984): 143-152, and "Flow of Television Programmes in Western Europe," University of Tampere, Department of Journalism and Mass Communication, Publications B, no. 14 (Tampere, Finland, 1984). The 1973 figures are presented, among other sources, in Kaarle Nordenstreng and Tapio Varis, *Television Traffic: A One-Way Street?,* Reports and Papers on Mass Communication, no. 70. (Paris: UNESCO, 1974).

3. William H. Read, "Global TV Flow: Another Look," *Journal of Communication* 26, no. 3 (Summer 1976): 69-73.

4. Nordic Council of Ministers, "The Nordic Radio and Television via Satellite," NU A (Stockholm, 1979).

5. Commission of the European Communities, *Television Without Frontiers* (Brussels, 1984).

6. See, for example, *Media Perspektiven,* no. 3 (1985) and the *Journal of Moral Education* 13, no. 2 (1984).

7. Michael Mosettig and Henry Griggs, Jr., "Things Fall Apart: TV at the Front," *Foreign Policy* 38 (Spring 1977): 67-79.

I have a court order
to evict you.

I have nowhere to go.

Independent Video
in Latin America

Karen Ranucci
interviewed by Julianne Burton

As a freelance journalist for North American television news (particularly NBC) in Central America, I was appalled to see the ways in which many television reporters working there gather news for the North American audience. Reporters descend on a given country when something "hot" is going on. Equipped with only meager knowledge of that country and of the background relevant to the event which brought them there, they do much of their reporting without leaving their hotel, attending government-sponsored press conferences and receiving press releases from the U.S. embassy. As their command of the local language tends to be rudimentary (if they speak it at all), generally these "news gatherers" write their scripts without making an effort to include the words of the citizens of the countries whose events they are reporting. If they incorporate local spokespeople, they must be English-speakers, since the networks refuse to use subtitles on newscasts. Such practices perpetuate a North American perspective on Latin American events and prevent U.S. audiences from getting a sense of what Latin Americans have to say about their own realities.

As a result, the opportunity to see how Latin Americans visually interpret their own reality is scarce in North America, generally restricted to the limited number of films by Latin Americans currently in U.S. distribution. In order to fill this void, I have been involved in assembling an eight-hour sampling of independent video and film produced by Latin Americans from nine countries, ranging from Mexico to Uruguay; the collection is entitled *Democracy in Communication: Popular Video and Film in Latin America*. The result of a year's travel throughout Latin America, *Democracy in Communication* documents the efforts of independent media producers and community groups who have turned to video as a tool for expressing their social and political concerns.

Once I began trying to locate Latin American video producers, I found that videomaking activity in the region was far more widespread than I had suspected. The video movement in Latin America is quite recent. Only in Brazil—which has had portapaks almost as long as they have been available in the U.S.—is there a large and well-organized community of videomakers, with national video festivals, journals, production guides, and so on. Although widely practiced, videomaking seems still to be in its infancy in the rest of Latin America, especially in those countries where repressive governments or restrictive state control of the airwaves discourage the circulation of independent views. It is rare for independent videowork to be broadcast nationally in Latin American countries.

The question of expense is very important. Economic factors often combine with political ones to discourage or limit independent production. While in the United States video is a very inexpensive medium, in Latin America tapes and equipment are quite costly. For instance, a Beta tape which would cost us $5, costs $20; a three-quarter-inch tape which would cost us $15, costs $45—the equivalent, in some population sectors, of an entire month's salary. Still, individuals and groups, determined to utilize the medium, are surmounting these obstacles. For many of them, video (unlike film) at least remains within the realm of possibility.

Democracy in Communication begins with a selection of off-air broadcasts from Mexican television which I edited together into a humorous montage. The "distancing " produced by the fact that these fragments from programs and advertisements are being broadcast in Spanish, and the estrangement of seeing North American personalities and products as they are viewed by Latin American audiences, inevitably produces laughter. I interpret this as an important step toward a critical perspective on television and

its impact on our lives. Moreover, Americans are generally unaware of the extent to which North American culture is packaged and sold abroad, or of the social implications such "value-transferring" practices involve. The fact, for example, that 100 percent of the cartoons seen on Mexican television are purchased from the U.S. has a tremendous social effect. This "pirated montage" provides a glimpse of the commercial context within and against which the other works in the collection—independent, popular, noncommercial, national rather than imported—are being made.

Amas de casa (Housewives), made by the Colectivo Cine Mujer, is an example of how groups working in Mexico choose to produce their tapes according to different standards and paradigms. In Mexico, because of monopolistic television control, the chances of getting independent work broadcast on TV are virtually nil. Independents recognize the limitations they face and have evolved other forms and uses for the video medium. Although it would be a wonderful organizing tape for women interested in forming a housewives' union, this tape was not in fact used in this way by the people who made it. Instead, *Amas de casa* was made on an *ad hoc* basis, for and with a specific group of women living in an impoverished Mexico City neighborhood. The women acted out a dramatization of eviction (which in fact they were facing); thus, unlike other kinds of video production in which the finished product is the most important consideration, this is a case where the process of production is

Still from *Varela in Xingu*, 1985, video, 13 min.

paramount. *Amas de casa* is representative of the way in which videomaking can catalyze and represent an empowerment process—here, among people who historically have been abused and exploited by landlords, evicted from their houses and turned out onto the streets without legal recourse. There was no need to write a script for these women; they devised their own dialogue from personal experience. The emotion they display is clearly the product of the frustration they've had to contain for too long. In the process of collaborating on the videotape, particularly the role-playing, they are unleashing their emotions in a very positive, unifying direction.

Another tape from Mexico also exemplifies the role of video in community empowerment. *Nuestro tequio (Our Tequio)* is a tape made by a group of Zapotec Indians from the state of Oaxaca who have been tenaciously maintaining their traditional culture in the face of persistent pressures to integrate into contemporary Mexican society. Their method of governance involves *asambleas* (assemblies) where whole communities come together to discuss important social and economic questions. Recently, groups of Zapotecs have been using video to document their community assemblies, not only for purposes of historical record, but also as a means of encouraging their people to look at themselves and their political process in a more self-conscious way.

Nuestro tequio is a bit of a departure from their other works because it attempts to depict a physical corollary of their communal process—the collective repair and reconstruction of a community building in Yalalag. Working without any official support, relying completely on their own limited human and material resources, they labored on the building over a three-year period. The video depicts hundreds of Zapotecs very proudly coming together from the surrounding villages to construct the new roof. After their workday was over, the entire community assembled to watch the video footage. The producers told me that the tape was very important to them because they could use it like a mirror within their community, looking at themselves from a different perspective and generating a renewed sense of appreciation for their customs and their traditional commitment to the welfare of the group.

The Zapotec video group, which has been operating since 1980, grew out of contact with a video group from Mexico City who went to Oaxaca at the invitation of several community members to conduct a media workshop. They subsequently lent their own equipment to the Indians, who shoot in half-inch, then take what they've shot into Mexico City where it is bumped up to three-quarter and edited. The four people who make up this group—three men and one woman—are seasonal migrants to the U.S. They use the wages they earn as farmworkers to buy what they need to keep their video production going.

Video Servicios is a group of Mexican video producers who have pooled their resources and talents to create a community video center. Their activities are limited, since they have no outside sources of funding. (Government and private funding agencies such as exist in the U.S. and Canada are rare in Latin America.) Members of Video Servicios share and circulate videotapes among themselves and have access to production and editing equipment at lower-than-commercial rates. They have occasionally been contracted by Mexican state television to produce specific programs. This is, in fact, the only way the state works with independents. Networks will take "bids" from independent producers on certain stipulated programs, often determining not only the general topic but the actual script in advance.

In this way, Video Servicios has produced a number of tapes for Mexican educational television, subsequently channeling any financial return from this activity into the production of tapes of their own choice. *El triunfo* (The Triumph) is a thirty-minute educational tape produced on their own. It grew out of their concern over environmental destruction in the jungles of Chiapas. The tape has been widely shown by environmental groups in their attempt to educate the population about the consequences of shortsighted government policies in the region. It argues, for example, that the creation of reserves is merely a stop-gap measure. *El triunfo* delineates the problem without proposing solutions; it aims instead to generate concern and involvement among those who view it.

Brazil is by far the most advanced of the Latin American countries in terms of its video production. Brazilian videomakers have been very inventive in expanding and challenging the generic boundaries of their medium. *Marley Normal,* by Olhar Electronico (Electronic Look), a

Still from *Algo de Ti* (Something of You), 1985, music video, 5 min.

leading independent video group, uses erratically rhythmic montage to condense a day in the life of an urban working woman into five minutes. The result—comic, poignant, and uncannily familiar—is the product of an unusual combination of documentary, fictional, and experimental modalities. Another work, *Varela in Xingu,* caricatures a TV correspondent and parodies traditional network news-gathering techniques. At the inauguration of a new tribal chief on the Xingu Indian reserve in the Amazon jungle, Varela spouts his clichéd, Eurocentric view of the Indians while giving the Xingu an unusual opportunity to retaliate by giving their impressions of (westernized) Brazilians.

Beijo ardente: Overdose (Passionate Kiss: Overdose), by the Porto Alegre video collective Olho Magico (Magic Eye), deals with the process of turning an old gas plant into a local cultural center. The tape was an effective tool in generating community backing and enabling the artists to win the necessary local and official support. Instead of a "straight" documentary about the artists' struggle to convince community officials to donate the building to their cause, Olho Magico substitutes an allegorical vampire story. Made with local actors and broad community participation, this forty-minute tape is a very successful example of an off-beat approach to videomaking as a catalyst for social change.

Panama has an annual National Music Video Competition, sponsored by Maxell Corporation; the organizers of this festival are interested in alternative music videos. *Algo de ti,* by Luis Franco and Sergio Cambefort of Boa Productions, was one of the winners of the 1985 event. Using the same surreal, dreamlike visual language as American-made videos, *Algo de ti* turns a love song into a visual parable of the horrors of life under a repressive military regime, underlining the passive complicity of individuals and institutions. Another music video comes from Peru. It uses images of Ayacucho, the regional center of the struggle between the Shining Path guerrillas and Peruvian government troops, over Rubén Blades's song *Desaparecidos* (The Disappeared). Fragments of interviews with relatives of disappeared persons disrupt Blades's poignant lyrics. Images of mass graves and troop convoys evoke a hyperrealism which stands in diametrical contrast to the approach used in *Algo de ti*.

El Salvador's Radio Venceremos is very important for assessing the role of video in revolutionary culture. In addition to their activities in radio broadcasting, they produce films and videotapes for internal consumption and also for export. Their internal tapes inform Salvadoreans of war-related developments in various regions of the country, giving isolated communities a sense of connection to political dialogue. They also use video in very practical ways: for teaching subjects like battlefield surgery or weapons maintenance, and as a means of circulating important messages from the military leadership. Radio Venceremos uses any kind of video they can get their hands on—VHS, Beta, three-quarter-inch, off-the-air—as well as 16mm and Super-8 film.

Radio Venceremos' *Tiempo de audacia* (Time of Daring, 1983), an intimate behind-the-scenes look at both sides of the military conflict, impressively testifies to the effectiveness and polish which is possible using "conglomerated" media. In both content and form, *Tiempo de audacia* provides an illuminating contrast to *Atlacatl*, the companion tape from El Salvador in the collection, a publicity tape made by the Salvadorean military forces about a U.S.-trained special forces brigade. The Salvadorean military has turned to video as an important propaganda tool, making music videos, for example, to convince young people to join the army. Needless to say, these promotional tools are frequently seen on broadcast TV. Coming on the heels of *Atlacatl*, which glorifies—almost deifies—the skill and bravery of this U.S.-trained unit, *Tiempo de audacia* presents the Salvadorean guerrillas' view of this same special forces brigade—not only the exaggeratedly macho bravura of their training but most notably their utter bewilderment, collapse, and despair in actual battle. One of the strengths of *Tiempo de audacia* is its ability to show how the war overwhelms individual fighters on *both* sides.

In neighboring Nicaragua, as is now generally known, there was no independent video production prior to the coming to power of the Sandinistas in July 1979. Since that time, many videomakers from Europe and the Americas have set up their own companies in Nicaragua. Various international sources have provided funds to train, equip, and support independent video production groups staffed by Nicaraguans. The Timoteo Velasquez Popular Video Workshop grew out

Still from *Atlacatl*, 1983, video/film, 22 min.

Still from *Tiempo de Audacia* (Time of Daring), 1983, video/film, 22 min.

of the Super-8 workshop organized in Managua by Bolivian Alfonso Gumucio Dagron under the auspices of UNESCO. *Testimonios* consists of the testimony of rural Nicaraguans about how their lives are affected by the contra attacks. *Las mujeres* (The Women, 1985) is another short tape by a women's video workshop which examines the disparity between male and female salaries on cooperative farms. Focusing on one farm where the men joined with the female coworkers to demand equal pay for all, the tape both questions government policy and suggests an alternative. Because of the strains and shortages imposed by the war economy, the workers were reluctant to stage a conventional strike. They were unwilling to put further strain on an already beleaguered economy. Instead, they continued to work, but refused to accept their salaries. By this means, they embarrassed the administration of the cooperative into recognizing and eventually granting their demand.

Aqui en esta esquina (Here On This Corner, 1985) was produced by the Nicaraguan government network, Sistema Sandinista de Television. It adopts the form of an American game show, but with one key difference: rather than being studio-produced, the show broadcasts live from a different community each week. The format pits one community organization against another in a friendly contest—arm wrestling, dance competitions, tug-of-war, races to reassemble a rifle, or whatever. The other component is a kind of talent show where local people get a chance to perform.

Finally, *Que pasa con el papel higlenico?* (What's Going On With Toilet Paper?, 1983) is a good example of how the government ministries are trying to use video in their own work. In this case, the Ministry of Agrarian Reform (MIDINRA) takes a critical look at questions of supply, demand, and distribution (including issues like hoarding and black marketeering), all related to one of the more humble but necessary commodities of daily life. Dozens of ordinary Nicaraguan citizens address themselves to the camera, giving their response to the shortage and opinions about what can be done to correct it. An antidote to dominant North American assumptions about the propagandistic tendencies of Nicaraguan government media, this tape is an excellent example of official self-criticism through video.

Latin American videomakers continue to produce tapes, despite the odds against them. They have realized that isolation makes their work even more difficult and, consequently, have begun to extend themselves to other Latin American videomakers through a number of international newsletters. But a critical problem remains the lack of distribution outlets. Many of the videos included in *Democracy in Communication* have been shown only in the communities in which they were produced. *Democracy in Communication* is an attempt to bring the voices, images, and perspectives of Latin Americans to a North American audience, a rare opportunity for us to see Latin Americans as they see themselves.

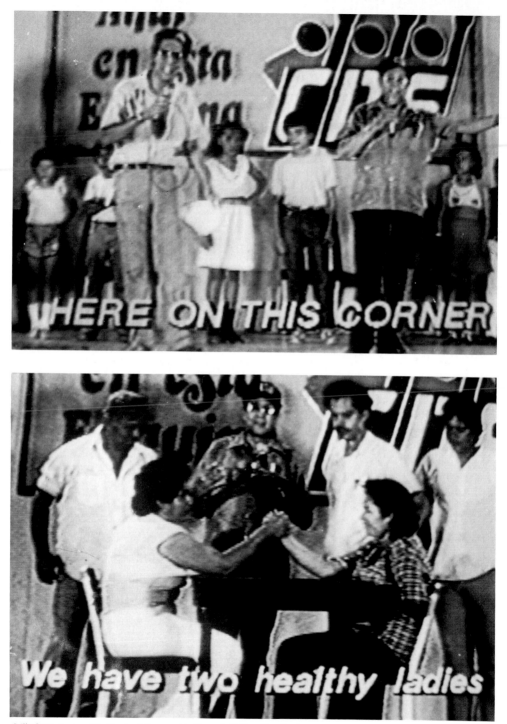

Stills from *Aqui en Este Esquina* (Here on this Corner), 1985, video, 5 min.

National Cinema and International Television: The Death of New German Cinema

Thomas Elsaesser

The New German Cinema (what remained from Oberhausen and what came after) has many kinds of energy. Alexander Kluge would be its synthesizing intelligence, Werner Herzog its athletic will, Wim Wenders its phenomenological power of perception, Werner Schroeter emphatically underscores its emotional side, Herbert Achternbusch is its rebellious stubbornness, and Volker Schlöndorff its craftsman. Rainer Werner Fassbinder, however, would be the heart, the beating vibrant center of all these partial impulses, these different aggregate states of its energy . . . He was the pounding heart. Now it has been stopped.

—Wolfram Schütte[1]

Decline, dispersal, death, disintegration: the metaphors abound by which to characterize the end of a movement, the termination of a career, and the closure of an epoch. In the case of the New German Cinema, Fassbinder's death in 1982 was—not only for the German cinema—an incalculable loss, and more historical distance will be needed before the importance of his work can be fully assessed. But even today one might argue that Fassbinder contributed more to the "death" of the New German Cinema when he was alive than after his death. His restless explorations of the different media, of the industrial conditions and financial possibilities of filmmaking: if they did not inaugurate, they at any rate accelerated the changes that led to the transformations of the New German Cinema into the German Cinema, and of the German Cinema into a form of filmmaking that is now neither quite cinema nor altogether television.[2]

Fassbinder seems to have been aware of these changes earlier than most of his colleagues, and able to expand his mini-studio to a one-person film industry. His immense productivity helped to build up an infrastructure of technical and artistic skills in several fields very quickly. Working in film and television, but also in the theater, his projects were often designed to stretch and extend the technical and organizational possibilities of his team. For WDR he was the first to create a popular television series that seriously engaged with political issues *(Acht Stunden sind kein Tag)* as well as leading in low-budget films with high production values *(The Bitter Tears of Petra von Kant)*. He took on subjects which required commercial and international finance, and in his work there is ultimately no opposition between the cultural mode of production and the industrial one: he used the cultural one *as* the industrial one.

Fassbinder had from the start aimed for the fascination that glamour could bring. This glamour required the existence, if only as a memory, of the international film industry with its typical movie mythology, and the view that the cinema itself is what brings audiences into the cinema. Fassbinder had a make-believe studio system, he had make-believe stars, and he was making make-believe Hollywood films. When he advocated the industrial model of filmmaking (as opposed to the auteurist one) in the late 1970s, he merely spelled out what he had himself practiced since 1968. By the time of his death, he was producing almost simultaneously wholly uncommercial films such as *In a Year of Thirteen Moons,* politically controversial films such as *The Third Generation,* big-budget and fashionable films such as *Lili Marleen,* very private but international art cinema such as *Querelle,* and prestigious national television such as *Berlin Alexanderplatz.* When he talked about the fact that films can ultimately only be made by taking risks, he had added "the capitalist way."[3] It is in this sense, more than in the genres he revived and imitated, that he finally achieved his ambition of making "real Hollywood" films.

One might conclude from this brief overview of Fassbinder's example that, broadly speaking, the surge in filmmaking in West Germany during the 1970s followed a classic pattern: on the one side a much-trumpeted national "new wave" that leaves a few auteurs as it ebbs away; and on the other, a transfer of power from cinema to television which implied drawing on and absorbing a considerable number of as yet unaffiliated directors, cameramen, and related personnel, first on a freelance basis and then in regular jobs. With the stabilization of this labor market in the mid-1980s, the New German Cinema vanished like Cinderella's carriage, leaving a vast number of individual films hardly ever shown in cinemas either in Germany or abroad. The internationally known auteurs, on the other hand, might arguably have made a name for themselves even without the

Rainer Werner Fassbinder

film-funding system or elaborate government-sponsored promotion campaigns. If this is the impression, then it is partly because the discussion of New German Cinema has often focused too narrowly on Germany itself.[4]

The International Situation

The *Autorenfilm*—the name by which the New German Cinema is commonly known—does not point to a particular genre or primacy of self-expression of the director, but is first of all a political concept. It was intended to create spaces for filmmaking outside those colonized by the international commercial feature film. In the early 1960s, the Hollywood product, together with its national variants, seemed to be the enemy. And while David did not actually slay Goliath at the box office, the New German Cinema was successful in establishing institutional structures— some would say cultural bureaucracies—that substituted for and bypassed the hierarchies of the traditional film industry.

But it seems clear that the success of the *Autorenfilm* was also due in part to a shift in the balance of power between the commercial cinema and its rival, television. This shift in the economy of entertainment affected not only West Germany but—to look no further—Europe as a whole. So, if the battlefront that prevailed at the time of the 1962 Oberhausen

Manifesto has disappeared, it is not the *Autorenkino* that can lay claim to victory, even though its erstwhile enemy, the domestic film industry, seemed to have been swept aside before its very eyes. For the forces that finished off the old German cinema were at the very same time in the process of also swallowing up the *Autorenfilm,* probably without even noticing that they were doing so.

Over the last decade, the entire picture has changed. None of the old oppositions really hold: not only *Altbranche* versus *Jungfilm* has gone, but commerce versus culture, Hollywood versus national cinema, *Autorenkino* versus *Anderes Kino,* and even "cinema" versus "television" are beginning to be antimonies of the past. In place of these polarities, we have the so-called new media—video, cable, satellite—which strictly speaking are not new media, but (to use the jargon) new delivery systems.[5] Because the club of those who have a stake in owning these systems is even smaller and more exclusive than the old film industry, their existence and the battles over control mean that all audiovisual products are affected sooner or later.

So far, the signs—in Italy and France, for instance—are that the emergence of media conglomerates clustering around satellite broadcasting and cable television in particular are effectively squeezing out whatever resists or does not fit into the global concept that the old *and* the new media are building up. They are reducing the diversity of programming on national television and further eroding the admission figures for cinema. If one takes a longer view of the present situation in Europe, one can see that in the current crisis of the *Autorenfilm,* it is the survival of independent cinema itself that is at issue, not because the *Autorenfilm* is the only possible or the most prestigious form of cinema, but because in its German variant it was an extreme and—for its time and on its own terms—very consistent concept for non-Hollywood filmmaking.

The Leading Players

We are witnessing in the 1980s the takeover battles by which the giants of the print media (newspaper, publishing) are acquiring the audiovisual media on a worldwide scale. The players in this very unevenly matched game are, firstly, international media barons, like the Australian Rupert Murdoch, the Canadian Ted Turner, the Italian Silvio Berlusconi, press lords in France, the backers of Radio Luxembourg, the Bertelsmann Verlag, Axel Springer, Gruner & Jahr in West Germany. They are not only fighting over respective shares in the cable and video business, but are also busy lobbying governments to amend protective legislation and persuading state monopolies like the postal services to grant licenses and become themselves suppliers of the necessary informational infrastructure.

Secondly, there are the national broadcasting networks and their commercial competitors: in Britain the BBC and ITA, including Channel Four; in West Germany, the relatively autonomous regional networks such as WDR, as well as the Second Channel, ZDF. As producers of feature films either from within their own resources (as has largely been the practice of the BBC and WDR), or by commissioning freelance and from independents (as in the case of Channel Four and ZDF), the television networks are in a strong—if precarious—position when it comes to supplying the new, deregulated market. WDR, for instance, has built up very extensive commercial relations with Germany's largest studio, the Bavaria Atelier Gesellschaft in Munich-Geiselgasteig (of which ex-WDR producer Rohrbach's transfer of post and change of tune are the clearest signs).[6]

Thirdly, there are national and international film distributors. In Britain these are: Thorn-Emi, Cannon, Rank, and the US Majors; in Germany mostly the US Majors, and small national distributors such as Constantin (Bernd Eichinger), Horst Wendlandt, Filmverlag der Autoren, Laurens Straub's Filmwelt, Theo Hinz's Futura, the Berlin Basis-Film Verleih. They compete with one another on two fronts: to supply the cinemas and to get their share of the video market. Effective control in the new media is determined by access to existing markets, not by the products. Yet access and delivery system together redefine the market for all products (including film), for all sites and spaces of consumption (including the cinemas), and in all countries (including those in which *Autorenfilm,* independent, art, or avant-garde cinema have a [small] stake in the overall media on offer). The consequences for the cinema are clear: certain films—usually Hollywood films—are heavily promoted only for their start in first-run theaters. Instead of counting on the second-run market, distributors now go straight into the video shops, usually within two or three months of the movie premiere—the haste being partly in order to discourage pirating. According to official figures, in Germany during 1987, more money was made with video cassettes than the gross turnover of all the film theaters. Germany shares with Britain the lowest percentage of the domestic cinema market (11.4 and 12 percent in 1984), and they also register the lowest attendance figures (about roughly half of those of France or Italy).

Finally, in the 1970s, United States film and television production became a relatively minor field of diversification for multinational corporations such as Gulf & Western, the Kinney Corporation, or Coca-Cola. Yet, however marginal Hollywood might be to the petro-chemical, food, or soft drink industries, it still dominates the international film industry, and also most of the world's television screens. In film production, the 1970s brought another major concentration of capital and resources: fewer films now attract a larger share of the overall investment, and very intensive marketing strategies create no more than a dozen mega-hits annually, with budgets so vast that they have allowed the industry to modernize its technology and keep abreast of advanced research (computerization, sound systems, camera robotics, special effects). The American film industry can thus act in many ways as a production site for developing prototypes, both in terms of manufacturing processes and of types of entertainment spectacles.

This American-style commodity-film blitz represents another form of colonization, a strategic occupation and territorial penetration to which the European film industries and independent filmmakers may not be able to respond. For in the reorganization and redefinition of the market there are several obvious casualties: the cinemas, for instance, unless they are first-run houses; the so-called noncommercial or 16mm market, affecting students and teachers of film; and, most importantly, the independent feature films—such as the *Autorenfilm*—which have rarely made it into the first-run theaters, and thus are unlikely to make it into the video market (exceptions being the few films distributed by US Majors: one-offs by Wenders, Fassbinder, Herzog, Schlöndorff, Margarethe von Trotta, Wolfgang Petersen, and recently, Doris Dörrie).

The New German Cinema:
An Invention of the Social-Liberal Coalition

What makes the situation complicated for the filmmakers is that the players are often very unevenly matched. Some, like the media empires, always play offensively, while others, like the national broadcasting networks, are usually forced on the defensive. This is especially true at times when they do not have a politically sympathetic government to back them up, as in Britain, where the present government has practically declared war on the BBC. Throughout Europe, deregulation seems to be the order of the day, partly because the national governments themselves are already in defensive positions vis-à-vis private enterprise companies. In Italy, the

Scene from R. W. Fassbinder's *Berlin Alexanderplatz*.

coalition governments are too divided and too much involved in playing political games with and via the media to implement any kind of restraints, and in West Germany, the Kohl administration is busy dismantling the media policy which the Social Democrat/Liberal coalition had built up over the years as mitigating mechanisms.

The kind of protection which the *Autorenfilm* received during the late 1960s and throughout the 1970s was prescient in two ways: it subsidized a "national" film culture, but it also created institutional structures that may be able to withstand the onslaught of the new media more effectively if a political response can be backed by an economically practicable program concept. Politically, the New German Cinema was the result of lobbyists like Alexander Kluge finding a sympathetic ear among Social Democrat and Liberal parliamentarians, who then included the cinema in their policies of rewarding national prestige projects (along with museums, music festivals, theater events, and international sports). Practically, the New German Cinema was financed by television, via co-productions that could also pass as cinema both in the specialized markets and at national and international festivals. (In the film festivals a television film could be upgraded to the status of international art cinema, if critics, journalists, prize-giving juries, distributors, or a television buyer from abroad liked it.)

This dual strategy—of working with the structures of government and of television—corresponded to a functional division in the purposes of the *Autorenfilm,* between its creation of a national cinema (which could range from re-presenting and re-writing national history, to the self-representation of special groups, such as women or gay subcultures) and its support of alternative forms of cinema altogether (avant-garde films, nonnarrative films, documentary, opera and music drama, dance theater, or film essays). In neither case does "self-expression" or the notion of the "author" play a significant part other than as an ideologically useful bargaining chip. An "author" was a necessary feature to give the work a cultural cachet within the specific political situation in West Germany, where film had to bid with (and initially against) the rest of the arts for a share of the overall cultural budget distributed by the States. In Britain, by contrast, to describe cinema as "art" or even "culture" would give it a bad name; this makes the terms "independent" or "freelance" the preferred currency when appealing to State sponsorship or television funding. To that extent, the "Autor" in Germany was not only a "Public Institution,"[7] but a strategic fiction. Although it created its own problems for filmmakers, in the German context the concept of the "Autor" had a peculiar potency and effectivity.

For with this concept (if not the term), West Germany was, during most of the 1970s, ahead of the rest of Europe in subsidizing film. By the time of the third revision of the Film Subsidy Law in 1974, the German film funding system was quite finely tuned, combining federal and regional funding, automatic subsidy, and project subsidy with Kuratorium, television co-production, and Berlin-Effekt. This complex funding system gave German filmmakers a boost at all levels, and across the whole range of film forms and modes, from the medium-to-big budget prestige film like Fassbinder's *The Marriage of Maria Braun* or Schlöndorff's *The Tin Drum,* to avant-garde and experimental films by Werner Schroeter, Herbert Achternbusch, Helke Sander, and Ulrike Ottinger.

So why does it now seem as if the Germans "blew it"? France and Britain have learned from the German experience and are currently more successful in keeping a stake in the national market as well as breaking into the international market. The German cinema, despite its better-than-average chances, however, was unable to build on the real but brief breakthrough afforded by the *Autorenfilm.* There is no shortage of critics offering reasons. Was it that the basis for a full-scale recovery had always been too small? Was it a change in government policy? Was it that the Americans killed some of the geese that laid the golden eggs—Wenders,

Still from R. W. Fassbinder's *The Marriage of Maria Braun*, 1979, starring Hanna Schygulla.

Herzog, Schlöndorff? Was it Fassbinder's drug overdose? Was it that distributors did not promote German films, but merely chased international box-office hits (which do not require a risky outlay when launching on the German market)? Was it the so-called telephone producers, who simply specialized in milking the subsidy system? Was it that film critics and journalists were too shortsighted, provincial, and masochistic to mount a decent public relations job, not just for this or that film or director, but for a broadly conceived production policy? Was it the filmmakers, who stayed on the defensive, dreaming of becoming *auteurs*—with Truffaut, Fellini, Scorsese, or Coppola as their models—or hankering after support from the international avant-garde, regardless of the changing conditions, and without fully grasping what was happening in their medium? Was it the public—in the sense that the generation that had supported the independent *Autorenfilm* during the 1970s had dropped out as an active cinema public, because they had become too old, too busy, or too lazy to bother to go to the cinema? Was it the cinemas that had turned into multiplexes showing films in a semi-pornographic environment, with bad projection, bad sound, and bad service? Or was it that the films themselves were not inventive enough, exciting enough, or intelligent enough to interest either a national or an international audience once the new had gone out of German cinema? Whatever the reason, or combination of reasons, instead of celebrating the New German Cinema's twenty-fifth anniversary since Oberhausen, journalists at the 1987 Berlin Film Festival behaved as if they were attending a wake.[8]

A Missed Opportunity or a Strategic Retreat?

Some of the complaints echoed those made by the old film industry, namely, that in all the years and despite hundreds of films, the German cinema still lacked an adequate industrial and technical infrastructure. Other gripes were similar to the ones raised during the years of the Young German Cinema, such as that funding had created too many first-time filmmakers and one-off films, forever passing off their home-movie-look as authenticity and red-hot inspiration. The criticisms of the industry-oriented faction came down to three: not only did the German cinema lack professionals, the films were, by international standards, often too cheaply made to employ properly trained technicians. Secondly, the German cinema lacked scriptwriters of experience, and therefore neglected narrative; it lacked a feel for dialogue and therefore for character; it had no sense of situation and therefore lacked drama. Consequently, despite a manifest demand on the part of the public for entertainment films with German stars and German settings, the independent cinema was unable to supply them, having developed no genres of its own, nor credible reworkings of others, and instead taken refuge in exoticisms, camp and kitsch fantasies, and lurid evocations of extreme states of mind. Thirdly, German films lacked popular support, not least because they were completely identified with the generation of '68, currently very much out of favor with those under thirty. A new generation of audiences—and filmmakers—now look at these films and find them boring, pretentious, vacuous.[9]

To these criticisms was added that the subsidy system has made German directors too obsessed with film policy. There is no aesthetic concept, other than a homemade kit of ideas borrowed from *Cahiers du Cinema* cinephilia of over thirty years ago or from Suhrkamp-ed Brecht. Even the political program of the *Autorenfilm* had collapsed, not just among the doubters but among its most fervent advocates and ideologues. A massive tome, *Bestandsaufnahme: Utopie Filme,* edited by Kluge in 1983 is, once the pretty illustrations and amusing anecdotes are discounted, his declaration of defeat. Elegantly and dazzlingly as ever he accomplished a complete turnaround, making it seem as if his position had remained the same by calling the *Autorenfilm* now *Zuschauerfilm,* and putting dubious

»Manchmal denke ich, Raumpflegerin ist nicht der richtige Beruf für mich!«

market research into catchy phrases the way he had once put Marcusean theory into catchy phrases.[10]

In defense of the German cinema of the 1970s, one might argue that France, once it had adopted virtually the same funding system as West Germany, could build on the advantage of a relatively healthy national film culture, which still functions both in Paris and in the provinces to get spectators into the cinemas, spectators who—because France has a quota system—have been brought up on French as well as American films. In Britain, too, even though all governmental aid (such as the Eady levy and tax concessions) has been removed, Channel Four's commissioning policy and the BFI Production Board—both modeled on the German example—are beginning to maximize the advantages of British television productions: better access to the international television market and thus to the new art cinema than many of their European competitors. Britain is also well-placed in the entertainment sector, thanks to its leading role in the pop music industry and because of the continuing American affection for British period dramas as the highest form of "serious" television.

The German cinema has none of these cultural advantages and no serious hopes of breaking into anything other than the prestige market of the art cinemas, as its domestic "commercial" successes underline: for the directors of the 1980s are not Werner Herzog or Wim Wenders, but Peter

F. Bringmann and Carl Schenkel, Dominik Graf and Peter Keglevic, Hartmann Schmige, Stefan Lukschy, and Christian Rateuke.[11] And the stars are not Hanna Schygulla or Bruno Ganz, but rock singer Marius Müller-Westerhagen, television comics Didi Hallervorden and Gerhard Polt, the stand-up comedian Otto, and—Jean-Paul Belmondo, ever popular comic adventurer whose *The Ace of Aces,* a Franco-German co-production made with Bavarian subsidy funds, was one of the biggest successes of the 1984-1985 season. In other words, precisely the sort of genres and stereotypes the New German Cinema had avoided like the plague are the ones that today please German audiences.

From Experience to Event

So, perhaps the New German Cinema did not "blow it" after all. If the mass audience prefers German versions of *The French Connection* or *Kojak,* of Marty Feldman or Louis de Funès, they might be better off with the real thing. American distributors could be left to run the show, or French directors and co-producers to collect the automatic subsidies for *The Ace of Aces* or *The Name of the Rose.* Many of the complaints against the New German Cinema, even where true, seem misplaced if they implicitly assume the vantage point of an ideal—the home-made mass entertainment film—which is either unattainable or undesirable in practice or as a norm that is about to become obsolete. The developments in the "new media" will rapidly lead to a concentration of the cinemas on highly professional, expensively made (and therefore American) blockbusters and prototypes, with national film industries in Europe supplying medium-to-low-cost broadcast and canned television entertainment. Already in 1982, filmmakers were up in arms over a suggestion that the European Community was thinking of prosecuting member states and forcing them to abandon their respective film subsidy schemes. French, Italian, German, and even Greek directors felt that it could not conceivably be in the interest of a united Europe to destroy nationally specific cultural or cinematic traditions by the stroke of a bureaucrat's pen in favor of more harmonization. "Every film must declare its nationality and its own cultural identity" according to Bertrand Tavernier, who condemned the multinational cinema of co-productions by pouring scorn on the prospect of "Sophia Loren playing a Berlin housewife, and Catherine Deneuve a Sicilian peasant." The Eurofilm of the future could join the Golden Delicious Euro-Apple: tasteless and bland.[12]

Thus, the independent German cinema, behind the times and out of

Heimat (Edgar Reitz, 1984), an eight-part epic produced by WDR (West German Television) that achieved international acclaim.

favor with its critics for failing to deliver one kind of product, may actually be ahead in another, perhaps more modest, but crucial area. Out of the two decades of experiment with film forms and collaboration with television, German filmmakers have acquired expertise in two "alternative" uses of the cinema, both of which are capable of further developments: they succeeded in combining film *and* television for what one might call, perhaps too pompously, nationally specific but internationally recognizable media products, such as Syberberg's *Our Hitler,* Reitz's *Heimat,* or Fassbinder's *Berlin Alexanderplatz,* in order to respond in the independent or cultural sector to what in the commercial field is the Hollywood superhit launched in the cinema, but which makes its money in other aggregate states. These film and television "events" also indicate how the political spaces that the independent cinema had won in the 1970s become, thanks to television and media-multiplication, larger occasions. In these instances, the critical reflexivity and introspection so typical of the New German Cinema can combine with that other experience of self—the history/memory/film-history-as-memory experience—without foregoing what was once so crucial about "going to the movies," namely, the spontaneous creation of a community (even though spectators are now sharing the same viewing time rather than the same viewing space).

Secondly, the German cinema has proved itself very inventive in "minor" formats and hybrid forms. The reason for its eclecticism and its borrowings from so many different cultural models—from pre-cinematic spectacles like the magic lantern to opera, melodrama, and the *Gesamt-kunstwerk;* from film essay to film tableau; from chronicle to allegorical mystery play; from documentary to requiem; from dramatic monologue to schizo-dialogue—lies in the desire to preserve the cinema as the site of self-alienating experiences, in contrast to television's essentially self-confirming and self-validating function. In this respect, filmmakers are inheriting the legacy of a wide cultural field, from literature to protest action, from history to case study. This requires nonnarrative as well as narrative forms, a cinema of gestures and expressions as much as a cinema of spectacle, and a cinema of the white page and *temps morts* as well as a cinema of *temps forts* and action. Although not a counter-cinema in the Straubian or Godardian sense, the New German Cinema responded in very different ways to the pressure of (cinema) history. Filmmakers are increasingly aware of the extent to which their works are "windows"—not onto the world, but on an already programmed screen. In Europe, films can no longer be made either just for the cinema or just for television, but *with* both and *against* both. In a situation where independent filmmaking's best chance might be to anticipate, test, and initiate the types of programming public television will need to compete and contrast with satellite television, the independent films are as much pilots and models of a cinema of the future as the high-tech prototypes out of Hollywood.

This might be the sense of Alexander Kluge's turnaround: that one has to think of the (German) *Autorenfilm* not as a certain kind of product, but as a certain kind of space. Throughout the 1970s, the emphasis was on defining this space as political in the broadest sense, having to do with different kinds of self-awareness, with rendering experience directly, with forms of subjectivity and sexual identity, but also a soul-searching, for instance, about Germany's recent history, about power structures in the family and questions of the environment. The inner logic of this cinema and its central strategy was undoubtedly to set against the politics of spectacle as practiced by Hollywood the notion of personal experience as political.

However, the more thoroughly spectacle comes to pervade personal experience and private fantasy, the more this strategy begins to look esoteric, purely introspective or merely morbid. The move of some filmmakers (not only in Germany: see Peter Watkins's *The Journey,* or Claude Lanzmann's *Shoah)* to undertake projects whose scale can generate television events is symptomatic in this respect. It can be seen as an attempt

Marita Brewer seems to age as Maria in the television epic *Heimat*. The story chronicles the fortunes of three families in the fictitious German village of Schabbach from 1919 to 1982.

to use film and cinema as release mechanisms for a discursive activity that crosses the boundaries of entertainment, and even of the arts. When a documentary film makes it from the review pages to the front of newspapers or becomes the subject of late-night talk shows, it underlines television's powerful potential for creating something like an instant public sphere. Compared to the packaging of experience as we find it in the movie mega-hit, which spawns everything from a novelization, a soundtrack album, or a new line in fashion, toys, or tee-shirts, the television event exploits the various aggregate states not of the commodity but of discourse, as the interest and emotions aroused by *Hitler, Heimat,* or *Shoah* cascade through television program grids, the press, and academic journals. Yet is this different in kind or only in degree, one might ask, from television news, which runs a "story"—Ethiopia, South Africa, Nicaragua—for a few weeks, until it switches to some other: Lebanon, the Gulf, the West Bank?

Thanks to the cooperation and cohabitation of television and independent filmmakers, such questions have been argued in West Germany at a fairly informed level of debate. Kluge, for instance, sees duration, the organization of time as the key to an "alternative" use of television: "In *Heimat,* the spectators are not really interested in Edgar Reitz, nor the Hunsrück, nor in artistic values; they want to test through their own feelings what life was like in 1919, 1933, or 1945, what their parents did.

Like standing by the window; it is raining, I look outside, and something goes through my mind. This kind of interest can be satisfied by pop songs, whose function it is to weave a carpet on which the spectator can fly—but we can do it best. If it is done well, it is the opposite of what television usually gives the viewer, because television is always obliged to make sense of things, to provide a commentary."[13]

Taking the total media environment as a political and cultural inevitability, Kluge's view is that as long as the spaces and windows of television exist, they must be used, in the name of a diversity that can only survive in and through television. Since 1984 he has been active in getting together a consortium which could make a "cultural" channel viable financially and politically attractive also to a conservative government. He may even be looking to the European Community, which has declared 1988 the "European Cinema and Television Year," designed to promote awareness of the achievements of the film and television industries in all the countries "from the Atlantic to the Urals."[14] If this public relations exercise has any value at all, it would have to start with the culture clashes still existing in the various nations and regions. This at least is the direction taken by ZDF, which for the occasion has commissioned and co-produced a series of films about Turks in Hamburg, a Basque family in Spain, a Welsh soldier fighting in Northern Ireland, a young gypsy in France, and a teacher working in a remote Kurdish village.[15]

Another scenario is at least as likely: promoting European film and television will help to soften up the national audiences for the multinational programmers. But even they are perhaps merely the side show, the publicly acceptable face of another offensive altogether. Kluge, in one of his handy phrases, talks of the "industrialization of consciousness,"[16] by which he means that the new media are only the vanguard of a more sinister move to turn public opinion itself into "corporate property." Given the strength of nationalism, regionalism, and the ecological movements in at least some European countries, this may seem overly pessimistic. There can be little doubt that in the current reorganization of delivery systems and their ownership, more is at stake than the profits to be made out of entertainment and culture. An industrialization of consumption is under way, of which television and the media are linchpins, allowing goods and services to circulate, from mail order shopping to banking, from education to medicine. If the arts become the musak of the system, destined to enhance a consumer-friendly environment at the point of sale, what role then for an independent cinema on television?

Notes

This article is based on a talk given at the Institute of Contemporary Arts in London in May 1987. Parts of it are taken from *New German Cinema: A History*, to be published by Macmillan Publishing Company later this year.

1. Wolfram Schütte, "Das Herz," in *Fassbinder*, ed. Wolfram Schütte and P. W. Jansen, rev. ed. (Munich: Hanser, 1982), p. 63.
2. See interview in *Der Spiegel*, "Wir sind nicht mehr der Jungfilm," June 18, 1979.
3. Interview in *Frankfurter Rundschau*, reprinted in Rainer Werner Fassbinder, *Die Anarchie der Phantasie* (Frankfurt: Fischer, 1986), p. 136.
4. This is the case, for instance, of the famous "Hamburg Declaration" of October 1979, reprinted in *medium* (November 1979): 27.
5. For an overview of the German "new media scene," see Kraft Wetzel, ed. *Neue Medien contra Filmkultur?* (Berlin: Verlag Walter Spiess, 1987).
6. See Günter Rohrbach, "Die verhängnisvolle Macht der Regisseure," *medium* (April 1983): 40-41.
7. See Sheila Johnston, "The Author as Public Institution," *Screen Education*, no. 32-33 (Autumn-Winter 1979-80): 67-78.
8. See "Der deutsche Film ist tot," *Berlinale Journal*, February 27, 1987.
9. For one of the most vitriolic attacks on the New German Cinema, see Andreas Mayer, "Auf dem Wege zum Staatskino?" (Parts I-III), *medium* (October-November-December 1977).
10. Alexander Kluge, ed., *Bestandsaufnahme: Utopie Film* (Frankfurt: Zweitausendeins, 1983).
11. See Hans Joachim Neumann, *Der deutsche Film heute* (Frankfurt: Ullstein, 1986), pp. 43-48.
12. See Ian Christie and Thomas Elsaesser, "Bring on the Clones," *The Guardian*, March 4, 1982.
13. Quoted in Kraft Wetzel, "Luftlöcher ins Packeis," in *Neue Medien contra Filmkultur?*, p. 250.
14. Martin Blaney, "Words Speak Louder Than Actions?" *Berlinale Journal*, no. 12 (February 23, 1988), p. 3.
15. See Dieter Krusche, "Schwierige Heimat—Europa im Blickfeld junger Regisseure," *Spiel im ZDF*, March 1988.
16. Alexander Kluge, "Warum Kooperation zwischen Film und Fernsehen?" in *Neue Medien contra Filmkultur?*, p. 238.

The New World Information Order and the U.S. Press

Francis N. Wete

Criticisms of the one-way flow of international communication were first conceived and elaborated in the 1940s while England was still a major economic power and when the United States was still militarily, diplomatically, and economically unchallenged.

Herbert Schiller has suggested that the policy of a free flow of information was "one of the very few indispensable prerequisites" for the "imperial ascendancy of the U.S."[1] He noted that the private interests of U.S. mass media organizations also were served by this policy. It was a propitious time to extol the virtues of unrestricted movement of information and resources in that Nazi occupation had traumatized Europe and a good part of the rest of the world, and thus, freedom of information and movement were highly desirable. Under these circumstances, Schiller notes, it was relatively easy to confuse truly national needs with private business objectives. Moreover, the decisive role played by the British worldwide communications network had not escaped attention in the United States: "It was against these finely spun, structural ties that an Ameri-can offensive was mounted. Conveniently the attack could avail itself of the virtuous language and praiseworthy objectives of 'free flow of information' and 'worldwide access to news.'"[2]

The underlying motive was to break the international grip of the European news cartels. Kent Cooper, executive managing editor of the Associated Press (AP) had written about the limitations Reuter, Havas and Wolff (now Agence France Presse, AFP) posed for the activities of the AP.[3] Cooper indicted the European news cartels for keeping the AP out of the race for dissemination of information to the world:

In precluding the Associated Press from disseminating news abroad, Reuter and Havas (French) served three purposes: (1) they kept out Associated Press competition; (2) they were free to present American news disparagingly to the United States if they presented it at all; (3) they could present news of their own countries most favorably and without it being contradicted.[4]

Both the U.S. press groups and government soon found others in the country who recognized the advantages that worldwide communications control bestowed on foreign trade and export.[5] *Business Week* commented: "In peacetime, reduced costs of messages will energize our trade, support our propaganda, bolster business for all the lines."[6] The British were not aware of American motives in this campaign. The *Economist* (London) reacted to Cooper's "free flow of information drive": "The huge financial resources of the American agencies might enable them to dominate the world . . . [Cooper], like most big business executives, experiences a peculiar moral glow in finding that his idea of freedom coincides with his commercial advantage . . . Democracy does not necessarily mean making the whole world safer for the AP."[7]

In 1946, William Benton, the assistant secretary of state who greatly influenced U.S. policy on communications after the Second World War, outlined the government's position on the meaning of freedom of communications:

The State Department plans to do everything within its power along political or diplomatic lines to help break down the artificial barriers to the expansion of private American news agencies, magazines, motion pictures, and other media of communications throughout the world . . . Freedom of the press—and freedom of exchange of information generally—is an integral part of our foreign policy.[8]

Having sought and secured government endorsement of their aims, the American Society of Newspaper Editors, meeting in November 1944, then declared: ". . . most Americans and their newspapers will support government policies

. . . and action toward removal of all political, legal, and economic barriers to the media of information, and . . . our Government should make this abundantly clear to other nations."[9]

At the constitutional conference of UNESCO in London, 1945, the United States chiefly was responsible for making the free flow of information a UNESCO objective. Article I, Section 2 of the UNESCO charter states that the Organization "will collaborate in the work of advancing mutual knowledge and understanding of peoples, through all means of mass communications, and to that end, [will] recommend such international agreements as may be necessary to promote the free flow of ideas by word and image."[10]

A year later, the United States tried to follow this mandate by proposing that the Organization establish a worldwide communications system at a cost of $250 million.[11] The British objected strenuously to the proposal, charging that the United States was attempting to use UNESCO "to blitz the world with American ideas," and the plan was dropped.[12] However, the United States did not give up producing material for UNESCO radio programs that even friendly editorial comment in Western Europe called "American propaganda." U.S. newspapers supported this effort, especially during the Korean War, "U.S. Looks to UNESCO to Tell Koreans Truth," and "UNESCO's Aid Sought Along the Propaganda Front." A reaction by the *London News Chronicle* struck a note of warning: "American insistence that UN-

ESCO enter the Cold War by spreading pro-Western, anti-Communist propaganda is providing a crisis which may wreck the Organization."[13]

Though fully aware of the commercial threat the free-flow doctrine posed to their own communications industries, faced with the United States' media power, the Western market economies, especially Great Britain, nonetheless supported the principle as a means of embarrassing the Soviet sphere and placing it on the ideological defensive.

In 1962, the U.S. General Assembly endorsed the principle that "development of communications media was part of overall development" and recommended that "technical assistance be made available for the purpose of improving media facilities." The U.S. National Commission for UNESCO statement in 1963 noted these actions "with satisfaction" and recognized "information media development as a necessity for economic growth."[14] Against this background came the decolonization decade of the sixties when some seventy former colonies gained their independence and became members of UNESCO. The new nations joined the international community with demands that threatened the status quo.

According to Joseph Mehan, the first reference to a change in the information order was made in 1969 at a UNESCO meeting in Montreal. The meeting introduced the concept of "two-way circulation of news and balanced circulation of news."[15] In 1970, at the 16th General Conference of UNESCO, the Director General was asked "to help member states in formulating their mass communications policies." This was the genesis of the current international information flow debate. For more than a decade, the resentments bred by the imbalances in the flow of information spawned a series of proposals to correct it. Of these, the Mass Media Declaration, the MacBride Report, and the International Program for the Development of Communications are easily the best known.

But when the communications debate burst upon U.S. public awareness at the 1976 UNESCO General Conference in Nairobi, most of what preceded it was largely unknown to all but a few academicians.[16] Charles W. Bray, deputy director of the International Communication Agency, explained the reason for this late start: "The reply of the U.S. was at first to stand aloof. The regime for information interchange had already been established, its name was freedom, and we saw no need for any declaration or arrangements."[17]

From the standpoint of the Third World, a good deal is wrong with the "old," and still prevailing, order. In terms of news and news coverage, the overwhelming majority of world news flows from the developed to the developing countries and is generated by four large transnational news agencies—AP, UPI, AFP, and Reuters. Moreover, the West dominates the use of satellites, the electromagnetic spectrum controlling the use of airwaves, telecommunications, micro-electronics, remote sensing capabilities, direct satellite broadcasting, and computer-related transmission.

Implicit in the quest for a new world information order is an awareness of the differences in media functions in various countries throughout the world. These differences are particularly evident in developing nations that are consciously using their communication systems as tools to promote national growth. A basic tenet that each nation has the right to determine what the communication system within its boundaries shall be, what shall be communicated and to what end, emerged in large part from the increasing concerns of the nonaligned nations.

Another basic assumption of the new information order is that the best technology for conveying information rests in the hands of the developed nations. Because information brings power to those who have it and control it most effectively, current technology concentrates economic, educational, and other informational power in the developed world. This state of affairs makes developing nations "knowledge colonies." For example, the developed nations have selected and claimed the best frequencies and left the rest of the world at a disadvantage in developing their communication systems.

Western opposition to the new information order has been led by the U.S. news agencies and journalistic organizations, which belatedly entered the debate in the mid-1970s. They began pressuring the U.S. government to air its views in UNESCO forums when it appeared that the government was not taking a strong stand against the Order's proposals.

U.S. press coverage of UNESCO conferences since 1976 has focused on the subject of the new world information order, almost to the exclusion of everything else. The main themes of the debate were represented in terms of "government control of information," "licensing of journalists," "censorship," "mandatory code of ethics," and other formulations believed to endanger press freedom instead of the equitable distribution of the capacity to communicate and a balanced flow of information.

On May 17, 1980, *Editor and Publisher* commented on the MacBride Report, which had not yet been published: "Whether you have read it or not, the IPI, ANPA, ASNE, IAPA, the World Press Freedom Committee believe there is enough wrong with it to constitute a threat to the existence of a free press everywhere."[18] "All the proposals are dangerous," said Allen H. Neuhrath, president of the Gannett Newspaper chain and chairman of the Executive Committee of the American Newspaper Publishers Association.[19] He said proposals such as those advocating for the media to promote social, cultural, economic, and political goals set by the governments—and creating a UNESCO agency that "could become an international organization to control and watch over the news media"—are "in opposition to the concept of freedom of the press."[20]

Sean MacBride wondered whether these critics actually read the report. The U.S. government had admitted on April 11, 1980, that the final result of the report would be "remarkably favorable to our interests. Censorship is gone, licensing of journalists and similar nostrums are gone; there is a robust commitment to a fully functioning free press. There is even a recognition of the right to access to diverse sources of opinion within a country, to which the Soviet delegate was alone in footnoting strenuous objection."[21] But, although the U.S. government and Western press associations reacted to the MacBride Report with caution, the U.S. press reacted with rage, panic, and considerable bias. With conspicuous uniformity, the U.S. media accused UNESCO of being the archenemy of freedom of the press.[22]

After the 1980 UNESCO General Conference held in Belgrade, the National News Council conducted a study of the U.S. coverage of that meeting. The findings of the study were reported by A. H. Raskin,[23] deputy director of the council. The council examined 448 news clippings and 206 editorials from newspapers in all parts of the country. About 80 percent of the news stories were from the Associated Press and United Press International (UPI).

During the six-week conference, no story treated any of the reports, speeches, or resolutions on UNESCO's basic activities in combating illiteracy, developing alternate energy sources, protecting historic monuments, broadening educational programs for scientists and engineers, and scores of other fields. By contrast, there were 173 news and feature stories and 183 editorials dealing with the debate over communications policy. The editorials all expressed apprehension about UNESCO's involvement in attempts to establish policy in matters affecting the worldwide flow of information. In 158 cases, the editorials were strongly hostile to the point of suggesting (in 27 papers) U.S. withdrawal from UNESCO if it persisted in moves deemed destructive of press freedom.

As Raskin notes, the tendency of the U.S. press to focus on negative aspects of the UNESCO role in mass media brought reactions not only by champions of the proposed new order but also by many who view the concept with reserve. Leonard R. Sussman, executive director of Freedom House in New York who spoke at Belgrade as representative of the Inter-American Press Association, expressed approval for projects involving technical assistance to Third World journalists. But the only things included in the AP account were his warnings to UNESCO to shun any moves toward licensing or monitoring journalists. "Every word in the account was absolutely accurate," Sussman said, "but it was unbalanced in its total effect."[24] He deplored the extent to which that approach is, in his view, characteristic of most of the reporting on the UNESCO information debate.

Sussman conducted an independent survey of U.S. newspaper coverage of the UNESCO Conference related solely to articles and editorials on the communications debate.[25] His survey showed that 38 of 63 news accounts examined (60 percent) were "unfavorable" in their general reporting of the conference, 5 (8 percent) were "favorable" and 20 (32 percent) were "balanced." Of the editorials of 37 papers he studied, 34 (92 percent) "strongly attacked" the work of the conference. One was "favorable" in his view and two were "balanced."

Sussman's assessment of U.S. press handling of the Belgrade developments is of particular interest because he and his organization[26] are in the forefront of the campaign against UNESCO's current role in the mass media:

The coverage was unbalanced because many reports of the events at Belgrade emphasized the dire potentialities of press controls as though they had already materialized. Votes taken or a consensus reached were faithfully reported. But all of these actions were directed toward further studies and meetings over the next three years. These actions unquestionably target the free press for future governmental restrictions or, at least, repressive standards however enforced. This is undeniably a threat—but too often the reports and certainly the headlines gave the impression doomsday had already arrived. Neither public understanding nor an effective defense of press freedom is helped by exaggerating the present state of challenge.[27]

Following the Belgrade Conference, in April 1981, a group of Western journalists met at Talloires in the French Alps and issued what has been called the Declaration of Talloires. The declaration expressed the Western media's objections to many of the fundamental ideas of the MacBride Report. It not only resurrected the original Western formulation of "free flow" but, as Kusum and Gross noted, conspicuously dropped the words "and balanced" (see note 33).

Without specifically referring to the report's critique of commercialization, monopoly, or bureaucracy, the signatories affirmed uncompro-

mising allegiance to "the importance of advertising as a consumer service and in providing for a strong and self-sustaining press." Omitting comment on the report's plea for the democratization of communication, they supported "the universal right to be freely informed" and opposed "any interference with this fundamental right." Without mentioning the report's comments on self-censorship, they called for the elimination of "censorship and other forms of arbitrary control of information and opinion." On ethics and licensing, they were very explicit:

There can be no international code of ethics; the plurality of views makes this impossible . . . licensing of journalists by national or international bodies should not be sanctioned; nor should special requirements be demanded of journalists in lieu of licensing them. Such measures submit journalists to controls and pressures inconsistent with a free press.

Within a year of the Talloires declaration, a group of prominent American international affairs experts issued a report on U.S. policy toward the United Nations. Among other things, the report deplores "the efforts by the Soviet Union and some Third World governments to legitimize under the rubric of a 'New International Information Order' government controls over the collection, transmission and publication of news by the press and other mass media."[28] The report hastened to add that this notion of what the new order entails is suggested by "leaders of independent news organizations" in Talloires and has been endorsed by the President and the Congress of the United States.[29]

Besides endorsing the Declaration of Talloires, the ad hoc group invited the United States to adopt a harder line at the United Nations:

We believe the time has come to reassess the capacity of UNESCO and certain other UN agencies, to function compatibly with their declared ideals and purposes. Where politicization, or gross inefficiency, has seriously impaired this capacity, and remedial efforts fail, the U.S. should consider alternative institutions. If these efforts fail, we should not exclude the possibility of withdrawing financial support or even withdrawing from the agency.[30]

This is the "free flow of information" diplomacy of the 1940s in reverse.

The AP indictment of the European cartels in the 1940s is ironic in the context of today's debate where the U.S. news agencies dominate the flow of world information. Third World countries are advancing arguments today similar to those made by the U.S. government and press in the 1940s—developing nations are kept out of the competition by the monopoly of industrialized countries; international news agencies present the Third World disparagingly, when they do; those international agencies present their own countries favorably without contradiction.

The U.S. media not only do not treat the new world information order debate in an objective manner, but also do not acknowledge or appreciate criticisms of their treatment of the debate. Their shoddy coverage of events exemplifies the very problem that triggered the debate over a new information order. William Steif, a Washington correspondent for Scripps Howard papers, commented, "my self-important peers are protecting their own interests much more than they are worrying about lofty ideals of 'press freedom' that they proclaim so fervently."[31]

It is normal that corporate media interests in the United States should be at odds with the demands for a new information order. It is also normal that the American government should defend those interests in U.N. forums when they are challenged by the diametrically different interests and aspirations of most developing nations. But the basic U.S. public notion of the new order and even of UNESCO is founded on a biased view of reality.

The new information order is not a scheme "to legitimize government controls" but an attempt to promote the decolonization and democratization of information capacities and contents, the question of controls being left for each society to decide. Moreover, the new order is not designed, as has been claimed, "to license journalists." Recommendation No. 50 of the MacBride Report states specifically that "the commission does not propose special privileges to protect journalists in the performance of their duties, although journalism is a dangerous profession" and to propose anything beyond human rights "would invite the dangers entitled in a licensing system since it would require somebody to stipulate who should be entitled to such protection."[32] As far as the MacBride Report is concerned, "Protection of Journalists" is but one of the issues requiring further studies.

The only other instance is when a French nongovernmental organization proposed that a commission for the protection of journalists be established.[33] It would have given journalists identity cards that could be withdrawn if they violated "generally accepted codes of journalistic ethics."[34] Thus, neither the MacBride Report nor the UNESCO secretariat nor any member state has formally advocated the protection or licensing of journalists.

A clear impression emerges that the ethics-licensing controversy is a tool devised by the Western press to distract from the essence of the new information order. Suggestions and proposals are treated by the press as though they were laws ready for enforcement. Besides, those suggestions "to license journalists" in order to promote the professional integrity of journalists and to develop a system of professional self-regulation are not different from suggestions made on the same subject in the United States. The Hutchins Commission and other groups in the United States have made proposals at various periods during this century to raise the standards of journalism by means of "government control" to an extent greater than has been suggested in the context of the new information order debate, particularly through licensing schemes for journalists.

The dangers of the present double standard by the United States in the debate over international communications were clearly pointed out in a report by the International Communications Agency in 1979.[35] It noted, for instance, that the United States has been a massive supplier of media products to the rest of the world, but it uses very few foreign media products itself. International news reaches the United States largely through AP and UPI. The U.S. television system is the second most "closed" to foreign programming in the world. "These facts, deriving from the success and dynamism of U.S. private media, may limit our ability to see the world (and ourselves) through others' eyes."[36]

When that limitation is accompanied by the need to defend a profit motive interest, perception of the world can be totally distorted. The campaign of the U.S. mass media has emasculated the fundamental purposes of the new world information order concept. The reception given the National News Council Report is a further indication of the U.S. media's determination to undermine criticism of their performance. Unless this attitude changes, the American public will continue to receive incomplete coverage.

Backed by the administration, this media campaign became the joint strategy of both the U.S. government and the press for dealing with the idea of the new world information order. Coupled with the threat of withholding financial support or even withdrawing from UNESCO,[37] it has torpedoed concrete action toward the new order.

Kaarle Nordenstreng suggests that this strategy has been determined by the balance of political forces on a world scale, putting the United States and the West on the defensive as a minority partner in the international community.[38] The three-pronged strategy entailed portraying the new order as part of an Orwellian design, gently blackmailing UNESCO, and offering assistance to Third World media facilities and training as carrots.[39]

It is worth noting that the U.S. sells more goods to developing countries than to Western Europe and Japan combined. U.S. media therefore need the fast-growing Third World markets just as the latter need U.S. assistance to build viable communications systems and effectively participate in the exchange of information across continents. If America is to maintain and expand its trade with developing countries, it has to be more sensitive to their problems than it has been in the debate over a new information order.

Notes

1. Herbert I. Schiller, *Communication and Cultural Domination* (New York: International Arts and Sciences Press, Inc., 1976), p. 24.

2. Ibid., p. 26.

3. Kent Cooper, *Barriers Down* (New York: Farrar & Rinehart, Inc., 1942).

4. Ibid., p. 43.

5. Schiller, *Communication and Cultural Domination*, p. 28.

6. Ibid.

7. Ibid., p. 29.

8. Ibid.

9. Ibid., p. 31.

10. UNESCO Charter.

11. Joseph A. Mehan, "UNESCO and the U.S.: Action and Reaction," *Journal of Communication* 31, no. 4 (Autumn 1981): 160.

12. Ibid.

13. Ibid.

14. Ibid.

15. Ibid., p. 161.

16. Ibid.

17. Charles W. Bray, Deputy Director of the International Communication Agency, speech made before the School of Journalism and Media Representatives, University of Seattle, Washington, April 11, 1980, p. 2.

18. "The MacBride Report," *Editor and Publisher*, May 17, 1980, p. 8.

19. "Press Groups Denounce UNESCO Plan on Media," *Editor and Publisher*, June 7, 1980, p. 11.

20. Ibid.

21. Bray, p. 8.

22. Mehan, "UNESCO and the U.S.," p. 160.

23. A. H. Raskin, "U.S. News Coverage of the Belgrade UNESCO Conference," *Journal of Communication* 31, no. 4 (Autumn 1981): 164-174.

24. Cited in ibid., p. 167.

25. Leonard R. Sussman, "Illusions at Belgrade UNESCO," *Freedom at Issue*, January-February 1981.

26. Freedom House and the Inter-American Press Association are affiliated with the World Press Freedom Committee.

27. Sussman, "Illusions at Belgrade."

28. United States Policy toward the United Nations ad hoc group, "The United States and the United Nations . . . a Policy Today," October 1981, mimeo released on March 16, 1982, p. 16.

29. Ibid.

30. Ibid., p. 17.

31. William Steif, "On the 'Objective Press,'" *The Progressive* 43 (January 1979): 23.

32. International Commission for the Study of Communication Problems, *Many Voices, One World* (New York: Unipub, 1980), p. 264.

33. Kusum Singh and Bertram Gross, "'MacBride': The Report and the Response," *Journal of Communication* 31, no. 4 (Autumn 1981): 113.

34. Ibid.

35. Jonathan Gunther, *The United States and the Debate on the World "Information Order"* (Washington, D.C.: Academy for Educational Development, 1979).

36. Ibid.

37. Since the writing of this article, the U.S. has withdrawn from UNESCO.

38. Kaarle Nordenstreng, "U.S. Policy and the Third World: A Critique," *Journal of Communication* 32, no. 3 (Summer 1982): 56.

39. Ibid., pp. 56-57.

Counterterror

Annie Goldson and Chris Bratton

Counterterror is a serial videotape comprised of four half-hour segments, each of which are being developed in collaboration with video groups in the following countries: El Salvador, Northern Ireland, Lebanon, and the United States. The purpose of this collaborative videotape is to investigate the meaning of the term "terrorist" in various countries where it is frequently applied and to examine the broader, global implications of the "discourse of terrorism." Rather than entering into the debates that surround the definition of "terrorism" (and which frequently revolve around the problems of cultural or political relativity), in *Counterterror* we are suggesting that the term functions within a wider discursive practice. That is, the term is consciously invoked by subjects and institutions (from which and through which the subjects speak, such as the political bureaucracy or the media), that have particular and profound investments in speaking and writing of "terrorism."

The fact that those who create and reproduce the discourse admit to the problems of defining "terror-

Personnel

El Salvador: *The Video Workshop of the University of El Salvador*
Lebanon: *Jamal and Lillian Farhat*
Northern Ireland: *The Derry Film and Video Group*
United States: *Annie Goldson and Chris Bratton*

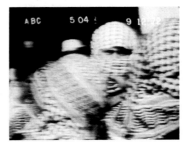

After Munich, ABC gives terrorism a face.

ism" does not prevent the term from functioning. Quite the reverse. Debate confers much-needed legitimacy on the discourse, while sheer repetition of the term (underwritten by institutional authority) naturalizes "terrorism," placing it within the realm of commonsense. Through this process, the label enters everyday language; its meaning becomes recognizable, available, and widely shared. It is therefore rarely scrutinized. Instead, its meaning is naturalized and therefore "fixed"—within flexible parameters. Indeed, the very indeterminacy of the term "terrorism" also operates in the interests of those who use the discourse. Its ambiguity and lack of precise definition provides "terrorism" with an elasticity through which power can be enforced. *Counterterror*, then, is about those institutions that create and manipulate both the definition of "terrorism" and the absence of its definition to further their own interests. It is a crosscultural exploration of why, how, and with what effect the discourse of terrorism is employed.

In *Counterterror*, we are proposing that the discourse of terrorism has been specifically designed to maintain repression within countries or communities whose labor, resources, and ideological alignment have sustained the wealth and privilege of the "Free World." In other words, we see the discourse as emanating from the advanced capitalist countries (led by the United States), that use as their object the Third World. This discourse, to use Antonio Gramsci's theory, is one mechanism through which the

White House responds to "terrorism in El Salvador."

Transcript of Statement by White House Spokesman Larry Speakes on Attacks in Salvador and Frankfurt. From the *New York Times*, June 21, 1985

Last night, senseless terrorism again took its toll on Americans, this time in El Salvador.

Of the 15 killed and 13 wounded, two were U.S. businessmen and four were unarmed off-duty marines not in uniform. They also killed 9 and injured 13 other innocent Salvadoran and Guatemalan men and women.

This atrocity, like the bombing early yesterday in Frankfurt, Germany, is further evidence that the war which terrorists are waging is not only directed against the United States.

It is a war against all of civilized society. This is a war in which innocent civilians are targets. This is a war in which innocent civilians are intentional victims and our servicemen have become specific targets.

This cannot continue.

We must act against those who have so little regard for human life and the values we cherish. And we must do so in concert with other nations who are democratic institutions and hold basic disdain for violence and the use of force.

We of the Western World must act

"ruling class fractions" can exercise "political and cultural hegemony over the entire society" (or in this transnational example, over societies).[1] This central premise will be examined in the tape in the light of the histories and relationships between a series of dominating/dominated countries: the United States and El Salvador; Britain and Northern Ireland; and Israel (underwritten by the United States) and sections of the Lebanese community. We are not attempting, as producers, to take a position on political violence as a tactic within a broader struggle. To do this would be to reproduce the dominant discourse of "terrorism" that uses the label precisely to efface the particular historical and political background of groups as diverse as the Red Brigades, the Tupomaros, the PLO, the IRA, etc. The issue of armed struggle, when it does arise, will be addressed specifically by the local segment producers according to their positions and experience.

The particular scenario on terrorism emerging from the advanced capitalist countries (and especially the Reagan administration in the U.S.) argues that there is a "terror network"—directed by Moscow and comprised of such regional proxies as Libya, the PLO, the IRA, the FMLN, the Sandinistas, and so on. This network threatens the very fabric of the free world.[2] In contrast to this view, we argue that the real terror network is a "counterterror network," a coalition that links the political and military interests in the United States and its clients in the Third World, the United Kingdom, South Africa, and Israel. This

"Senseless terrorism" requires "investigative assistance."

together as we did over a century ago to wipe out piracy from the seas and as we did 45 years ago against the threat of tyranny.

In response to the death of our marines and private citizens in El Salvador, the President today has directed the Secretary of State and the Secretary of Defense, with the help of our intelligence services, to immediately provide whatever assistance is necessary to President Duarte's government in order to find and to punish the terrorists who perpetrated this act.

To this end, the President today has directed that the United States expedite the delivery of security assistance items on order by the Salvadoran Government and be prepared to use the emergency authorities of the President to furnish the Salvadoran armed forces with additional military assets which will help them prosecute their campaign against the Communist guerrillas.

Their hope that terrorism will weaken our resolve or support for the revitalization of democracy in El Salvador is futile. If other U.S. military assets can be effective in this regard, then this government will provide them.

The President expects the Congress to support these measures and will be consulting with the appropriate legislative committees of the Congress on network, commanding the power and wealth of advanced capitalism, is based on the sharing of military and surveillance technology, intelligence operations, and strategy. In short, it is a collaborative effort to enforce their order.

Although the very structure of *Counterterror* emphasizes transnational collaboration, here we are focusing our brief discussion on the discourse of terrorism as it has been produced in the United States. Therefore, the following argument will refer only tangentially to the use of the label "terrorism" in the United Kingdom, Israel, or elsewhere. We have chosen this emphasis on the United States, first, because President Reagan, whose position represents a convergence of significant military, business, and political interests, has become the chief proponent of the discourse. This is not to say that the United Kingdom and Israel play an insignificant role in this process of naming; rather, they have become the beneficiaries of the amplification granted the term by a United States president, and have appropriated the discourse to suit their own political agendas at this juncture. But, second, we are concentrating on the United States because, as U.S. residents, we are more familiar with the development of the discourse here. Its effects within Northern Ireland, El Salvador, and Lebanon will be better represented by the producers in the final videotape.

In this article, then, we will outline the relationship between three specific institutions within the United States/advanced capitalism

The massacres at Sabra and Shatila refugee camps, Beirut, 1982.

what additional steps can be taken in El Salvador and elsewhere to end the external support for Salvadoran terrorists that they receive from Nicaragua and the Communist bloc . . .

Upon his return, the Vice President is to convene a Government-wide task force to develop recommendations for the President's decision on how all available U.S. resources can best be brought to bear in dealing with this problem.

Finally, the President wishes the American people to know that what we do in this circumstance must not be done in pointless anger. These events call for reasoned responses to lawless actions by those who do not abide by the norms of civilized society.

As for the President, he believes that our actions must be appropriate and proportionate to the criminal acts which have been taken against our citizens. Those who are responsible for such lawlessness and those who support it must know the consequences of their actions will never be capitulation to terrorist demands. We are both a nation of peace and a people of justice. By our very nature, we are slow to anger and magnanimous in helping those in less fortunate circumstances. But we also have our limits. And our limits have been reached.

that maintain the discourse of terrorism: political and military institutions; the conservative academy (academia, advisory groups, and think tanks); and the media (in particular, television).

Political and Military Institutions

If, as we believe, the discourse of terrorism is structured to support the interests of the United States in the Third World, a counterterrorist policy is essential. In effect, however, this policy is used to preclude, and if necessary, to subdue uprisings within client states and to create consensus at home.

The Reagan administration, in the name of counterterrorism, has realigned the institutions of military, judicial, and legislative power. This realignment has to be located within a more general program of massive military expenditure, and represents the most recent step toward maintaining the global hegemony of the United States at a time of international economic crisis.

Counterterrorist policy is the latest instance of a history of political repression which escalated after World War II.[3] Since the 1950s, the United States has marked specific Third World countries in Latin America, Asia, and parts of Africa for penetration as sources of cheap labor, available resources, and open markets. Anti-imperialist insurrections in these regions—popular uprisings against exploitation—have had to be constantly managed and suppressed. Direct U.S. military intervention has been used occasionally and remains an option for

Report of a contra attack in Nueva Guinea, Nicaragua, 1986.

El Salvador

The Reagan administration has continuously depicted El Salvador as a country locked in a struggle between elements of the "far right" and the insurgency movement of the "far left." It claims that U.S. financial backing has transformed El Salvador into a Latin version of "democracy," a viable model for the entire region. In fact, the political system that Washington has tried to install has been a "centrist" regime that has worked with the military to crush both popular resistance and the guerrilla movement, and to continue repression of the majority.

By the late 1960s, unemployment, poverty, landlessness, and state violence were rampant in El Salvador and tensions grew between the workers and peasants and the oligarchy. Broad-based movements comprised of students, campesinos, women, workers, and church members stood up against the dictatorship and by the mid-1970s the guerrillas had become a major force. The government responded to the demands for change by increasing the repression—El Salvador was marked by massacres, disappearances, torture, and massive human rights violations. It is estimated that as of 1982, forty thousand Salva-

the future. However, popular dissent has been met with other strategies, such as covert action and counterinsurgency warfare. The latter includes the funding, training, and equipping of police forces and paramilitaries in the Third World, countries which then become, in effect, client states of the U.S. The result of this support has been the institutionalization within these countries of military forces engaged in savage wars against their own people. Counterinsurgency—based on the training of U.S. advisors—entails tactics that range from the suspension of basic civil liberties to torture, assassinations, disappearances, and wholesale massacre.

The economy of representation . . .

While maintaining its interests in the Third World, the United States has had to struggle to manage dissatisfaction at home. After the Second World War, consensus had to be created for rearmament or, perhaps more accurately, the permanent war economy. There have always been real and perceived internal threats to the policies of the United States government, namely minority and working-class dissent, as well as organized political opposition to its expansionist policies. A campaign of political repression against these threats can be traced directly from the 1950s. Redbaiting, blacklisting, witch-hunts, and spy trials were the most visible methods used by a growing national security bureaucracy. During the 1960s and 1970s, massive surveillance operations such as COMINTELPRO indicated that government-sponsored political oppression was continuing

doreans had been killed. The most notorious murders were carried out by the "death squads," since proven to be drawn from the armed forces and the government.

Ronald Reagan's representation of El Salvador as a democratic success story disavows the current political reality. In consigning the left to the margins, the administration has denied the huge popular support that the guerrillas enjoy, their successes in the city and the countryside, and the willingness of the FMLN, the guerrilla's umbrella organization, to form an alliance with progressive democratic elements—most notably the FDR, which is comprised of parties that have been banned from the political process in El Salvador. The U.S. administration has consistently failed to mention that the rebel movement has been attempting since 1981 to implement peace talks so as to achieve a negotiated end to the conflict, an attempt that has been constantly thwarted by U.S. interference.

The central motivation of the Reagan administration in installing the "centrist" government to stave off the "evils at both ends," has been to eliminate the armed resistance, which by 1980 had won significant support. The United States, citing national security and that the bureaucracy was expanding. Today, within the United States, the alleged menace of "terrorism" has justified the introduction of a multitude of tactics to contain dissent, such as a greater emphasis on secrecy of information, the tightening of immigration laws, the extension of surveillance operations by permitting the CIA to operate inside the country, the spy "show trials," and so on.

. . . two histories/two minutes.

Permanent war, both hot and cold, has been supplemented by a state of permanent emergency where the apparent "extraordinary threat of terrorism" justifies "extraordinary responses." Therefore, many military operations are carried out in the name of combating "terrorism." These include direct military intervention, the bombing of Tripoli, and the underwriting of Israeli aggression against the Palestinians; and covert activities such as the funding of the contras and the attempted assassination of the leader of the Huzballah in Beirut.[4]

These aggressive policies, we believe, spearhead the real "terror network," a coalition of the political and military interests of the advanced Western powers. Counterterrorist policies facilitate the aim of transnational capitalism, which is to concentrate its riches at the expense of the poverty of vast numbers of people. By doing the police work in the Catholic communities of Northern Ireland, in West Bank refugee camps, and in the townships and homelands of South Africa, the counterterror network is maintaining, through terror, a status quo based on North American class privilege.

interests and recognizing the success of the FMLN, feared another Sandinista revolution. In addition, Washington had come under increasing pressure to improve the human rights record in El Salvador. In the most expensive elections ever held in Central America, the U.S. maneuvered the success of the Christian Democrats, headed by Napolean Duarte. In the administration's view, this election result should have isolated the FMLN/FDR politically, driven a wedge into the rebel alliance, and forced the left to negotiate on Washington's terms. The far right would also be compelled to obey U.S. plans, making requests to Congress for more economic and military aid more attractive. However, the plan failed. Duarte, although tolerated by the military and private sector as the only guarantor of the large amounts of military aid, was unable or unwilling to challenge the power of the armed forces and did not implement any significant social changes. The death squad murders, which never completely ceased, began to rise again.

Each new tactic by the United States, military and political, has failed, and only the current amount of aid—currently $2 million a day—has stopped the country from collapsing.

The Conservative Academy

In *Counterterror*, we argue that the conservative academy functions to legitimize the "discourse of terrorism." Largely, this has been accomplished by individuals working through universities, think tanks, and private research institutes producing books, articles, publications, symposia, conferences, and curricula.[5] As we discussed above, what "terrorism" actually is remains disputed, but it has, nevertheless, been fully constituted as an object of study. The validity conferred upon the concept by academia can then be employed by other institutions, particularly those of government, but also those of media—and from these institutions it passes into the language of everyday life. These reverberations grant the discourse greater power.

The effects of this discourse are not limited to the classrooms or contained within the lecture halls. Its consequences in the Third World, for example, are very real. The facade of neutrality or independence that gives these institutions their credibility generally allows them to dissociate themselves from these consequences. But a closer examination reveals the shared interests that connect such institutions with the intentions of a United States administration determined to maintain its position as a global power.

The Rand Corporation and the Center for Strategic and International Studies (CSIS) at Georgetown University are two of the many public policy research institutes within the United States. At

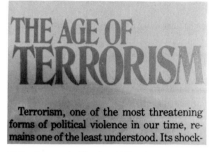

Walter Laqueur's *The Age of Terrorism*.

"Terrorism is a bit like pornography, there's no real definition, but everyone knows it when they see it."
—*Dr. Walter Laqueur, Center for Strategic and International Studies*

"I think it's possible to define terrorism objectively so long as we define it by the characteristics of the act itself, not the nationality of the perpetrator and not the nature of the cause, but the quality of the act. An act of terrorism is first of all a crime . . ."
—*Brian Jenkins, Rand Corporation*

"The whole notion of objectivity says that the truth lies exactly midway between two extremes. In Northern Ireland this is a nonsense. There couldn't be a moral balance in a situation where you've got a historically disadvantaged community which is actively resisting that disadvantage and other people who are maintaining this disadvantage. Even if the notions of objectivity and balance have meaning—and I don't believe that they do—they still wouldn't produce a fair account of what is happening here, for the very simple reason that what is happening here is not itself fair."
—*Eammon McCann, journalist, Derry, from Northern Ireland segment of* Counterterror, *analyzing media coverage of the North.*

Rand, 84 percent of the research is directly commissioned by the Departments of Defense, State, and Justice. The claim of these centers to independence obscures their formal relations to government. (CSIS has provided various administrations with high-ranking appointees, including Jeanne Kirkpatrick.) Moreover, this so-called neutrality hides a web of informal relations, shared interests which dictate the boundaries of acceptable research. Therefore, the topic of the "terrorist mind" or "why women turn to terrorism" would be deemed suitable by both government and institution, while an investigation into the underlying discourse of terrorism would never be considered.

Contemporary studies of "terrorism" have as their direct antecedent government-funded research of the 1950s and 1960s. Most relevant here is work done after 1966, during the escalation in Vietnam, which showed an increasing concern with the sociological and psychological characteristics of guerrilla organizations.[6] At the same time as assisting the practice of social counterinsurgency, science was investigating the problems of managing domestic dissent. Now, as then, such research provides a "scientific" analysis of possible threats to the hegemony of the United States both internally and abroad. In so doing, it attempts to predict the movements of dissenting populations, and therefore provides the military and political institutions with the information necessary for continued domination.

Northern Ireland

Northern Ireland was created in 1923 by British partition. At the outset, it was constituted as sectarian and undemocratic, denying basic political rights to over one-third of its population, the Catholics. Since 1977, the British have instituted as one facet of their long-term strategy in the North, the policy of "Ulsterization." The British had taken the lead, and consequently the most visible role, in fullscale counterinsurgency warfare. "Ulsterization" put the Ulster Defense Regiment (UDR)—the locally recruited branch of the British Army—and more importantly, the Royal Ulster Constabulary (RUC), the "police," on the front line.

By placing the UDR and the RUC in the limelight, the British government intended to give the appearance in England ("at home") that events in the North were in fact a local conflict. More to the point, they criminalized the struggle, lifting it out of the register of the political and rendering it a problem of "law and order."

However, a closer look at the situation reveals, again, the role of the British government. The RUC, for instance, is not a local "police force" but is an institutionalized, sectarian paramilitary, trained, financed, and maintained as an agent of British imperialist interests. The result of the RUC presence, along with that of the UDR and Protestant paramilitaries, continues to benefit not only Britain, but also the Ulster industrialists, business people, and landowners united in the Unionist Party. Together, these interests maintain a system based on discrimination and poverty.

The Media

While it is an oversimplification to suggest that the media is merely an organ of the ruling class, it has to be analyzed as part of the existing social structure, that is, a structure based on class inequities.[7] The media has definite shared interests with the ruling classes, which run the gamut from the class of its owners (and the editorial power that they enforce), through its central reliance both on its commercial sponsor and hence on an audience of active consumers, to a direct investment in technology.[8] It is also beholden to certain institutional conventions that have been established in its history and development under advanced capitalism, including, for instance, how the news is structured, the rules of narrative and the interview, and the central role of objectivity and neutrality.

All these factors come into play when the media's coverage of "terrorism" is considered. Yet, these are precisely the issues that are avoided in the clamorous discussions that connect the media to "terrorism." Rather, the arguments that arise after each incident of political violence are variants on the issue of media responsibility—that is, its vulnerability to terrorist manipulation, its role as the precipitant of violence or its position as a de facto player in foreign policy, and so on. The "solutions" offered range from a complete ban on coverage (working on the assumption that if there is no coverage, there will be no incidents) to the more moderate suggestion of

Peter Jennings report on terrorism.

NBC Guidelines for the Coverage of Terrorism

A basic factor common to many terrorism situations is the desire of the terrorists to publicize a complaint, or a "cause" or simply themselves. Consequently, there must be a delicate balance of our obligation to keep the public informed, our obligation to avoid being used and our obligation not to exacerbate or sensationalize the situation. Of course, the final news judgment must remain with NBC News.

The basic standards which govern our coverage of civil disturbances also apply to our coverage of terrorism.

Hampering negotiations between terrorists and the authorities will be avoided to lessen the possibility of making the situation worse.

NBC News will not attempt to interview terrorists or hostages until authorities have the situation in control. Even then, any attempt requires approval from the President or Executive Vice President of NBC News.

Live interviews with terrorists require approval by the President or Executive Vice President of NBC News.

Generally any direct communication from terrorists or alleged terrorists is to be reported to the authorities promptly.

guidelines directing responsible journalism. The media grimly bears the criticism, not wanting to appear unpatriotic, but asserting in the name of the Fourth Estate its independence. The institution, after all, is understood to be a crucial ingredient in a "democracy" in that it provides the "objective truth" to a voting public. If apparent strictures are placed on the media, those who gain so much from the United States model of democracy, that is, from advanced capitalism, may find that their interests are challenged.

That the mainstream media might use its coverage of "terrorism" to critique the effects of "democracy" within the Third World is rarely considered. Instead, it reduces the question surrounding the representation of "terrorism" to those of sheer spectacle. In so doing, it continues a process that it is eminently suited for: the evacuation of history. The social and political factors that have led up to incidents of violence are excised—little mention is made, for instance, of the historical role of the United States in the sponsorship of Third World conflict. Nor is there any attempt to question why violence that the developed world instigates or underwrites— the murder of thousands of Nicaraguans through the funding of the contras, or the invasion of Lebanon, for example—does not qualify as "terrorist." Furthermore, this lack of historical analysis within the media suggests that "terrorism" is indeed an enormous threat that has to be met with massive military expenditure and a strong military

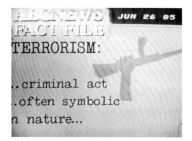

Defining terrorism on the news:
a few cogent phrases, a few iconic images.

response. In fact, to name a country/community "terrorist" becomes enough to justify aggression against it, regardless of the political circumstances. Finally, then, despite the laborious discussions about the media's relationship to "terrorism," it continues to produce the discourse because it, too, is invested in its continuation.

Popular Culture

In addition to interrogating the institutional basis of the "discourse of terrorism," *Counterterror* will present the rise of community video as an expression of "popular culture."[9] That is, the videotape will be constructed of works that are based in opposition to the mass media images that are exported to the Third World.

As has been illustrated in studies in international media, a very small number of countries account for a substantial share of all media influence. The leading media producing country in the noncommunist world is, by far, the United States. It is particularly influential in the export of American television. Because of the sheer volume of U.S. exports, the American model of programming—a mix of commercial, accessible forms, that are based in entertainment—has proved extremely influential in both the Third World and in the smaller developed countries. Underwriting its consumerist form are several basic assumptions: that there is a need for continuous daily output, that news services must be "objective," and that the audience is cosmopolitan.

Lebanon

The divisions inherent in Lebanon's sectarian sociopolitical structure have made it susceptible both to its ambitious neighbors and to the political and economic strategies of colonial and imperialist powers. Israel, from the time it was established in 1946, has viewed Lebanon as a "soft border"—a point of entry that would allow Israel to break the Arab circle that surrounds it. The expressed desire of the Israeli military has been to create a Maronite Christian state in Lebanon under Israeli tutelage.

Repeated incursions into Lebanon prepared the Israeli military for the fullscale invasion of 1982. The official rationale for what was to be a "two-week strike," a brief "war on terrorism," was to eliminate the supposed PLO military threat headquartered in Beirut. However, it became evident that the stated "strike" was in fact total war—twenty thousand Lebanese and Palestinians, mostly civilians, were killed. An estimated three thousand were massacred at the Sabra and Shatila camps alone, after Palestinian militias had carried out a negotiated withdrawal. The extent of the slaughter suggests that Israel's intention was not to curtail the military threat of the PLO, but to eradicate completely Palestinian political culture, to destroy the nascent Palestinian state—comprised of refugees left stateless after the Zionist settlement of Palestine—that was developing in Beirut. The invasion of 1982 widened into a continuing war as the Israelis encouraged, even as they were forced to withdraw, the politics of sectarianism. This has resulted in a war by proxy, with the Maronite militias continuing the aggression against Lebanese and Palestinians.

In much of the developing world, however, these assumptions have made American-style television inappropriate. The images transmitted overseas are, for the most part, relevant only to the minority elites. And it is these sectors of Third World society who identify with, and who are supported by, the advanced capitalist countries. These same minorities also control the security and police forces in the Third World. And it is their attachment to advanced capitalism, the ideology of which is transmitted through the mass media, that gives them their direct investment in subduing insurrection in their own countries. For it is the working-class communities within these countries that provide the labor and the resources that underwrite the wealth of the developed world, and therefore the privilege of these elites.

The video groups that we are working with from El Salvador, Northern Ireland, and Lebanon have intimate links to their communities, working-class communities that have had little or no purchasing power and that have grown up emulating a media lifestyle that they could rarely attain. In addition, these communities have themselves been represented as communist threats, terrorist threats, and barbarians: backward, unfortunate. But just as they understand the role they play in the production of the products represented in mass media, so they are producing representations of their own, articulating a cultural and political position long suppressed.

Notes

1. Antonio Gramsci, "State and Civil Society," in Selections from the Prison Notebooks, ed. Quintin Hoare and Geoffrey Nowell Smith (London: Lawrence and Wishart, 1971).
2. On several occasions Ronald Reagan has used Claire Sterling's thesis of "Soviet-sponsored terrorism"; she outlines this theory in The Terror Network: The Secret War of International Terrorism (New York: Holt, Rinehart and Winston, 1981). Edward Herman's valuable work, The Real Terror Network (Boston: South End Press, 1982), is a critique of and rejoinder to Sterling's hypothesis. Herman proposes that it is the U.S., through its funding and support of National Security States in the Third World such as Indonesia or Chile, that perpetuates real terror.
3. See Michael Rogin, Ronald Reagan, the Movie, and Other Episodes in Political Demonology (Los Angeles: University of California Press, 1987). Rogin locates political repression as central to an understanding of American political structure—ascribing its effectivity to its construction of suitable "enemies."
4. Cited in Bob Woodward's recent book, Veil: The Secret Wars of the CIA, 1981-1987 (New York: Simon and Schuster, Inc., 1987).
5. Amos Lakos, International Terrorism: A Bibliography (Boulder, Colo.: Westview Press, 1986), lists over 6,500 titles of journal articles, books, and documents written on the subject of "terrorism."
6. Carol Brightman and Michael Klare, "Social Research and Counterinsurgency," in Communications and Class Struggle, ed. Armand Mattelart and Seth Siegelaub (New York: International General, 1984).
7. James Curran et al., eds., Mass Communication and Society (London: Edward Arnold, 1977), has useful articles offering a class analysis of media. See especially those by Golding, Murdock, and Barrat-Boyd.
8. See Herbert Schiller, Mass Communications and Empire (Boston: Beacon Press, 1969). Schiller is exemplary in tracing the emergence of mass communications through the various business, political, and military institutions in the United States.
9. Armand Mattelart posits "popular culture" as a culture of resistance developed in opposition to mass media or dominant culture. See Communication and Class Struggle, Vol. 2: Liberation and Socialism, introduction.

When Speculative Logic Ruptures

That paralyzing deficit you experience almost every day now—around the time the market closes—it's so . . . unproductive, isn't it?

In just a moment . . .
the world might pass you by.

Are your futures permanently devalued? Will
you rise again, slouch out of the desert, blink
away this mirage of graven images?

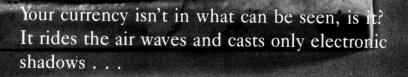

Your currency isn't in what can be seen, is it?
It rides the air waves and casts only electronic
shadows . . .

Bolster your image.
If necessary divest yourself of nagging worries.
Kick back.

Satellites, Video, and the News

Peter Fend

Ocean Earth is the first company to produce news reports with data from satellites. The company was begun in 1982, with a Falklands survey for the BBC and NBC, then a Beirut study for CBS. During the course of our analysis numerous intelligence discoveries occurred (e.g., detecting routes of attack), but so did interference from governments. Since 1982, including the four years when Ocean Earth was the only supplier of satellite-derived reports to television, the company found that reporting from space is more a political than technical challenge.

As a technical means of public observation and verification, satellite monitoring for news has been a "worry" for governments, and all the more so for governments in adversarial positions. Sales of authoritative information to the media in such countries usually entails a full-scale distortion. A sale to broadcast TV news in the United States, a cold-war superpower, does not mean getting the story broadcast. It means getting some of the "pictures" (as the trade-lingo goes) broadcast, with another story added. Take the case of coverage for CBS of the Iran-Iraq war.

In October 1984, seven months after beginning efforts to obtain civil-grade satellite data for the Iran-Iraq war zone (this lag time being typical of the long struggle to get data for sensitive sites), Ocean Earth handed over its results to a long-expectant client, CBS. The initial response was enthusiastic. Several days later, after review of the material with the State Department and the Defense Department, the story was telecast—but in a form considerably moderated, even reversed. Although the information reported was correct, critical facts were omitted, and the conclusion was the opposite of that presented by Ocean Earth's analysis.

The basic fact discovered by Ocean Earth was that Iraq, with Soviet assistance, had been building a massive river barrier along the border since before the commencement of the Iran-Iraq war, that is, before 1980. Iraq had begun to direct this barrier into Iran, cutting off Iranian land

Overall view of the Iraqi water system in July 1984 as broadcast on the *CBS Evening News*.

access to Iraq and to Iraq's allies Kuwait and Saudi Arabia, and blocking access to the original border river, the Shatt-el-Arab, by diverting most of that river into Iranian territory. From 1984 to 1988 the barrier grew larger, extending deeper into Iran. Feeder canals were built to supply flood waters to first one, then a second, and finally a third channel.

Despite repeated telecasts worldwide of the steady advances of the Iraqi constructions—all with fresh Ocean Earth satellite evidence—CBS News ran only the one story on the subject, on October 10, 1984. Headed "Last Stand Ditch," this short news bite suggested a Custer-like last stand by Iraq. This view was opposite to the truth, and opposite to information made available by Ocean Earth—information confirmed several years later by reports that surfaced in the Iran-contra hearings. What had been under construction for over seven years was described by CBS as being built in seven months, since the "last Iranian offensive." Iran's 800,000 casualties, which by then had shrunk to 30,000, were attributed to a battle "last February." What was being extended northwards by thirty miles, then spilling across the border into Iran, was simply excluded from the computer graphic overlay on the satellite photograph. By cropping out spillage into an excavation in Iran, the CBS viewing public saw only a defensive barrier and not the essence of the system: expansion.

The ultimate achievement of the Iraqi excavation, a ten-channel, mile-wide flood raceway receiving waters from the Tigris and Shatt-al-Arab in Iraq (even from rivers in Iran) is targeted on Iran's principal river, the Karun. The flood raceway will cut through the Karun and form a new channel for the Shatt-al-Arab, clear through to the Persian Gulf. By 1987, this project was set to receive floodwaters, smash through the Karun, and shift the border—defined as the Shatt-al-Arab—east inside Iran. It threatened not only to deny Iran access to its prime ports and oilfields, but also to cut through the dikes Iran had used so effectively early in the war (these appear as a giant chevron in 1981 satellite photos) to flood the land and thus bog down Iraq's initial offensive. ABC's defense correspondent ran several revealing stories on this development, with Ocean Earth imagery contracted from the higher-resolution French satellite. But the report had damaging consequences: the French publicly accused Ocean Earth of "l'overselling," their satellite company strictly warned ABC against future reports without official clearance, and the data was declared contraband. Ironically, the illegal data ended up in protective custody in a (now unidentified) country leaning toward the only political stance suited to truthful news reports from satellites: neutrality.

Dan Rather reporting Ocean Earth findings on the Iran-Iraq war on the *CBS Evening News*, October 24, 1984.

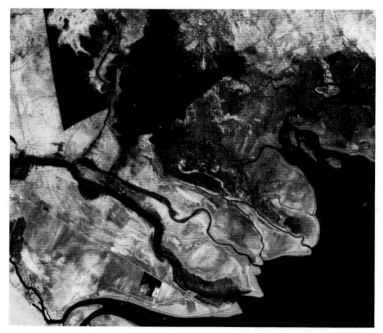

Close-up detail of Iraqui defense system detected by Ocean Earth's analysis of satellite photographs.

Overall view of the Iraqi water system in May 1987, over two years after the CBS news broadcast, showing advances in the "defense" system, including flooding of the "tail" reservoir.

Close-up of the mile-wide, ten-channel flood raceway constructed by Iraq at its junction with the Karun River, May 1987.

Big Brother Goes Bicoastal:
An Interview with Jay Chiat

Carol Squiers

Jay Chiat is chairman, co-founder, and principal owner of Chiat/Day, a Los Angeles-based advertising agency with offices in New York and San Francisco. Born in the Bronx and raised in New Jersey, Chiat entered advertising in 1954 writing copy for recruiting ads for an Air Force contractor. He opened his own firm in 1962, and in 1968 Chiat merged with the fledgling ad agency of Guy Day to form Chiat/Day.

A small agency with a Southern California base, Chiat/Day produced prize-winning ad work throughout the 1970s. But it was one particular ad in 1984 that propelled the agency to national attention. That spot, titled "1984," was a sixty-second television commercial for Apple Computers. Broadcast only once—during the 1984 Super Bowl—the commercial features legions of gray humanoid drones who march in lock step. Looming over them, the giant televised image of an Orwellian Big Brother declaims about the triumph of uniformity. Suddenly, at the back of the hall, a young woman in a red track suit breaks free from a squad of riot-geared thought police. Running full tilt toward Big Brother, she hurls a sledgehammer that shatters the huge projected image. Filmed by British director Ridley Scott (*Blade Runner*, *Alien*), the commercial reportedly cost over $500,000 to make and another $800,000 to run during the Super Bowl. Within ten days, however, Apple had reportedly logged over $100 million worth of orders for their new Macintosh.

The following year, Chiat/Day attempted to repeat their success. This ad—known as "Lemmings"—was also shown only during the Super Bowl and features mindless conformists. Only in "Lemmings" these conformists are dark-suited American business people with briefcases and wearing blindfolds. They march in single file across a windswept heath and, reaching a cliff, each plunges over the edge. Only one young man stops and raises his blindfold. Presumably this illustrates the moral: one can either look into new office machines or continue with business as usual. Although it was extraordinarily compelling to viewers, "Lemmings" was almost universally panned by the advertising industry.

Today, Chiat/Day continues to produce intelligent and provocative ads for such clients as NYNEX, Drexel Burnham, Nike, Reebok, Porsche, and Mitsubishi.   — C.S.

What is advertising according to Chiat/Day?

Howard Gossage was an advertising idol of mine on the West Coast. Very few people know about him, but he had a small agency that did marvelous work. He didn't actually define "advertising," but he said, "Nobody reads advertising. People read what interests them and sometimes that happens to be advertising." I don't know whether that functions as a definition, but I think that it's a marvelous description.

In other words, advertising is just another communication.

Advertising is a potpourri of art and marketing, and good advertising doesn't suffer from the process that's required to produce it.

Do you think many advertising people consider themselves to be artists? Do *you*?

No. I don't think that it's a case of being an artist. Instead, it's a case of the art portion, which is minimal, making the difference between mediocre, better-than-mediocre, or occasionally good or great advertising. But it is an infinitesimal part of a particular ad. It could be the way the film is directed or the premise that's used, or a particularly brilliant photograph. Or it could be a very simplistic idea like the Nike outdoor billboards that we did; they worked because they moved from advertising toward art.

Didn't those Nike ads, or at least the kind of advertising Chiat/Day is known for, inspire something called "event advertising"?

Marketing always happens after the event, or the positioning happens after the success, never before. I think "event marketing" grew out of the fact that we seemed to do advertising that achieved more than passing interest, both negative and positive. As a result of that, the advertisement itself probably gets more attention than it deserves and/or other advertising gets, so that it makes it an event. And if you understand the dynamics of that, then you can manipulate it occasionally to the client's advantage.

Chiat/Day, "Lemmings," 1985. Television ad for Apple Computers.

So, for example, an ad like "1984," which really only ran once because the client, Apple Computer, wasn't confident that it should run at all and therefore kept canceling the original broadcasting schedule until we had only one spot left. Then, in the hindsight of history, it became "event marketing" because we only ran it once. So it was "preplanned" about two days before the Super Bowl because we couldn't sell that spot to any other client.

At around the same time, January 1984, you also did a Mitsubishi campaign, where you convinced them to cancel their entire fall print budget and run only one $300,000 television spot. Is that true?

I don't know whether we convinced them to cancel their print budget, although that was the effect. What we said was it would be more effective if we ran this ad for TV, because theoretically people who watch TV are driven more by that message than they would be by print. And Mitsubishi had historically been a print advertiser. It was really a media decision, not a grandiose scheme to scrap something that was good. Even now we use print, and even when we use print we use it in an interesting way.

Do you prefer doing television or print ads?

I grew up as a print writer, so I have an affection for print. TV is easier to do—it's easier to write short things. Every ad needs an idea. Then you have to develop copy for print ads and that's harder to do. With television, the most effective ads usually have the least amount of copy because it's a visual medium. Very few people walk away from a television ad remembering the lines from the ad. They might remember a slogan, but they rarely remember the copy because they're watching the visuals.

Would you say that your ads rely more on emotional or rational appeal?

I think they begin rationally but they also try to influence emotionally, to give them an edge—the difference between art and mechanics. The best ads are those that combine both. We have a term for it: "relevant distinctiveness." We try to make the ads look both relevant, which is the logic, and distinctive, which is breaking through the clutter. So they have to be relevant—significant, understandable—and distinctive so that they stand apart from the rest of the clutter.

How do you measure the effectiveness of your ads?

In a lot of conventional ways, using pre-testing and post-testing. For instance, we're running a Nissan campaign right now which is really being villified in the press, especially the trade press. So DRI independently conducted a telephone sampling to see if everyone hated the campaign as much as the trade press did. In a sample of about a thousand people, they found that 70 percent liked the campaign. Another 15 percent didn't like the campaign at all, and the other 15 percent was fairly noncommittal. So, here was a case of the general press picking up the trade press—because advertising is hot now and a media event by itself. In fact, the campaign has been fairly successful according to DRI research and our own research with dealers who have indicated that people have come into the dealership because of the advertising.

How do you explain the discrepancy between the negative portrayal of the ads in the press and the positive response by the audience?

First, I think the trade-press writers pretend to be students of advertising, which they have to be in order to be critical. Secondly, most of the people who write for trade publications, including advertising trade publications, are not usually the target audience of a particular campaign, but are probably better educated, more cynical—

And less affluent.

Yes, that's a nice combination, and therefore they are angrier. I think

Chiat/Day, "Rock Drills," 1987. Television ad for NYNEX.

we have such a high profile that we're fair game, deservedly so in many cases.

Who are some of your clients now, national and international?

Reebok, which has a British logo because it was founded in Britain in the late 1800s, but is licensed to operate in the U.S., and has a British partner. NYNEX is a regional account for the Yellow Pages, in New England, New York, and New Jersey. Home Savings, which is in about fifteen markets now—they just bought Bowery here. Yamaha, which is national. We just were awarded Nissan in Canada—so that makes us international.

So you don't do any ads that actually function as ads outside of the United States?

Yes, we had done some for Apple, such as "1984," that were picked up by the European agencies. That ad worked pretty well internationally, it's kind of a universal message. It wasn't changed at all except for the accent of the voiceover.

What do you think about the theory of global advertising, which Saatchi & Saatchi have been promoting as the wave of the future?

I ran into Ted Levitt, who is the inventor of the premise and is a consultant for Saatchi & Saatchi. He kind of smiles when you mention "global advertising" to him. It's another case of doing the marketing plan after the event.

The "event" was the publication of his theory?

Yes, the event was the publication and the marketing plan is based on the fact that Saatchi uses it to pitch business. It's much easier for an international client to believe that they can press one button and have all their marketing problems go away. The reality is that they can't do that.

Can't one ad be made for all markets?

Well, you work for Saatchi and I'm at British Airways and I only have to deal with you and can ask you if the advertising in Zimbabwe is doing all right and you assure me that it is. The reality is that it's usually not.

So you don't believe in this concept of global advertising?

No. And I've looked at Coca-Cola advertising from around the world. Now, Coca-Cola is probably one of the most simplistic products you could advertise for, right? With the exception of possibly China and Russia—where Pepsi has the franchise—Coke is pretty much all over. This is a company that's trying to be global, and they have an international task force that works on adaptations of Coke's ads. The reality is that the ads probably don't work in half the places.

What do you mean by adaptations?

They change the ethnicity of the cast, the language, and reshoot the ad using the same premise. But it's like translating a joke from one language to another—it's not funny in translation. You have to deal with cultural issues, the translation itself, and sometimes even the visual aspects of the presentation. You can help it somewhat by having someone from the country adapt what you're doing. But if they try to make the adaptation accurate, it probably loses a lot of its charm. I've never seen a locally adapted campaign of an American or British advertising campaign adapted successfully enough that it was applauded or won anything at international advertising festivals. The advertisements that always win are those that were generated locally, in a particular community.

So Saatchi & Saatchi's "Manhattan Landing" for British Airways was not a prizewinner?

Chiat/Day, "1984," 1984. Television ad for Apple Computers.

I thought it was a solid B-plus or A-minus; it was an impressive production. I admire the fact that they've done what they've done, in terms of their size—they're the biggest agency in the world—and certain parts of the London agency do very good work. But with the exception of a British writer they have here who's done some good public-service work, I haven't been that impressed.

You've said in interviews that you were influenced by the ads that Doyle Dane Bernbach did in the sixties. What was it about these ads that you liked?

They were so simple. Everything else was complicated and garlanded with unnecessary accessories. Like models standing in front of something. Or using the product in an environment instead of just laying the product out. Their Volkswagen campaign had a car sitting in a blank seamless background, and a great headline and a marvelous piece of writing. While in ads for General Motors, the car is shown pulling up in front of a country club because they want to try to make a Plymouth look important. So people are standing around in gowns and tuxedos with some inane headline like "The Quality Lives On." It's just advertisingese that nobody believes. It was an incredible breakthrough to simply tell the truth and see if people would respond.

What you mean is that those ads were trying to provide a context for the product in terms of social and economic class.

They were using all of these fake issues to get you to aspire to the product, when in fact you could get back to Gossage's comment that people do not read about anything that they're not interested in. If you don't care about something, then you won't read about it—whether it's an editorial or advertising. You become interested in certain things that you haven't been interested in before when they break down. For instance, if your refrigerator breaks down you start noticing refrigerator ads—how much they cost, their features. You start paying attention to the marketplace.

Your ads are only appealing to people who are in the market for a product?

No, that's not what I said. We're appealing to people who are interested in the thing that we're talking about, and that doesn't mean that they're in the market for it. It means that if we can figure out a way to make the product interesting, we can enlarge the number of people who are interested in the product or service.

And you do that by the way your ads look and the way they're written?

Hopefully. I say that we "try to do great work" because there's a critical difference between doing it and trying to do it. Trying to do it means that you can't excuse not doing it. You can't say the client wouldn't let it get through, it tested badly so we changed it, etc. You have to be relentless. If you get a good piece of work turned down by the client, you can't go back with an inferior piece of work. You have to go back with a piece that's as good or better, that you can get through.

Do you actually do ads yourself?

Occasionally.

What do you do?

Nothing. I think what I do is create the standards and say "no" to stuff that isn't good enough.

Were you involved in the "1984" ad?

Yes, a little bit. The ad was originally a print ad—we were trying to put together a campaign that at that time was primarily print. The art director was Mike Moser, who's still at the agency, and a writer whose name

Saatchi & Saatchi, "Manhattan Landing," 1985. Television ad for British Air.

escapes me. The headline on this print ad was "Why 1984 Won't Be Like 1984." I really liked the ad so we developed it further and did the copy. A few months later, Brent Thomas, who was an art director at Apple, was trying to do a couple of TV spots to introduce Macintosh. He saw the print ad and that triggered the Orwellian theme. That's how the TV ad was created. In London, Ridley Scott insisted we put some words in the mouth of Big Brother. Our copywriter, Steve Hayden, didn't want to do it but Ridley kind of forced him to write that copy.

The "1984" ad was very popular. The "Lemmings" ad was panned by the trade. Do you think that the reason for that is that in the "1984" ad there was a kind of predictable politics? In other words, the IBM versus Apple fight was played out as the U.S. versus Godless totalitarianism?

That IBM versus Apple argument happened after the event, at a sales meeting when Steve Jobs gave a speech indicating that it was an anti-IBM ad. But the ad was not created with the intention that IBM represented Big Brother. The symbolic essence of the ad was really that the computer company itself is Big Brother, and that Macintosh was a *friendly* computer. The post-research on the "Lemmings" ad scored higher than "1984" in the message being received, understood, and acted upon by the target audience. You have to remember that the reality is that the product didn't work in an office situation. Macintosh didn't have the power or the software. So we introduced the Macintosh office because Steve Jobs was convinced he had to do that to top the others. If you bought this product you probably wouldn't be able to convince your boss to buy more of them. The only thing that kept it going was the advertising, the "myth" of the product rather than the reality of the product. It's only this year that Macintosh has started to work. That's why it's selling—because it's a dynamite product now that it has the software. We knew the reality of the product, and that it had to be directed at the rebels—the guys who didn't want to be IBM. They wanted to be seen as independent. This was the only way of keeping the product alive until they developed the software.

Were more office computers sold after the ad ran?

I don't know the actual sales figures, but the sales were in the toilet at that time. Then the press picked up on the ad and established it as a failure. And it wasn't just the trade press—talk about "event marketing."

You got bad PR from everywhere about it?

It was pretty much universal. Even Lee Clow, who was as responsible as anyone for doing the ad, believed it was bad. I was the only one who thought it was a good ad. And everyone I show it to today—now that there's none of the furor that surrounded it then—is knocked out by it.

Do you think viewers had great expectations for it because you actually ran print ads to announce the TV ad?

We just ran one ad during the Super Bowl. There was a buildup, but there was also a crisis going on between Jobs and Scully—unknown but suspected by us—an incredible internal war going on at Apple.

I want to return to the issue of global advertising. In 1984, Maurice Saatchi predicted that by the end of this decade, most small advertising agencies would be wiped out or gobbled up by larger shops and that the world advertising market would be dominated by about six mega-agencies.

I think he's probably as accurate as he is inaccurate, depending on the interpretation. A lot of the smaller agencies that were doing great work decided to sell. I think you have more agencies now in the U.S. that are breakaways and probably more now in what they call the third wave in England. First, you had the original agencies, the American multinationals like Thompson, McCann, and Ogilvie. They all had offices in England. The British decided that they could do this better, so they broke away and formed agencies. That was the second wave. Now you have a group of smaller agencies spinning off, starting all over again. Those are third-wave agencies, five to ten years old. There are a lot of them in the U.S. Some of them are owned by the intergalactics, some of them are not. The point is that for the first time in ten years you're seeing some new agencies start up, aside from the occasional and sporadic one.

Does this mean that you think what Saatchi said is true?

You can evaluate what he said and say, "yes, that's true," and you can deliver the statistics to prove it. Or you can say, "no, he's wrong," and you can also make that statistically sound.

I understand that you are starting a chain of fast-food restaurants.

It's something I wanted to do. I've worked for about six fast-food clients and I've never felt any of them paid much attention to any suggestions I made about operations. So I thought I'd see if my ideas made sense by putting my money where my mouth is. The name of the chain is Sañwiches.

Are you going to do anything unusual with them?

We're going to have clusters of TV sets in the restaurants, which we'll use to sell advertising to other fast-food chains—so they can advertise to our customers.

A business would buy space on these TV sets?

If you're a McDonald's or Burger King or Wendy's or Pizza Hut or any of these, you'll want to reach this target audience.

Why would you want your competitor right there under your customer's nose?

First of all, I think it would be funny and exciting and that's part of the ambience and the environment that we want to generate, something that's contemporary. TV certainly is—along with advertising—one of the most contemporary of all forms. Even if it's bad, it's contemporary, right? It's reflecting the mood of the nation. And then, you can't get the person to eat every meal in your restaurant every day. That's the trouble, most of them think, "God, I don't understand why someone doesn't come into my place five times a week." Most people don't go *home* for dinner five days a week.

Going Global

Transcript of a report broadcast
on the MacNeil/Lehrer Newshour
September 29, 1987.

Paul Solman: This is Coca-Cola's newest ad, it's called "General Assembly," and it pictures teenagers from two dozen different nations. "General Assembly" will debut this fall all over the world in sixteen different languages and more than fifty countries. This ad represents the latest stage of what was once a heresy on Madison Avenue, but is now the the hottest trend in advertising—global marketing.

Ted Levitt, Harvard Business School: Increasingly, all over the world, more and more people's preferences regarding products and services and qualities and features are getting more and more alike.

Solman: Several years ago, this man, Harvard Business School professor Ted Levitt, stunned the advertising community by announcing what seemed to him pretty obvious.

Levitt: Increasingly, all over the world you find the same market segments repeated over and over again.

Solman: So, the yuppies of Paris, for example, behave in much the same way and have much the same taste as the yuppies in Peoria, or anywhere else. You sell to all of them as if they constituted one segment of a global market.

The first ad agencies to go global would get a big jump on the competition. But for years, ad agencies resisted global marketing. The agencies and their clients were used to making money the old-fashioned way; different ad campaigns for apparently different markets. In America, Kentucky Fried Chicken sold as cheap, fast food. But in Japan, it was being marketed as an authentic high-quality product.

[Film clip of commercials in different countries] This ad is still multinational. Each country unique, each marketing campaign uniquely tailored. But multinational marketing may be a thing of the past.

Levitt: Well, the multinational corporation is precisely what it says it is. It's a corporation that thinks the world consists of a multiplicity of separate and distinct nations and separate and distinct markets in each one of those, and is organized and managed around each one of those separate markets, with a consequence of very high costs of doing business. Whereas global really is a step beyond that: where you're organized and operated to treat the world—or major segments of it—as being a single or similar category.

Solman: In the world of marketing, a product is not just a piece of chicken or a pint of soda, but a set of associations, a mystique. Advertising doesn't just communicate these intangible qualities, it creates them, and hence advertising itself becomes part of what you're selling. In global advertising, that means you're selling similar associations, similar dreams.

[Clip of Coca-Cola ad] This Coke ad, featuring pro football great Mean Joe Green, ran in the U.S. in 1982. It was a hit in this country, with its connotation of Coke as the hero's magic elixir, but heroes and hero-worshippers sell everywhere.

[Clip of same ad in Brazil, Argentina, etc.] In Brazil, Argentina, in Thailand, Coke had caught the global wave. But in the early 1980s, despite Coke's efforts, there were still major hurdles for global marketing to overcome. In most countries, television was still monopolized either by state-run, or at least heavily regulated stations. In almost every country, the state rigidly controlled the type and amount of advertising. In West Germany, for example, the state allowed only two minutes of advertising per hour. In France, you couldn't run a computer ad, presumably because it would compete with the French state-owned computer monopoly.

But national restrictions on advertising like this were beginning to give way. A wave of deregulation was sweeping the globe and opening up TV markets from France to the Philippines.

Bob James, McCann-Erickson: In a very short span of time, you've had two or three things happen that are going to really enhance marketers' ability to advertise on a global basis. First is pan-regional advertising, which comes from the satellites, and second is the opening up of more commercial time in each and every country.

Solman: And so, a company like Pepsi-Cola could now produce an ad with rock star Tina Turner and any local rock star anywhere in the world. Make one ad teaming Tina with Puerto Rico rock idol Wilkins. And anybody else for that matter. Tina doesn't mind. She knows that she and her partners are simply selling the excitement and energy that appeals to the Pepsi generation every where. Pop culture, particularly American pop culture, has homogenized world taste. And so now advertisers are simply exploiting that sameness for themselves.

And that brings us back to Coke's "General Assembly" ad, the newest instance of global marketing. For those who favor global marketing, this is the realization of an age-old dream: one world, united by common tastes and a common propensity to consume. But those who deplore global marketing may see something different: one small industry, Madison Avenue, homogenizing the world and destroying precious cultural diversity in the process. Both sides would agree, however, that globalization is here to stay. And that will mean more global products, more global ad agencies, and more global ads in the future.

Scene from *The Twonky*, 1953, a film about a TV set that comes to life, walks, does household chores with electronic beams, and hypnotizes anyone who tries to stop it.

The Third Window:

An Interview with Paul Virilio

Cahiers du Cinema,
with a preface by Jonathan Crary,
translated by Yvonne Shafir

Any theorist labeled a theorist of "media" or "technology" tends to unleash a peculiar mix of both enthusiasm and virulent disdain from other intellectuals. And the stakes in such debates often seem to have a theological gravity (though, of course, the actual questions center on the body, power, the real). In this way, Paul Virilio has incited a range of intense responses to his work, even though he has shunned the more visible and oracular public stature of Marshall McLuhan or Jean Baudrillard. But the anger he arouses in many leftists (see, e.g., *Social Text* 17, Fall 1987) may be proportional to the inadequacy of Marxist categories for describing the effects of contemporary technology. Thus economic considerations, for example, have little part in his writing; in fact, for Virilio technological culture is no longer explainable by recourse to models of increasing rationalization, efficiency, or accumulation.

Virilio keenly senses the futility of any "theory" of technology, that such an attempt is foredoomed to banal oblivion in the face of accelerated technological change. Thus the volatility of Virilio's style is not inadequate to the dynamics of his object. And to the exasperation of some, he rejects systemic or theoretical discourse in favor of more aphoristic and epiphanic expression. None of this should obscure Virilio's standing as a strikingly innovative thinker and clearly, much of the strength of his work, beginning with his book *Bunker Archaeology,* has been the staking out of radically novel vantage points from which to survey his chosen fields. But it must be stressed that, for Virilio, technique is always a function of specific political relations of territory (space) and movement (time). These new relations he has articulated in a series of provocative historical typologies and periodizations.

Thus Virilio's interest in television and the VCR, in the following interview, is based on seeing them as part of a new paradigm defining the use and control of time. If capitalism can be said to be an issue for him, it is capitalism's reconfiguration around this issue of temporality and its remaking of the human subject to conform to new temporal imperatives. A crucial part of Virilio's work is the chronicling of the mutation of human perception of duration and space and the conditions for these changes. Anyone who has used a VCR has likely had the experience of frustration and impatience when watching real-time broadcast TV that it *can't be fast-forwarded*. It is at such moments that time becomes a qualitatively new substance, commodity, and affect.

The mobility of Virilio's thought diagrams the shifting gap between human beings and the new forms of movement or inertia imposed on them. He is a cartographer of obsolescence, charting the effects of speed by what is left behind: the body and social life. He insists on the state of dereliction that is always the flip side of the quest for ubiquity, instantaneity, and hyperperception. But of course these are not all new problems. Walter Benjamin wrote in 1937, ". . . traffic speeds, like the capacity to duplicate both the written and the spoken word, have outstripped human needs. The energies that technology develops beyond the threshold of those needs are destructive. They serve primarily to foster the technology of warfare, and of the means used to prepare public opinion for war." Fifty years later, Virilio is delineating the contours of this same divergence.

—Jonathan Crary

With VCR recording, there has been a lot of talk about the collection of images, cinephilia, fetishism of the fragment, etc. But above all, this discussion concerns time. Don't you think that in the final analysis, these kinds of gadgets are more than just machines that record time?

I believe that everything revolves around the management of time: for a long while already we have been dealing not with the distribution of space, but with the distribution of time. And these machines effectively permit the distribution of time itself. It is no longer just a distribution of time in the sense of leaving on a holiday, the H-hour, or transport strikes, but in the sense of daily life: manage your own time yourselves.

The prerecording VCR is something of an anticipated calendar. The role of the time gauge in the history of societies is extraordinary: consider the diversity of means since the calendar system: the clepsydra, the solar screen, the watch, the digital display, etc. I believe that the prerecording VCR (or the VCR with prerecorded transmission, I don't know exactly what it's called) participates in this, participates in this organization of time itself. There's no doubt that the distribution of time is the role of technology today; in the organization of society, but also in the organization of the family. The machine, the VCR, allows man to organize a time which is not his own, a deferred time, a time which is somewhere else—and to capture it.

But there are two levels of programming: on the one hand the decision to settle in, on a particular day, at a particular time, in this deferred time which has been regenerated by the VCR. On the other hand, there is the choice of a particular prerecorded program, as opposed to another such program.

Like I was saying, "I see for you." Thus the idea of a prothesis takes on a visionary character. It's no longer "I speak for you," but "I see for you." That means, "I bring you another day." The notion of day has always fascinated me; not in the sense of the light, to be born, etc. The technology of the VCR creates a day, an additional "false-day"; you have a secondary day which comes into being for you alone, just as in the secondary residence whose heating turns on of its own accord when it gets cold. That's just like a day that emerges for you, which is staged; there is a sort of electronic cosmography.

There's also a substitute for travel. The secondary residence used to function through the automobile medium: the two-fold nature of habitat made possible by the car. The VCR works in the same way. It creates two days: a reserve day which can replace the ordinary day, the lived day. And I'm astonished to see certain advertisements where the VCR is represented in the form of a vehicle: you see the VCR—I don't know which—on a Montlhery-type track, as if—because of the energy crisis—the car had been replaced by this engine. In other words, the new windshield is no longer a car, it is a TV screen. There is therefore a much more precise alignment to be made between the deferred day and the deferred residence.

To bring up once more an important idea from The Aesthetic of Disappearance, might one say that the essential function of the VCR is the production of a program of absence?

Oh yes, absolutely. What interests me the most in the technique are the interruptions, the montage. In some way, the interruption of direct vision produces a perception of time proper, a nonfascination. If you could watch continuously, without any picnoleptic breaks, as I mention in the book, without absences in the strict sense, well, you'd become completely fascinated and fall asleep. So these interruptions are absolutely fundamental for us if we are to be conscious of time proper; that is to say, conscious of the identity of lived time. Technology plays the same role, but it feeds off the system of interruption, creating out of it a new system through cinematographic montage, through videographic sequences, or, we might say, through the to and fro of cars, because I always connect these two media: the automobile and the audiovisual. What goes on in the windshield is cinema in the strict sense. It seems very important to me to join them rather than separate them, because speed is what interests me.

There are two speed effects and two effects of vision: the videographic effect and what I've called the "dromographic" effect, an effect of duration. There's a coupling together and a parasitism of these effects: not only are there biological and physiological interruptions in perception, but also electronic and technical interruptions, etc. But what we are trying to do, and what subliminal effects have already done, is coupling. In other words, effects of subliminal speed aim, in my opinion, to replace physical interruptions. We're really in the middle of an absolute manipulation. It's really, "I see for you," and "I have duration for you"! It's this technically organized duration which thinks for me. Before it was a duration which was organized by my own rhythms, by my biorhythms, which allowed me to be myself. I often say this: one is not only large, small, man, woman, tired, or fit, one is also "speed." To be alive is to be speed and speed itself: Guy Drut and I . . . it's not the same. So you can see that there's a "dromological" identity (my term) which technology has disturbed and hopes to finally replace. In subliminal conditioning, it's clearly replacement which is being aimed at.

"Total control remote control puts a world of excitement at your fingertips."

The most frightening thing is surely "I have duration for you."

Of course, because taken to its extremes, this duration is our very thought. To think is to establish a relationship with intensity. We know that very well. What's a fever? It's an intensity. What does it mean to be down? That's just another level of intensity. And on top of that, another electronic intensity is inscribed. Thus, I would say, problems of subliminal fever or hallucinations come into play. I believe that we don't put enough emphasis on this: the conclusion that "technology" doesn't give us any greater intensity, but that it interrupts us differently. That is very important, I believe. When you look at the city, what tires you? What are the causes of stress? They're the interruptions. When you're in a car, for example, the car gets stuck in a traffic jam. In other words, when there is an interruption which seems exaggerated, imposed. Thus every technological object creates interruptions in the biorhythmic system. But you never hear anyone talk about that. Except for those interested in stress.

And so it's a magical idea—constructing a great chain for the express purpose of eliminating these annoying interruptions. That's the idea of giving more.

That's been the goal of every power: to create the day, that is, to take God's role. *"Voir le jour,"* in French that means "to be born." Every absolute power—and I said this in *The Aesthetic of Disappearance*—has wanted to be master of the day: Charles Quint and many others. Technology fully assumes the idea, I believe, that one can create a day through one's own power.

Perhaps we ought to talk about unwinding or procession. In the second to the last issue of Cahiers, *there is an interview with Jean Eustache, for whom the VCR acts like a sleeping pill: he turns it on and falls asleep as the tape goes on . . .*

Perhaps at the moment you start to watch it you're put into an infantile position, you recover the "hypnagogic" side, you return to a childhood in which you walk tendentially reassured by a teddy bear, or a panda . . . I believe that these factors are in play there . . .

And this "procession"—well, it's the tape which allows for it. To me, the idea of a tape has always been interesting. You go from a pinpoint image to a topological image. Ancient images presented themselves as a unique space, a container; like a reliquary, like a frame in the sense of what's in it, with the portrait of the beloved. Whereas with cinema, with video, you enter the topological space of the tape, where the reinvention of the walking or running track comes into being. When you drive down a highway, or when you take a Roman road, or a road in the desert, you don't realize how extraordinary an invention this unwinding strip is. There is a very beautiful text by Julien Gracq, *La Presqu'ile,* where he talks about the road and I think that everything he says can also be said about the "unwinding" of the videotape.

But in reading isn't there also a procession?

Well, no, it's not the same. There is rupture, there are pages you have to flip through. With film, either movie or video, and despite the interruptions of the montage, you have a continuity.

And on the other hand, the material object, the reel, the reeling up, seems to me very interesting because it was necessary at the beginning of it all and is still there. It is there in the databanks, it is there in the camera when it is filming, it is there also in the machine gun . . . Moreover, there is a very close similarity between the first techniques—you will talk about this more in *Cahiers*—between the Gatling gun, the photographic revolver of Janssen, and cameras. The Colt .45, the chronophotographic gun—all these things are tightly bound up with each other . . . So for me, well, the film is interesting because it seems to me to be a way of revealing an element between the subject and the object, which has been ignored up until now: the journey, the trajectory, absent from philosophical and literary discourse . . . despite Stendhal's inspired phrase: "A novel: A mirror

Tobe Hooper, *Poltergeist*, 1982. Steve and Diana Freeling (Craig Nelson and Jobeth Williams) are baffled by a mysterious force which irresistibly draws their daughter (Heather O'Rourke) to a television set.

which extends the length of a path." That is a sentence about video.

But you yourself, in terms of video, you're really talking about a window?

It's the new window, in effect; because we have recovered the dimension which I would call the architectonic of the electronic, the optoelectronic image of those kind of things. Enter: the third window. The first window is the door-window: no building exists without a door. By definition, if there is no door, then it's not architecture, it's not a human habitat. Thus, the door-window is the first opening which produces man's habitat, structures his day: diurnal/nocturnal . . .

The second window, which appears very late, is the window which only gives us the day—light only—a window through which one doesn't enter. What enters through it is only an abstraction—the sun, direct vision.

It's very surprising to me to see how the window has evolved. It was miniscule at first, a clostra, then it becomes larger, growing and increasing in volume. It turned into a bay-window, that is literally the window-screen, which then became part of the vehicle.

At this point, the third window comes into its own: like in the American films or in the films of Wim Wenders (rarely in French films) where the TV is going continuously, for example. It doesn't function at all as a medium like radio or newspapers, but as an architectonic element: it is a portable window, insofar as it can be shifted. It's part of the organization of a city, a definitive, final, terminal city. The movement from television to informative video, the games, the machines, and all those gadgets, to an architectonic video or television creates a topology of an image of the world. You know that when you change the program on a computer screen, for example, automatic cartography: you have a map, you press, you want to see the map of the Paris region, it's drawn up at top speed by a little luminous cursor—it appears—then you have a slide which enables you to aim at the place you want to see. You put the slide at the point and then you change the program—so that the spot is enlarged and you can keep on going like that till you have got all your information. And when you change, the image gets fuzzy and restructures itself and you call this a "window." So you can have the window of the building in which you have the screen window plus the electronic window.

At the same time, these are more and more like blocked and sightless windows.

Yes, and also manipulative windows which deal with an image which has not been established inertly. But already these veils, these Venetian blinds, these shutters and all that, alot of things are at play in the filter, the filter of the window.

Anyway, there's still that problem—for both the producer of images and the spectator—of confusing the maps, of mixing up the representations of the real (direct or deferred; documentary or fictionalized, as in docudramas, etc.), of playing with time (time proper or astronomical time).

Let's not forget the term "day" *(jour)*: journalism means, in a sense, "to create a news-day," to bring information to light (day—light). The day doesn't exist in itself. It exists at an alternance between diurnal and nocturnal, but it's no big thing really. With the appearance of gazettes and the newspaper, a time proper appeared, a time of news and information. Information monopolized by one caste. The Electronic Logic is simply this— that the primitive newspaper, on paper, turns one day into the video and the VCR. We've really been given a day. In this there's a sort of anticipated life, or a life held over from elsewhere: the story of Amanda Lear with her mirror in which she could see her vision deferred—that is, eternally young, well that's a crazy image. It's really the morgue. The electronic morgue.

Embalming?

Absolutely, and there's always something of that in the practices of the VCR, I believe.

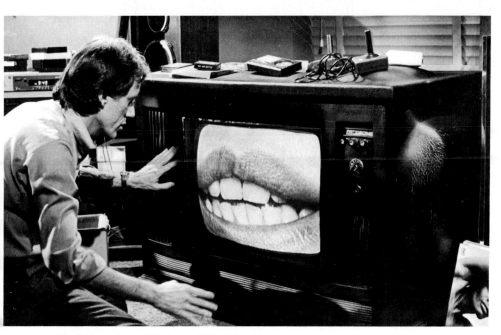

David Cronenberg, *Videodrome*, 1983. After Max (James Woods) becomes a part of "Videodrome," very strange things begin to happen.

Similarly, what's really interesting in what you have said about Howard Hughes are all of his manias: having a cinema at the foot of his bed, circumnavigating the globe, always the same hotel room or the same car, this corresponds completely to the uses of the VCR today.

It's the same. It's identifying oneself and identifying one's body, animal or human, with a territorial body; that is, creating an osmosis between geography and one's own body: *being* the body of the world. That, I believe, is man's very ambition. A quasi-maternal ambition. From which springs the idea of woman as a symbol, the womb, the earth-mother, the "I am in the Other." Here again you see the topological order, that is, seeing oneself from the back, and even seeing oneself from the front, the other side, which in my opinion is sexual. Whilst Euclidian geometry is masculine, topology is feminine: oriented and supple-surfaced, and so deformable, with all the possibilities of reversal that electronic technique permits. That's what I wanted to say when I was talking about the discovery of the earth-mother cult—the birthing side.

Many people use the slow-motion effects in replaying VCR programs such as football games. A bit in the Marey mode. Not necessarily to replay the most interesting or spectacular sections, but mainly to re-play, to re-create.

They want to live the organic time, the time it takes for plants to grow. They're unsatisfied with the time given them to live, that is, their own speed. They not only want to live the body of the world, but other times, which are those of the sprouting of plants (Painlevé, the time of germination, or the time of clouds, the accelerated time of Einstein, the Tempestaire, etc.). They try effectively to be identified with a geographical body, but also with different types of geographical time. Vegetable, mineral, etc. It's a ubiquitous desire to see the time belonging to other species. This is no longer the secondary residence, but infinite residences.

I saw at the exhibition *Images and Magic of Cinema*, the camera which produces one million images per second. There was a text, a little blurb, and I said to myself: it's extraordinary that this machine is only used in ballistic firing tunnels. There are special cameras and apparently you need astronomical speed to see the movement of the engine which propels itself into the ballistic tunnel; so there is somewhere a "will-to-be" projectile.

I think that there you really touch on the mystic character: it has to do with sainthood. It's really ascension, projection—from which you get the reference to Hughes as technological monk.

It's aviation which enabled Hughes to cheat or play with time. With the VCR, it's even easier.

Certainly, but on the other hand, in order to identify the territorial or geographical body with the physical or physiological body, you have to mix the two media: the automobile (in the sense of aviation in Hughes's case) and the audiovisual (as in cinema or TV). You have to understand that you're faced with a mixture. They're inseparable.

That's where I completely disagree with McLuhan. In order for there to be an identification, there has to be a fusion of both. Thus, simply speaking, the automobile medium lags way behind audiovisual media as a production of speed. The one has the speed of light, and the other has only the speed, let's say, of sound (in the case of the car, since Stan Barret broke the land speed record in December 1979, breaking the sound barrier).

Speed is nothing other than a vision of the world, and for me Hughes is a prophet, a monstrous prophet, moreover, and I'm not at all crazy about this guy, but he's a prophet of the technical future of society. That absolute inertia, that bedridden man, a universal bedridden man as I called him, that's what we're all going to become. All those who are not conscientious objectors.

So where is the monstrosity finally to be found?

To reduce the world to nothing. To want to be the world is to reduce it to nothing. The world is the field of action for man's liberty. If you reduce it

Not Evolutionary, Revolutionary.

to man, that is, to a total global appropriation, ubiquitous, panoptic, as Foucault would say, there's no more world, and so no more liberty, so one goes off and kills oneself somewhere. This desire for possession, of the identification of one's own body with the body of the earth, is thus a suicidal desire which, moreover, very well explains Hughes, who is really a suicide in his hotel room, eating at the same place every time. It's the idea of the bedridden person . . .

But how is the difference manifested between those that slide with this bedridden attitude and those who, on the contrary, resist it?

I believe that very few finally resist this. Few resist because in order to significantly resist technology, it's necessary to look into its enigma, and I deliberately choose the word enigma. Those who are against technology, against the nuclear, which, as it happens, is my case, are so mostly in a moral, moralizing way, not in a speculative way. In my opinion, this is what we have to watch out for. Technology is an enigma which necessitates our interrogation, our speculation. Here we are back at the Sphinx, not the Oedipus of psychoanalysis, but the being who moves . . .

That's what I'm concerned with—looking at a technological object as an enigma and not asking myself how it works; looking at what is hidden, what is unknown in the midst of the known, and not what is unknown in the midst of the unknown. I'll use an example to make this clearer. A few years ago, a review asked me to write an article about *la technique* and after some reflection, I told them: "That's it! I've got it! I propose to write you an enigmatic description of an airplane that I saw in the aviation museum, the Alpha-Jet; I'm going to describe the Alpha-Jet to you in my own way." They responded with: "That's of no interest; there are already lots of technical blurbs written about it." And I said: "Well, you just haven't understood, because I'm not going to talk about a machine with wheels, made out of rubber . . . It's not that. I'm going to try to work on, to penetrate, this enigmatic object. I know very well how it works, just as everybody does. There are wings, there are things and gadgets, but it's not that, it's rather how it presents itself to me today, how I see it. Why can't you do with the Alpha-Jet what people do with the ruins of a Greek temple? Don't you have the right?"

You see, here you come up against something which perhaps explains the absence of resistance to technology: that is, we believe we understand it. And when there's opposition, it's only moral: that's bad, we don't want that. But I feel like saying: I don't even know if it's bad. I don't know what it is. So, let's try and get into it.

That's a bit like what you're doing at the moment with the VCR—not explaining at all the way it works.

Absolutely. And in a certain way, Howard Hughes gives us the clues; not through his investigations, but through his life: in his own way he "translates" this, and that's the reason he interests me. In fact, there are several people like that who've interested me. Sarah Krachnov, for example: she's the American grandmother who in six months crossed the Atlantic one hundred and sixty-seven times to enable her grandson to escape the psychiatrists. This little kid was seven or eight; his father wanted him to undergo analysis or psychiatric treatment, and the grandmother said no, it's out of the question. She took the kid and she did Amsterdam–New York, New York–Amsterdam . . . like that for six months without ever leaving the hotel room, the plane, etc. And the kid's father tried to join them, but never caught up with them, and she died after six months because of the time-zones, finally . . . Well, this woman for me is a marvelous heroine. She lived precisely this deferred time, and a different time in which her son couldn't catch up with her. Those are the characters, and there are many more, who "translate," I really believe, the enigmatic character which I was talking about . . .

So I'm surprised to what extent we have a claim towards the accumulation of knowledge without being conscious that the more knowledge accumulated the greater the increase in the unknown. The question of technology is posed here, because it's considered a manner of making knowledge usable and functional, and instrumental in the strict sense. But it's also the means to increase the unknown; you see it with the nuclear. We've created a maximum unknown, and now we're faced with the situation of not knowing what to do with it. We've got the end of the world at our fingertips, the red button.

The problem of the unknown interrogates us about science and philosophy but also about technique, and I'm passionate about the unknown which is finally produced. I'm more interested that we produce the unknown than that we produce machines. In the end, the machine which has just appeared interests me as a revelation of a new mystery, a new enigma. And not as the resolution of a problem in order to go faster.

Then the mystery gets thicker every time?

The mystery gets thicker every time, an effect induced by technology which, in my opinion, is technology itself, you see. Moreover, it's the same thing for speed, which remains one of the great mysteries of technology. If the factory produces cars, the cars produce speed, and speed—I don't know what that is. You claim to know about the car, so you don't get interested in speed. You say "the Industrial Revolution," that is, the thing which has enabled us to produce, to multiply objects of the same, to create ten thousand similar objects—so you claim to know. But what interests me is that we've created, especially with the car, a means of producing speed. That is, an unknown which is there. It's there, we have its traces, its signs, its effects; effects of image, effects of light, effects of visual transformation, effects of transformation of the body itself, of time itself, etc.

What interests me is taking technology indirectly, from the angle of intensities.

Somewhere, therefore, it's necessary to look into technology. Why then aren't we looking into it? Why do those people who resist technology reject it so brutally? I believe it's because they claim to know it, and that's the worst thing. They know how a car is made, a microprocessor, etc. But the fact of knowing how to produce does not imply a knowledge of what one's doing; there's a very clear rupture. I produce a house because I'm an architect, I produce a tape recorder because I'm an electrician, I know how to do it, but I do not know what it is.

Video and the Counterculture

Patricia Mellencamp

V ideo entered the U.S. cultural vocabulary in the mid-sixties as a technology *and* a discourse. Like the wartime and postwar merchandising of the 16mm film camera (the portable, trusty Bolex developed for a single operator to record World War II for movie screens), Japanese video technology was mass-marketed during and after a televised war: Vietnam. This portable, electronic technology was coupled with a mystical/futurist metaphysics informed by the historical avant-garde or romanticism, and, as a result, Video Art, Guerrilla TV, and just plain video were portrayed as personal, innovative, radical. Ideally, it was hoped, simultaneity, feedback, delay, satellite capacity, and electronic visions would foster—like drugs and random sex—new states of consciousness, community, and artistic, political structures. With its immateriality, easy operation, reproducibility, and affinity with mass culture, video was imagined as challenging the status of precious art objects and the institutions of art (and commercial television)—Peter Bürger's twin claims for the historical avant-garde.[1]

Technological determinism prevailed: portable and affordable video equipment promoted artistry, populism, and utopianism. Like historical revolutionary movements, the political and artistic/social countercultures of the 1960s held an instrumental conception of technology, viewing the medium neutrally rather than as a system of social relations and discourses (including gender and economics). With a fervent idealism, in the face of commercial programming and cold war politics and containment, "video" would bring global salvation via access, circumventing institutions and going directly to individuals of conscience.

As the sociologist Armand Mattelart argues, we must concentrate on techniques for the fabrication of culture developed by popular revolutionary movements.[2] Although a middle-class, white (although intersecting with the Civil Rights Movement), educated, affluent, youth movement in the U.S. can hardly be labeled revolutionary, the counterculture did at least signal a generational crisis in the smooth transmission of culture through institutions, including academia, the media, and the family. It did present alternatives, among them video. In the late 1960s, counterculture practices of video emerged simultaneously in collectives on both coasts. People's Video Theater, Videofreex, Raindance, Global Village, and Video Freaks were all founded on a belief in liberation via the democratic pluralism of television—anyone could control the means of production, anyone could and should be an artist. I will take Mattelart's advice and analyze (rather than patronize) the techniques of their "fabrication of culture."

Ant Farm, a zany and ambitious group with outposts in San Francisco and Houston, was created in 1968 as "an army of termites in the subsoil of American officialdom."[3] Founded by Chip Lord and Doug Michaels, and soon joined by Hudson Marquez, Curtis Schreier, and others, this underground collective was a "family consisting of environmentalists, artists, designers, builders, actors, cooks, television children . . . university trained media freaks and hippies interested in balancing the environment by total transformation of existing social and economic systems."[4] Along with the denial of hierarchy, their collective work was "education reform, communication, graphic design, life-theater, and high art." Their techniques included "systematically resorting to psychophysical information and states of mind. Such states are achieved by the use of 'grass' which brings the community closer and releases creative energy."[5] Free association was encouraged by their "trips." Ant Farm sought commissions and won awards for architectural projects (including an organic concrete house outside Houston, various inflatables, and a design for a convention center for the 1976 bicentennial), toured universities, and made videos.[6] The climactic moment of the group's work was the purchase of a black-and-white Sony portapak in 1970 (like so many seventies videomakers, without an editing system).

Radical Software was the magazine of the video movement distributed by the Raindance collective in New York; but the bible was *Guerrilla Television*, a book commissioned in 1970 by Holt, Rinehart and Winston (the counterculture fascinated the official culture which resisted and incorporated it) as an Ant Farm design project and written by Michael Shamberg of TVTV (Top Value Television), later the producer of *The Big Chill* (an apolitical, whining appropriation of the counterculture as upper-middle-class, adolescent ennui and sexual/protest nostalgia, somewhat similar to *The 60s Without Apology*). *Guerrilla Television* (an exaggerated title of alle-

137 B

Video death-ray at California test site, 1952.

giance to international struggles and the End the War Movement) predicted
that media power would pass to the people. One vehicle for distribution
of media power was the video van (that ubiquitous, traveling home of
the counterculture, the circulating locus for nomadic fantasies and adventures, particularly sex, drugs, and rock 'n' roll, now returning with a
vengeance as RVs, Recreational Vehicles, cluttering the landscape). Video
vans spread the video gospel in a proselytizing/pedagogic return of the
agitprop trains and steamers of the Soviet constructivist filmmakers (who
would have loved the speed of video but been dismayed by the problems
of editing). Like the Soviets, video vans encouraged audiences to participate
in productions, and preached the new visions of society. In 1971, Ant
Farm's "Truckstop Project" (with allegiance to working-class travel, yet
visiting universities—a locus critical to the counterculture as well as video)
was "on the road" for two months in a "customized media van with
antennae, silver dome, TV window, inflatable shower stall, kitchen, ice
9 inflatable shelter for five, solar water heater, portapak and video playback
system."[7] (Counterculture tourism: The ecology movement combined
with technology and unfettered mobile domesticity. Would any of this
have been possible without the German VW bus or van?) Much has been
said about video techniques; Ant Farm was insightful in addressing auto-
technique although their car work focused on the fifties—the Cadillac El

Dorado, the first "to sport the famous tail-fin" and perhaps the 1955 early doo-wop rock hit by the Cadillacs, "Down the Road."[8]

Ant Farm often collaborated with other groups, among them Video Freaks, T. R. Uthco (Doug Hall, Jody Procter, and Diane Hall for *Eternal Frame)*, and TVTV (Top Value Television)—funny names of anonymity, identifying shifting groups, but against the cult of the individual or artist/ star. Disbanded in 1977, TVTV taped the last Apollo mission and inter- viewed the astronauts. (Chip Lord, an Ant Farm member, called NASA "a technodream state."[9]) With funds from cable-TV companies, the expand- able group taped the Democratic and Republican conventions in Miami (with a good review for the former in the *New York Times*).[10] Unlike the networks, they used portapak equipment, producing "alternative" readings of the events, including a critique of network journalism. The result, *Four More Years*, is an unsettling trailer for Reagan's presidency, completely unfathomable and impossible then; the presence of Vietnam veterans, pro- testing outside the convention, poignantly marks a very different history. An analysis of this work must, however, wait for another occasion. Fortu- nately TVTV, like hundreds of counterculture groups, also disbanded a few years after their 1975 move to Los Angeles. I say "fortunately" because Deirdre Boyle writes of *The Big Chill:* "Although the film was based on its director-writer Larry Kasdan's friends, it could have been about TVTV."[11]

Ant Farm's policy was to record real or imaginary events, disregarding distinctions. Although stated as a position of opposition to technocratic society and mass-mediated culture, their attitude toward mass or popular culture, like their response to technology, was ambivalent or postmod- ern—using it while condemning it. By undermining the authority of print or book culture and posing audiovisual culture as a positive alternative, they tipped the poles of high versus low, or elite versus mass culture. Aspects of the historical avant-garde reverberated in Ant Farm; they em- braced the mystic drug culture; they attempted to intervene in everyday life by using technology; and they challenged the sanctity of the art object and the author/artist (imagined by Ant Farm as a worker, a builder, a constructivist, a member of a group of divergent interests and talents: "Ant Farm accepts only worker ants, and by regulation, no queen ant or leader ant is admitted.")

Perhaps more significant for women, however, was the counter- culture commitment to communes and collaboration (for Ant

The Videofreex giant TV screen inflatable used for outdoor showings (with a video projector).

Farm read: Ant Colonies), eradicating the historical inequities between home and work spaces as well as hierarchies of labor and reward—thereby presumably undoing gender prescriptions. In terms of clothing, makeup, and hairstyle, gender was under question if not under direct siege, at least in appearances if not yet in power structures. Although modernized by technology, these groups of the sixties resemble prior utopian, communitarian experiments which drew upon socialism, anarchism, free love, and feminism, calling for local, voluntary cooperation and the organization of producers' and consumers' collectives. As Dolores Hayden reminds us in *The Grand Domestic Revolution,* earlier reformers advocated kitchenless houses, apartment cooperatives with childcare facilities, and shared communal rooms. These nineteenth- and early twentieth-century experiments challenged two characteristics of industrial capitalism: "the physical separation of household space from public space, and the economic separation of the domestic economy from the political economy."[12] Both principles were presumably reinstated in the seventies by Ant Farm.

The massive, U.S. postwar selling of the private home in the fifties signaled a defeat for these earlier dreams and practicalities. Like the development of nuclear power, suburbia spread by the development of 50 million low-technology, single family homes[13]—separate, private spaces connected by electricity, radio, telephones, and (from 1949 to 1954) TV, which housed three-quarters of all U.S. nuclear families. These very private homes of a bath-and-a-half and a barbeque were tied to industry and to credit-via-mortgages; wives were "Mrs. Consumer" or "home managers" married to "homeowners." As a 1920s home economist wrote:

There is a direct and vital business interest in the subject of young love and marriage. Every business day approximately 5,000 new homes are begun; new "nests" are constructed and new family purchasing units begin operation. . . . The founding and furnishing of new homes is a major industrial circumstance in the United States.[14]

Few of us remember that our space and its furnishings were once critical political issues, not only for earlier reformers but in women's "consciousness raising" groups of the sixties and early seventies. Like the plethora of "labor saving" appliances in the fifties, today's new techniques are marketed to keep us complacently in our home—among them the personal computer and the VCR. Those of us with modems who teach television and write about it may soon never have to leave home. These domesticated machines have turned the home into a double workplace (housework and "real" work) as well as leisure center, without eliciting any analysis of the implications of this new spatial (and economic) politics which separates the private from the public sphere via consumerism and electronic self-sufficiency. I will return to domestic technologies in the conclusion. Now, however, a brief sketch of intellectual premises of the sixties and seventies.

Among other things—including an assault on various institutions maintaining the family, the military, and capitalism by dropping out, turning on, protesting, or experimental lifestyles—the sixties and seventies counterculture was a response to the increasing privatization and consumerism of daily life, filled with "consumer durables" and labeled "upward mobility." Theodore Roszak was analyst and guru in *The Making of a Counter Culture*.[15] In opposition to technocracy and scientific discourses, including nuclear war and the military, Roszak proscribed a visionary culture of psychedelic drugs, Oriental mysticism, alienation (not Marx), and communitarian experiences—an adversarial culture of romanticism whose heroes were Blake, Wordsworth, Emerson, Thoreau, Tolstoy rather than Marx, and Jung rather than Freud.[16] In the sixties, the famous global village of Marshall McLuhan, under the slogan "The medium is the message," was an electronic utopia designed with the architecture of Buckminster Fuller and accompanied by the conceptual music of John Cage. (Fuller's architecture now adorns the Milwaukee airport, accompanied by muzak—a very different marriage.)

Two events in 1969 addressed this confluence: a thirty-minute tape, *The Medium is the Medium,* produced by an educational station, and the Howard Wise Gallery exhibition, *TV as a Creative Medium.*[17] Modernism's electronic triumverate and their disciples, inspired by Timothy Leary, proclaimed the new god of visionary liberation: SONY.

Along with the stoned, high, and radical romanticism of these Canadian and U.S. visionaries, other more political discourses were imported. One was particularly influential: Hannah Arendt's introduction to Walter Benjamin's *Illuminations,* published in 1968 as an essay in *The New Yorker,* with the full translation in 1969.[18] That same year, the Museum of Modern Art staged *The Machine as Seen at the End of the Mechanical Age,* arguing in the catalogue that "electronic and chemical devices— imitat[ing] processes of the brain and nervous system,"[19] were continuing the historical trajectory analyzed by Benjamin in his famous 1936 essay— the passage of techniques of reproduction from manual to visual and now mathematical, the brain, replicating the passage from photography and cinema to television and electronics. Indeed, Benjamin's writing suggested domestic television as much as cinema (for example, in his quotation from Paul Valéry):

Just as water, gas, electricity are brought into our houses from far off to satisfy our needs in response to a minimal effort, so we shall be supplied with visual or auditory images, which will appear and disappear at a simple movement of the hand, hardly more than a sign.[20]

Remote control and rapid channel switching are "hardly more than a sign." Benjamin's emphasis on exhibition versus cult value and his distinction between distraction and contemplation described U.S. videomakers on the road in their vans (as well as the Soviet filmmakers who influenced Benjamin): "the original meets the beholder halfway . . . in new situations and liquidates traditional cultural heritage."[21] The importance of alternative systems of distribution and exhibition, Benjamin's "new situations," cannot be emphasized enough. Too often, critics, fetishizing the commodity by focusing only on production, enact precisely what they attack.

Although not directly manifest in art works and criticism until recently, the fusion of avant-garde and romantic claims of video's spokesmen reflected the influence of Benjamin and of contemporary French theory. These theories, imported into the U.S. in the late sixties and seventies like Japanese video equipment and business practices, solidified a French connection intensified by the events of May '68. Roland Barthes's scandalous "theory of the text" heralded the plural subject and heterogeneity. According to Barthes, meaning was not located in the author/artist but in a process between text and reader, a co-creator of meaning. The text demanded reciprocal interaction, unraveling, deciphering. The author was displaced from center stage; the text was center-framed; and the reader/spectator/viewer was elevated to the position of active participant rather than faithful translator. Criticism was a game with at least two equal players. Because a "multiplicity" of interpretations was possible, entrenched, authorial meanings were overturned. Some of us did not mourn the passing. As the civil rights and anti-war protests momentarily altered the poles of power, criticism's hierarchy was also challenged. Video's desire for interactive, participatory TV coincided with theory's reciprocity and the claims for active "readers" rather than passive consumers of meaning.

Along with Barthes, Michel Foucault argued for the dispersion and multiplication of powers and sexualities; Foucault analyzed micropowers and microtechniques, focusing on the margins of culture. Rather than wardens and kings, Foucault researched discourses of prisoners and ordinary citizenry, careful, however, to repress and indeed deny the importance of gender to marginality. Like the women's movement and "guerrilla TV," Foucault's "countercultural" position argued for a drastic alteration of power/knowledge, an interrogation of relations of domination/subordination, and a shift from the center of official culture to the periphery of subcultures (Foucault would be employed later, for example, by Dick Hebdige's depiction of subculture).

Amidst the sixties and seventies unraveling of power and knowledge, theory itself was practiced *as* political activity. Barthes wrote of France in 1968, "power, itself, as a discursive category, was dividing, spreading like a liquid leaking everywhere."[22] In the U.S. and France, college students occupied buildings, went on strike, attacked "the system," and contributed to ending an incomprehensible war by making it public. While it is true that the political premises of theory—like the clothing and hair length of the counterculture which seem ancient, unreal, except on television reruns—have been abandoned by theory clones (proponents of generic, watered-down, easy theory), its practice and politics are still better ways to make sense of the world than what it attacked. At the same time, concealed by all the new terms was the similarity between the emancipatory claims of modern theorists and the romantics/radicals. Both ignored gender as

When a broadcast TV crew goes to an event, they stand above the crowd and tell you about it (Sander Vanocur of NBC at an anti-Cambodia demonstration in Washington, D.C.).

When you go to an event with a Porta-Pak, you shoot in the crowd and let environmental sound and people speak for themselves (a Raindance videotape of the same event).

a historical determinant. Although deconstructed, intellectual patriarchy was maintained, though in ways that were more difficult to discern and label. The famous theory of the subject endorsed and minutely studied in so many "feminist" books is gradually coming into focus—like Jimmy Stewart playing George Bailey in *It's a Wonderful Life*—as quite clearly male, with gender relations, like power, intact.

Thus, most of the U.S. population was and is excluded, as subjects, from theoretical debates. While real advances for women did occur—the devaluation of the institutions of female virginity and marriage (both very fashionable today, like the fetishistic fascination with babies, including Baby Jessica, and the babies on the wretched *thirtysomething* and *A Day in the Life*—the titles are cute giveaways of cloying women and whining banality), the passage of *Roe v. Wade* and the availability of birth control and abortion, the advances of the women's movement as support and activist groups (as strategies of collaboration and support turn, academically, to competition, careerism, and envy), the return to school and the job market—the heterosexual couple, although shaken up by the bumpy, experimental ride of women's consciousness raising groups, the subsequent divorce rate, and collective living, has emerged unscathed, nuclear, and private, reassuring patriarchy that it, like capitalism, has reasserted control. Today that old story of uncovering the biological, "real" father is rampant on soap operas—Lacan's name of the father returning in the eighties with a real vengeance. Bearing children is a critical production for ambitious, tenured female academics and executives, an old-fashioned, real way to get up all those messy, imaginary distinctions between penis and phallus which I never cared about or understood in the first place.

Manifestations of counterculture in the sixties and seventies, as text or lifestyle, theory or practice, with its gentle avoidance of feminism on both fronts are both appalling and appealing to me. While the advances of the women's movement were significant, the equivocation toward women still continues. Video's opposition to commercial TV was always slippery if not false, as video artists immediately sought and gained access to large TV studios, albeit "educational" stations, in New York, Boston, and San Francisco, with quiet commitments to sponsoring corporations and government foundations, particularly funneled through the Rockefeller Foundation, abandoning the portable sounds and struggles of the streets for the electronics and engineered effects provided by corporations, always with the mission of being broadcast to mass audiences—not necessarily negative. In a symptomatic after-effect, network television contributed to ending the war as well as the counterculture through familiarization and recuperation rather than argument. In 1987, rather than video politics (video meaning shared precepts, a common politics), video means leisure and industry—video bars, videodrome, video dating, the video column of *Time,* rock video, video movie rental at "Video Visions" and other cassette supermarkets, and most importantly, amateur home video equipment, and the circulation of video pornography, the latter a mass subculture, a real paradox.

Finally, without the intent to heroicize a spirit of an age, or to portray a nineteenth-century drama of generations, but with the advances of the women's movement in mind, the countercultural stance against polarities, particularly the reassessment of private versus public spaces, art versus commerce or life, word over image, the book over cinema or TV, mind over body, as well as hierarchy among media, cultures, genders, and nations are important, perhaps—in the dazedly conservative U.S.—now more than ever. However visionary, apolitical, and in the end patriarchal, the moment was a brief space in which, to quote Althusser, "the ideological state apparatus did not reproduce itself automatically."

E*ternal Frame,* a 1975 performance and videotape made by Ant Farm and T. R. Uthco, is a simulation of a catastrophe—the *film* of John Kennedy's assassination in Dallas. The recreation dissects representation, moving from the grainy film image imprinted in our memory, through the copy of their preparations, rehearsal, and performance to a model—the videotape. Thus, it shifts from film to television, without a "real" except the Zapruder film which it takes on its own terms, i.e., without incorporating the point of view of the assassin. The "bad" copy matches the "bad" original which is only an image—an indelible one. That historical image—along with the spectatorial mechanisms of disavowal or suspension of disbelief (reception)—is the real mystery (rather than who killed Kennedy and how, the usual concerns brought to bear on the footage). The videotape works through a series of contradictions, not the least of which is a definition of "art": it argues for television as history, as a set of social relations *and* as a challenge to historiography and mastery which can provide a truth, a real. At the same time, the performance and the tape grant answers and closure, and reveal mastery through professionalism—the satisfactory perfection of their recreation and its effects. The made-for-television movie, *The Trial of Lee Harvey Oswald,* the first in a series of planned restagings of history as courtroom drama, conducted by "real" lawyers interrogating experts, witnesses, and culprits and based on "real" evidence and documents, is a simpler investigatory simulation—looking for an imaginary real rather than interrogating its displaced representation.

The resemblance of *Eternal Frame* to the work of Jean Baudrillard is not coincidental, given the period and the common source of McLuhan; however, this work preceded the boom in Baudrillard's books in the U.S.: *In the Shadow of the Silent Majorities* and *Simulations* (imagine *Simulations* as the script for *The Last Judgment* co-starring Yves Montand as Charlton Heston, with Baudrillard in a cameo as a working-class god quoting Cecil B. DeMille). While a tragically paralyzed Baudrillard is awaiting the apocalypse (a process initiated by the postwar European invasion of U.S. mass culture and thought, signaling an end to mastery and classical education, lucidly pointed to by Meaghan Morris in her essay in *Seduced and Abandoned,* a celebratory Ant Farm critiques catastrophe, collectively signaling the conclusion of sixties rhetoric of youth and generational crisis. Fredric Jameson suggests that "for many white American students—in particular for many of those later active in the new left—the assassination of President Kennedy played a significant role in delegitimizing the state itself," with Kennedy's "generation gap" setting off "political discontent" of American students.[23] This positioning of "Kennedy" with the U.S. left—glaringly emergent in the obsession of many lefties with uncovering the conspiracy of the assassination—is also undermined by the tape's irreverence. The tape also marks another ending—of a cultural politics of collaboration and alternative distribution.

As the poster announcing the showing of the videotape to a San Francisco art audience cogently states, *Eternal Frame* is "An Authentic Remake of the Original JFK Assassination." Earlier, the artist/president, Doug Hall, declared:

I am in reality nothing more than another image on your television set. . . . I am in reality nothing more than another face on your screen, I am in reality only another link in that chain of pictures which makes up the sum total of information accessible to us all as Americans. . . . Like my predecessors, the content of the image is no different from the image itself.

"I am in reality an image" embraces the imaginary as a dilemma rather than the tragedy implicit in "The space of simulation confuses the real with the model."[24] This is, of course, the "hyperreal" in which all is statistic, memory bank, or miniature, abolishing representation. While

Production still from Doug Hall, Chip Lord, Jody Proctor, *The Amarillo News Tapes,* 1980, color video, 28 min.

Kennedy's death was, as the tape asserts, both a real and an image death, far from liquidating representation, it enthroned the film image: *Eternal Frame* critiques that powerful hold of the image as history on our memory and emotions.

For Baudrillard, furthermore, simulation is infinitely more dangerous than an actual crime "since it always suggests . . . that law and order themselves might really be nothing more than simulation."[25] (This was the premise of the conspiracy theorists after Jack Ruby's crime. If we take this in an opposite direction, nuclear war had better be a simulation.) The crime and danger of art are boredom or bad taste, often disguised by numerous platonic philosophers of false versus serious art as an issue of realism. A middle-age man, outside the theater after seeing the videotape (and near the end of the tape) speaks for Baudrillard's insistence on denotative distinctions, his desire for referents (so comically analyzed by Morris): "They didn't use anything original at all." They should have "either told what happened or made up their own story. . . . They took a theme of a real man getting killed and they played little games with it. . . ."

As the tape suggests, the assassination of Kennedy, but particularly the circulation and repeated viewing of the amateur/tourist movie footage endlessly rerun on television and scrutinized by real and amateur detectives for clues (the classic instance of close, textual analysis of film—pre-Raymond

Bellour), signaled the end of imagined mastery via brave individuality. Because it had been recorded, the image, allied to reality and tragic drama, would yield an answer, a truth, if, like the riddle of the Sphinx, we would only get closer, deconstruct it. When deconstruction failed, recreation or simulation was the next logical step—a cultural shift analogous to the move from cinema to television as the dominant theoretical object or cultural metaphor.

It could also be argued that the assassination, in 1963, linked to film footage and not initially covered by the networks, was the first and last time for a united television audience: everyone compulsively remembered and minutely described, again and again, like reruns, where *they were,* in real life, and where they were in relation to television, representation, a cultural moment when television and our daily lives were still separate but merging. (We still remember that Dan Rather was physically there *and* on television.) While our emotional experience of the event came from television, our bodies remained distinct from television; "meaning" occurred to us in specific places. The constant coverage realized television's potential for collective identification and national cohesion—television's dream that by informing us and setting a good, calm, and rational example via the anchors, the populace could be united, soothed, and finally ennobled by the repetition of and patient waiting for information.

Covering catastrophes is the ultimate test of the top anchorman's mettle, his stamina measured by words, information, and calm demeanor. Television fancies that if we have enough news, if it stays on the air with us, a vigil like sitting up with a sick or dying friend, we will behave like adults. Or, the stock market coverage of "Black Monday" demonstrates that television can also, like computer trading, panic us, creating a need *for* television. What was innovative then has become protocol which we have come to expect and which plays into and creates those expectations. The Challenger catastrophe exploded these dreams of technology as unifying a dispersed audience, symbolically fragmenting the national audience—like the unseeable and horrific imaginary nightmare of these human astronaut bodies, knowing and alive, for seconds, plunging at unfathomable speed into oblivion; the technological catastrophe, our telescopic, distanced view of an abstract speck, from outside, collided with the personal drama of a mother and father watching—and then, in an instance and a glance, *knowing*—their teacher/daughter/mother blown up in space; we were truly in the position of voyeurs, catching a glimpse of something private we shouldn't have seen and, unlike the Kennedy assassination, unable to really see what happened. While verbal facts and accounts detailing the horror of error, carelessness, and technological failure were piled onto that distant fragmentation to "explain" it scientifically, we imagined, from the audio-tapes, the personal nightmare and terror inside the shuttle. Did they know? For how long? Afterward, like conspiracists searching, the ocean floor was combed, in mourning, for the fragments of bodies and machine—to retrieve the real. NASA's role was investigated as a trial of errors rather than as murder, with videotaped evidence endlessly repeated. Seeing was not believing in this instance. The difference between these two events is profound, and historical: the horror of Kennedy was in what we saw; the terror of Challenger was what we could not see.

Baudrillard's prognoses of culture elided with nuclear catastrophe can be linked to television's instantaneous capacity to present "live" coverage of (death) events, both shocking and mollifying the audience, mediating and exacerbating the effects of the real—rerun and transformed into representation. We can await "live" catastrophes on TV, signaled by ruptures in the flow of programs, a disruption of time, TV's constancy. Catastrophe argues for the importance, the urgent value, the truth of television and its watching which will be good for us—providing catharsis, or better, mastery, via repetition of the same which is fascinating, mesmerizing. Catastrophe coverage thus functions "beyond the pleasure principle" as an essentially verbal rendering of *fort-da!* hinged on a visual detail, like Baby Jessica's cable or the thirty-second explosion or rifle shots, to acknowledge then alleviate fear and pain. (Think of Barthes's obsession with the photograph of his mother in *Camera Lucida*.) Perhaps masochistically, pleasure, aligned with death rather than life, comes from that game of repetition, with catastrophe as potent TV, coded as exception. For once, this doesn't come from TV techniques, which are usually of extremely poor quality—shaky, minimal, indecipherable images, awkward editing glitches, missed cues and connections, filler speech and delimited language, endless repetition of the same facts and simple arguments—like muzak, yet live, overwhelming regular narrative programming as we wait, with the anchor, either for further events and analysis or a conclusion before TV normalcy can return. The intrusion of the real is also the taking over by the news division of entertainment. If the network merely breaks, momentarily, the crisis was not in the U.S.—our catastrophes demand twenty-four-hour coverage, nation over narrative.

After this riff of speculation, *Eternal Frame* revisited. After a rerun of the brief "original" (the Zapruder film is shorter than I remembered, a clip lengthened by history and stop-frame analysis), the re-enactment of the assassination becomes, as the viewers acknowledge, "more real" (i.e., with fewer errors or deviations from convention and expectation) until it is encapsulated as "art" and replayed for us as image, which it always was. After the artist/president, Hall, declares Ant Farm's position in a presidential address, the first rehearsal of the assassination occurs in a car in front of rear-screen projection, which flattens depth like a 1940s Hitchcock automobile ride. The studio is replaced by location shots in Dallas, the scene of the real and artistic crime. The rehearsal is intercut with backstage costuming and interviews with Jack (Doug Hall) and Jackie (Doug Michaels) who comment on dress rehearsals, acting, and masquerade. Sexual difference is brilliantly inscribed as a simulation— Jackie is played perfectly in a pink suit and hat, and with minimal gestures. The hesitant actors, leery of reprisal, believing their act to be scandalous or sacrilegious, emerge, restage the event for passersby who deeply enjoy it, and rerun their final color re-enactment as a rhapsody six times from various angles, becoming "authentic."

In *Eternal Frame*, the clever interplay between valorized documentary conventions of late 1960s verisimilitude (black-and-white versus color, wild sound, camera movement, direct address, and the cinema-verité style of the backstage and on-the-street interviews) document the arbitrariness of film conventions of realism. The interviews with the actors are critical moments of a presumed real. That the actors' feelings are "simulated" rather than heartfelt is an unsettling suspicion. The level of the real intensifies when the tourist audience reacts—at one moment with tears. This audience of casual passersby recreates that historical audience which lined the street (and Zapruder's film) for Kennedy's motorcade, later to become witnesses, critics, and stand-ins or extras for the nation-audience. Thus, the real players simulated an image, turning a film into a live performance which is measured by historical audiences against the famous footage as reality or later in the tape against standards of "art." That both memory and aesthetics, or history and art, are slippery calls emerges in the irony that the standard of the real is a bad "original" film, famous because of its singularity and hence "aura." Its existence is the ultimate amateur filmmaker's fantasy and nightmare. ("This is really bad taste," echoes Hall when watching their rear-screen footage on a television monitor.)

The distance between the *Eternal Frame* and Baudrillard can be measured by their conceptions of the audience. Baudrillard's mass audience is passive, fascinated, silent, outside; Ant Farm's series of inscribed audiences

News photo of the assassination of President John F. Kennedy in Dallas, Texas, November 22, 1963.

Still from the Ant Farm and T. R. Uthco video, *The Eternal Frame*, 1975, a reenactment of the Kennedy assassination.

are vocal, actively involved in critique (or, surprisingly, disavowal), yet producing not merely consuming or escaping meaning (like the end of representation, one wonders how this might be possible). One position is conservative, humorless, and without irony, predicated as it is on a model drawn from commerce; the other is refreshing. The spectators in Dallas compared the live performance to the real thing, recreated, they imagined, as a tourist attraction(!) rather than "art": "I saw it on television after it happened. . . . It looks so real now. . . . The characters look so real." Shots of these tourists photographing the recreation remind us of the anonymous maker of the original: just a person in the crowd. "He's re-enacting it. . . . I'm glad we were here. . . . It was so beautiful." An incredulous Doug Hall says: "I thought the most interesting thing was watching the people enjoy it so much. . . . How could they enjoy it so much?" This is the critical question of catastrophe coverage.

However unexpected this response of spectator enjoyment was by the performers, who drastically misjudged reception and pleasure on many accounts, *Eternal Frame* nonetheless incorporates response. Its various audiences exist in a dialogue with the work, acting as a corrective and participant/observer. The "live" event was edited into a videotape for a San Francisco art audience which responded with remarks later incorporated into the tape: "bad taste but impressive," causes "bad dreams," "disturbing but entertaining . . ." Reception alters interpretation. This sophisticated construction of and respect for audience resembles Gilles Deleuze's model of simulation. In his reading, the simulacrum circumvents mastery because it already includes the spectator, the angle of the observer. Thus, the spectator is in tandem with the maker and can transform and deform the images. Deleuze argues that the simulacrum "subverts the world of representation" and is not a degraded copy but a positive one which denies privileged points of view and hierarchies.[26] Clearly another modeling of power is at stake—one which might unsettle "classical" scholars as well as patriarchy's parameters. Particularly intriguing in Deleuze is the inclusion of the spectator's point of view in the very definition of the simulacrum—a position which is in line with Ant Farm and divergent from Baudrillard, who posits the "mass" outside as a skeptical force of negativity.

Yet I must ask whose point of view is incorporated in theoretical models. For whom is divergence and decentering positive and joyous? To answer, I will remember where I was, not in 1963 but in

Doug Hall as the "Artist-President" in *The Eternal Frame*.

1975, the year of the making of the tape. I was in Milwaukee, collaborating
on the first of what would become the six controversial film theory conferences. The urgent and then scandalous context was the emigration to the
U.S. of semiotics, psychoanalysis, and marxism, then precious and exotic
imports. After conquering theory's riddling prose, the theoretical analysis
of the representation of women in classical cinema became an insightful
project of vast influence; in many ways, it has come to represent one
interpretation of film theory, *en toto*. However, amidst all the debate on
protocol which would avoid power, and despite the vociferous assertion
of the centrality of feminism to *all* papers and topics, we were talking too
fast and neglected to note the masculine ecology: finding ourselves lacking,
we proceeded to analyze that! Brilliantly! While dissecting women's luminous presence as onscreen objects, we failed to protest our offscreen absence
as subjects in film theory and history alike. The effects of our failure to
acknowledge the gender of discourses of sexuality, including psychoanalysis, are now apparent and urgent. During the sixties, feminism was taken
for a liberating joy ride. In the late seventies, it was seduced by language,
including a materialism strangely bereft of history; we were so happy
then to be at the party that we forgot to look at the expiration date of
the invitation. Now feminism is spoken for at best, or worst, betrothed,
elided, or erased as generic or dismissed as accomplished, old-hat.[27] We

must again ask the crucial questions that we overlooked then: who is speaking, to whom, for whom, and about whom? The gender of the answer makes a difference.

Rather than going back to the future, I will now fast forward to the past and back on my own analysis and argue the bleak underside of visionary video politics and its "instrumental" view of technology. Because the issue of consumer capitalism, like gender, was repressed, the ultimate dream of TV populism—the home market or audience—is returning as dystopia. Furthermore, the bodies "which need extension," reproduction, and recreation via technology are male. Baudrillard's "obscene" perfectly describes a contemporary manifestation of portable, video, consumer culture, which is for women very "rough trade." At the Merchandise Mart in Chicago last summer, the now multiple video gods—JVC, Panasonic, Mitsubishi—devalued by competition, hawked their allures and wares at a collective ritual which travels to major cities in the U.S. each year, culminating in the orgiastic gathering in Las Vegas. When it comes to crude commerce, Baudrillard is right: the ritual was perversely fascinating and frightening. Dominated by the huge "seeing eye" of an enormous surveillance image/screen, the cavernous, echoing space was filled with suited businessmen eyeing and fondling the merchandise: old and familiar sexual technologies, the software of women and the hardware of video equipment. Burlesque collided with electronics.

The female carnies, garbed in flashy costume, used an old technique to sell a newer one, interlocking technologies and sexualities. That gender was technology and technology was gendered was literalized in each manufacturer's miniature show: the male figure was robotic; the female was a "real" tease, a come-on; masculinity was the modern, high-tech machine, that place of invisibility and power, watching, taping while the low-tech women sang "Buy Me"; video and the female body were available, multiple techniques for sale. Consumer rape: (1) the powerful realization of the dream of accessibility and pluralism and (2) politics and art gone sour, taken into the home market—was metaphorically re-enacted in a quiet scene on the lower level. A line of men with downcast eyes had very patiently formed. What awaited them, at the end? Pat Robertson and the new, electronic fundamentalism? The demeanor of devotion, including silence, provided clues. However, another object of desire was being worshiped: at the end of the line was a female porno star, provocatively auto-

Still from the Ant Farm and T. R. Uthco video, *The Eternal Frame,* 1975.

graphing her image, flirting, available, with cascading, enormous breasts spilling everywhere—an image now real. The private home as the modern theater of pornography might not have surprised the counterculture.

At the risk of my own determinism and given that technology is not neutral, it could be argued that the way portable video equipment is currently being produced and marketed parallels the fetishistic history of the home stereo system; both have been taken into social/gender relations. Unlike machines marketed for women, machines addressed to men often have excess power, e.g., 160 mph sports cars, rifles, machine guns and hand-held missiles, and the unearthly decibel levels of stereos. Washing machines or vacuum cleaners with excess power become either sitcom jokes, as in *Mr. Mom* or *Lucy,* or a horror film nightmare. For women's machines, excess power is rarely a desirable, salable component. As well as being excessive, machines marketed for men are often infinitely extensible—there's always more to add, to buy, to build—linkages to the "do-it-yourself" frontierism.[28] Might one profanely suggest that these extensible machines evoke multiplicity, plurality, and are endless texts which demand endless mastery? In relation to stereo, the system—like certain theories of diffuse pleasures and sexualities which exist without referent or example—has become the dominant text. The content of the record is secondary, something which needs mastery by a system (like the actuality, the details of politics and events and personal experiences need mastering by a theory) which can jump over all those messy facts of oppression, cultural difference, and history.

It is not coincidental that the television set was introduced in the fifties into the American home as a piece of furniture, a woman's dilemma and resistance handled by extensive campaigns in *Good Housekeeping* and other women's magazines; it was imagined as a potentially disruptive element which, however, could be smoothly managed by spatial redefinitions—the building of family rooms (TV as a baby needing a nursery, just like the home computer needs its own space) near the kitchen and accessible to Mom and food, or located in rec-rooms away from the rest of the house.[29] In this appeal to women to determine a *pre*determined space, Dad controlled the programs and, like Archie Bunker, lounged comfortably in the front-row-center comfortable chair in numerous ads. Mom sat in straight-back chairs, darning, or she served Dad by turning the dial in this antediluvian era before remote control. Now that we are purchasing infinite "home-entertainment systems" of component TV parts (including stereo systems) rather than singular pieces of furniture, Dad has become the major buyer and assembler—not an uninteresting historical development.

Rather than providing the mass, plural, utopian, alternative market for art (although attempts are being currently made), home video is a family plot. Video is about the private home and the nuclear family, another replication in technology of ideology, of privatized spaces of unequal economics and labor. That the private home is represented in much current, nostalgic cinema as a combination of utopia and dystopia, with television playing an essential role in this Spielbergian contradiction, is not surprising. Perhaps we can take a lesson from Lucy—continually trying to escape domesticity while trashing consumption in the process. Down to the minutest detail, we must argue, again and again, that the personal is the political. And mean it, thereby reclaiming our work of the sixties and seventies, rapidly being deflated and recuperated in the eighties.

Production still showing crowd watching filming of *The Eternal Frame* in Dallas.

Installation for showing of *The Eternal Frame*.

Notes

1. Peter Bürger, *Theory of the Avant-Garde* (Minneapolis: University of Minnesota Press, 1984).

2. Armand Mattelart, Xavier Delcourt, and Michèle Mattelart, *International Image Markets* (London: Comedia Publishing Group, 1984).

3. *Domus* 522 (May 1973): 28.

4. *Design Quarterly* 78/79 (1970): 6-18.

5. *Casabella* 376 (1973): 30.

6. They also had plans for a mobile university in a Ford truck and called themselves "environmental nomads."

7. Linda Burnham, "Ant Farm Strikes Again," *High Performance* 24 (1983): 27. This short piece contains a useful chronology of Ant Farm projects.

8. See Bernard Gendron's essay on Adorno and the Cadillacs in *Studies in Entertainment: Critical Approaches to Mass Culture*, ed. Tania Modleski (Bloomington: Indiana University Press, 1986), pp. 18-36.

9. "TVTV: Video Pioneers Ten Years Later," *Send* (Summer 1983): 18-23. I cannot find my source for the Lord quote; it is not in this essay.

10. Deirdre Boyle, "Subject to Change: Guerrilla Television Revisited," *Art Journal* 45, no. 3 (Fall 1985): 229.

11. Ibid., p. 232. I suspect that the reason I so intensely dislike this film is because it is only about masculinity as arrested sixties male adolescence—needless to say, a tedious and boring topic.

12. Dolores Hayden, *The Grand Domestic Revolution: A History of Feminist Designs for American Homes, Neighborhoods, and Cities* (Cambridge, Mass.: The MIT Press, 1981), p. 1.

13. Ibid., pp. 23, 25.

14. Ibid., p. 285.

15. Theodore Roszak, *The Making of a Counter Culture: Reflections on the Technocratic Society and Its Youthful Opposition* (Garden City, N.Y.: Doubleday, 1969).

16. Alec Gordon, "Thoughts Out of Season on Counter Culture," in *Contemporary Cultural Studies*, ed. David Punter (London: Longman, 1986), pp. 185-211. This essay has directly and indirectly given me many ideas—not all of which are quoted in my text; I recommend it.

17. Barbara London, "Video: A Selected Chronology, 1963-1983," *Art Journal* 45, no. 3 (Fall 1985).

18. Walter Benjamin, "The Work of Art in the Age of Mechanical Reproduction," in *Illuminations*, ed. Hannah Arendt (New York: Schocken Books, 1969).

19. Katharine Dieckmann, "Electra Myths: Video, Modernism, Postmodernism," *Art Journal* 45, no. 3 (Fall 1985): 195.

20. Benjamin, p. 219.

21. Ibid.

22. Roland Barthes, "Lecture in Inauguration of the Chair of Literary Semiology, Collège de France," *October*, no. 8 (Spring 1979): 3-16.

23. Fredric Jameson, in *The 60s Without Apology* (Minneapolis: University of Minnesota Press, 1984), pp. 182-183. The impossibility of realizing a movement of *collective* protest and principles, precariously perched on the cult of individuality—and a very wealthy one at that, from the upper class no matter how the actual, family history is figured as Irish Catholic—is apparent.

24. Jean Baudrillard, *In the Shadow of the Silent Majorities, or The End of the Social*, trans. Paul Foss, Paul Patton, and John Johnston (New York: Semiotext(e), 1983), p. 84.

25. Jean Baudrillard, *Simulations*, trans. Paul Foss, Paul Patton, and Philip Beitchman (New York: Semiotext(e), 1983), p. 38.

26. Gilles Deleuze, "Plato and the Simulacrum," *October*, no. 27 (1984): 47-56. As Chip Lord recently informed me, the screening in San Francisco (with a screening in New York the same day, November 22, 1975, the anniversary of JFK's death), was at the Unitarian Church, an event promoted by a local TV news station. Lord: "We traded them a copy of the Zapruder film for this plug on the air, but of course they described it as a 'Who Killed Kennedy?' presentation, so the audience included conspiracy buffs from the public at large as well as an invited art audience. I would imagine the disappointed school teacher who you quote was one of them. And our copy of the Zapruder film came from conspiracy theory sources and was originally bootlegged out of the *Life* magazine lab."

27. In *The 60s Without Apology*, Stanley Aronowitz writes an Odyssey of the sixties student movement and surprisingly asserts that: "Third and perhaps most important was the formation of the new feminist movement about which much substantive has been said." Exactly what has been "substantively said" remains unstated. To his credit, he immediately acknowledges the "sexism of the male new left" and states that women leaders "took a great deal of abuse and suffered humiliation. We were, simply, a male elite." A bit later he writes: "The feminist movement became more than the property of a generation; it represented, mobilized, and embodied a large fraction of women as gender." Women *as* gender? What is that, in his construction, except women as sex? After this lonely, tricky paragraph, Aronowitz never returns to the subject—presumably still not having read women's "substantive" writing.

Fredric Jameson writes the Iliad of continental, intellectual marxism during its wartime adventures in the U.S. academy, declaring that "the historian should reformulate her vocation . . . to produce the *concept* of history." Suddenly, in this marxist paradigm of knowledge, which has not the slightest relationship to feminism or women's lives and histories, Jameson asserts: " . . . what began to emerge . . . was a whole new political space, a space which will come to be articulated by the slogan, 'the personal is the political,' and into which—[here's the critical part] in one of the most stunning and unforeseeable of historical turns [like a woman, 'stunning' and unpredictable, at least to men], the women's movement will triumphantly move at the end of the decade, building a Yenan of a new and unpredictable kind which is still impregnable at the present moment." "Impregnable" is, to say the least, an ill-chosen adjective.

There seems to be a new assumption: that feminism is an entity about texts—there, an available commodity, or a "natural" resource, like air, which belongs to all of us, automatically, without personal or scholarly work. Free-floating feminism can thus be pulled, in a rhetorical sleight of hand, out of the air or marxist magician's hats as a citation of "political correctness." This is merely another way to silence women's voices. (The flip side of feminism's eighties commodification emerges in, for example, *L.A. Law*, and *The Witches of Eastwick*; another usurpation is, of course, to write in drag, *as* a woman or male feminist.) To study, to *use* rather than exchange via patronizing or impersonating, feminist argument is the glaringly obvious solution.

28. David Punter, "The Unconscious and Contemporary Culture," in *Contemporary Cultural Studies*, pp. 252-276; this essay also influenced my thinking about these issues—particularly the "gendering" of technology drawn from Punter's work on stereo systems.

29. Lyn Spigel has discussed this in papers delivered at the Society for Cinema Studies Conference in New Orleans (1986) and at the television conference in London in the summer of 1986.

Broadcast Feminism in Brazil:

An Interview with the

Lilith Video Collective

Julianne Burton and Julia LeSage

The Lilith Video Collective is the producer of the first feminist series broadcast on Brazilian television, a five-hour television series called Feminino Plural (Feminine Plural, 1987). It is one of a growing number of women's video production groups in Latin America who attribute their genesis to a dual commitment: to video as a medium and to feminism as a politics. The group is thus representative of a larger phenomenon which is changing the face of media production in Latin America.

Based in São Paulo, Lilith Video began in 1983 with three women: Jacira Melo, Marcia Meireles, and Silvana Afram, all of whom had a prior involvement with both the feminist movement and image making. Because until very recently there has been minimal access to formal training in video production— even in São Paulo, the economic and communications center of the country, where there are over one hundred and twenty independent video producers— the group learned by doing. Maria Angelica Lemos, who organized the first national Video Mulher (Video Woman) festival, held in Brasilia in March 1987, is a more recent addition to the group. She is currently preparing a dissertation for the Communications Department of the University of São Paulo on the role of video in the grass-roots political movements which have become so widespread in Brazil during the current decade.

Feminino Plural, virtually an audiovisual encyclopedia of women's issues, is as remarkable for its unflinchingly comprehensive examination of social issues at the point of individual, personal impact as for its stylistic variety and inventiveness. In general terms, the programs are characterized by their racial/ethnic mix, their unconventional use of female "emcees," their emphasis on natural settings and verdant exteriors, the predominance of close-ups which convey intimacy rather than invasiveness, their commitment to reproducing the uninterrupted discourse of their social subjects, their clever use of classical musical themes as punctuation, their varied but always fluid pacing, and their often experimental montage techniques.

This text is based upon conversations conducted in Portuguese and Spanish by Julia LeSage and Julianne Burton at Cocina de Imagines, the First Encounter of Latin American and Caribbean Women Film and Video Makers, held in Mexico City, October 1987.

All of us who are part of the Lilith Video Collective belonged first to a larger group, SOS/Mulher (SOS/Woman), which was formed to combat violence against women. SOS/Mulher was an extremely important organization because it was the first to treat violence against women not as a private, personal issue, but as a public, social problem. In addition to organizing demonstrations, we advocated concrete solutions, like the creation of all-female police stations to attend to the needs of battered women. This demand got a lot of media coverage, which meant that more and more women sought us out—some in need of help, others anxious to work with us.

In 1984, when the state Council on the Condition of Women was formed to address issues which Brazilian feminists had been rallying around for a number of years, the women's police stations *(delegacias)* were among the first demands made to the government. They became a reality. The main reason that media coverage remains extensive is the staggering number of women who come to these centers for help. On a typical Monday at the São Paulo women's station, for example, you might have between two and three hundred women coming in to file complaints. The staff of the *delegacias,* women drawn from the police force, perform a number of functions above and beyond conventional police duties—directing the women to shelters if necessary, providing access to medical and psychological care, legal counseling, and so forth. Today these *delegacias* exist throughout Brazil.

We all come from an urban generation that was brought up on television. Because we have always loved TV and felt that we learned a lot from it, we seem to have been very attentive to the form itself, though this is such a deep-seated phenomenon that it's very difficult to talk about. Clearly, there's no single, unified method. With each tape we make, we end up discovering a particular dynamic, so that the language used—the very rhythm of the work—is tied to a large degree to an approach which we perceive to be intrinsically motivated. For example, in *Women in the Canefields* (1986, Umatic, 30 minutes), we got up at five o'clock in the morning and went with the women to the canefields, where we stayed with them under the burning sun until late in the afternoon. It seems both logical and appropriate that the rhythm of the camera and the editing reproduce the slow, repetitive agrarian rhythms characteristic of the countryside and the often laconic pacing of the women's testimonies.

Our first video dealt with the rights of working women and, in particular, with how the gap between existing laws and actual practices impacts upon women's lives. The tape is basically a reportage consisting of women workers interviewed at the gates of their workplaces, discussing certain rights and requirements not yet covered by legislation: unequal pay, the double day, lack of adequate day care, etc. But (and this characteristic of our work was already present at the start) all these issues had to be articulated by the women themselves. We have always based our work on the condition that the women who we are taping are their own spokespeople, without the intervention of anyone pretending to speak on their behalf.

Since *The Rights of Working Women* (VHS, 1984, 20 minutes) was made at the invitation of and in collaboration with the newly formed São Paulo State Council on the Condition of Women, production was predicated upon the pre-existing possibility of distribution. The tape immediately became part of the concrete political project which had enabled it to get made in the first place. It has circulated widely among urban and rural women's unions, thanks to the efforts of the women from the Council, who continue to show it at meetings of workers' groups, using it as a catalyst for discussions.

Our second tape, also made for the Council, was called *Health Care for the Working Woman* (VHS, 1984, 15 minutes). Similar in approach and composition to our first effort, it was an educational tape which focused on basic issues as viewed and experienced by working women themselves, seeking to generate awareness of problems.

These were the first videos made about women in the context of the Brazilian union movement, whose resurgence coincided with the slow transition from military to civilian rule. Video was still a novelty at that point, and the attention which the unions were beginning to give to women's concerns was also a new development. As soon as each of these tapes was finished, the Council had a dozen copies made for distribution among the various unions. As the demand rose, more and more copies were made. There are two main union groupings in Brazil—the Central Unica dos Trabalhadores and the Central Geral dos Trabalhadores. Naturally, these are divided by significant political differences, so it is important to note that our tapes have been very well received by both camps.

Initially, we had agreed to make five videos for the Council on the Condition of Women: one on day care, another dealing with women workers in rural areas, a third on black women and questions of racism, a fourth on menopause and aging . . . We only made the first three; the fourth was made by a friend of ours whom we invited to take over because the funding had finally come through for the television program *Feminino Plural,* the fifth part of the CCW project, which we began shooting in January of 1987.

It took a long struggle with the state funding agencies to win the backing necessary to realize this project. Although this television series was better funded than our earlier projects (we actually got *paid* for this work—a welcome novelty), the situation still left a lot to be desired. We had a maximum of five or six days to produce each hour-long program—including taping, editing, and post-production.

We decided upon the topics we wanted the series to address—menstruation and early sexuality, attitudes toward pregnancy and motherhood, aging, women and work, (lack of) adequate childcare, sexual violence against women, racial discrimination as it affects women—

and then divided them up among ourselves so that one of us was in charge of each subject. In addition, we each took responsibility for a general task: Marcia was managing director, for example, while Jacira was in charge of scripting. Scripting began with a briefing session. Each theme had its own idiosyncratic development, but a four to five page treatment was developed for each of the five hour-long programs, followed by a lot of collective discussion to determine the particular approach, look, and rhythm of each program.

Through her work with Olhar Electronica, Marcia has had ample experience making tapes for broadcast television. She feels that the commercial nature of the process usually generates excessive rigidity and compartmentalization. During the production of the *Feminino Plural* series, we were constantly asking ourselves whether the fact of shooting for broadcast television was changing the way we worked. It *was* a different experience, yet at the same time our approach was fully consistent with our previous independent work in that we tried to discover a particular rhythm which would be specific to each separate program—the topic's own inherent rhythm. The biggest difference for us was that we had to compartmentalize, and we had to allow for the commercials.

Feminino Plural has two types of interviews—those caught on the fly, and those which are the product of prior contact and discussion. Obviously, the gravest cases—the woman who tells of her rape, the pregnant teenager—were ones with which we were already familiar. What accounts in large part for the quality of the interview material in these programs is our close ties to various feminist groups. Ordinarily, such a tight production schedule might have precluded the depth and variety which our material displays. Most of the women who give testimony in this series were preselected by the various women's groups with whom we were in contact.

With each of our earlier productions, we had taken care to develop the "video competency" of everyone working with us. We weren't simply concerned that they understand the technology; we wanted to educate them about the nature and the potentialities of the medium. While making our initial tapes, we had worked with officials from the Health Commission, the Labor Commission, the Commission on Violence, and so on. We would encourage consultants from these government agencies, from union groups, or whatever, to go with us on the shoots, to the editing sessions, and so on. This principle was not without its price. It isn't easy to work under these conditions: you have to be very flexible, and very patient. But when we began to work on *Feminino Plural,* we had the incalculable advantage of already having well-established lines of communication with representatives of all sorts of agencies and organizations who already understood our methods and our goals.

Generally, though not always, we omit our own interventions when editing interviews in order to create more of a monologue effect. What we were seeking in *Feminino*

Plural, consistent with all our earlier work, is not a question-and-answer, give-and-take kind of interaction, but rather a form of personal testimony in which we create a situation which allows the speaker to talk uninterrupted, to present herself and her thoughts at her own pace and in her own way.

Feminino Plural was the first production where we opted to supplement first-person testimony with occasional dramatizations. Jacira and Marcia both have worked in theater and are very interested in the possibilities of fictionalization in a documentary context. The fictionalized sections of *Feminino Plural* were developed in collaboration with Cecilia de Melo, an actress who belongs to one of the leading experimental groups, and a local feminist writer, so that dramatizations were the result of a happy combination of many talents. We were pleased with the results, and with the way the testimonials and the dramatized reconstructions worked together.

An index of the general success of the series is that it has already been broadcast twice in São Paulo, as well as in ten other states throughout Brazil.

Distribution still lags far behind the actual demand from women's groups, unions, scholars. And every time International Women's Day comes around, things really get out of control. In 1985, a few groups in São Paulo began to organize small videotheques. The Women's Information Center (Centro da Informacao da Mulher), the Women's Network, and the Council formed lending libraries of their own. These videotheques continue to operate, circulating catalogues of their holdings to women's groups all over Brazil. Until now, this is how most of our work has been distributed. Unfortunately, it is a pretty precarious arrangement.

We would like to see Lilith expand into the areas of training and distribution. We are seeking international backing for our distribution initiatives. Since 1983, there has been substantial videomaking activity throughout Brazil, though São Paulo remains the most concentrated area. Within the many kinds of grass-roots political movements which have sprung up throughout the country, most of which had incorporated video into their activities, women's production has been the most extensive. We would like to assemble all the tapes made by women on women's issues (they currently number well over a hundred) and devise ways of getting them to the groups that can use them rather than waiting around for people to discover and request them.

The independent popular movements in Brazil are producing an extremely rich body of independent video. These new groups are not simply of great social and political significance; we believe that they are also of great cultural significance. Brazilian video production is unequaled in Latin America in terms of both quality and quantity. Yet on the formal level, we think that the work that is currently being done still leaves a lot to be desired.

For information about distribution of works by the Collective contact: Women Make Movies, 225 Lafayette Street, New York, NY 10012.

Loss: Separation
Subject: Natalie Cortlandt

Natalie Cortlandt continues to pay the price for the fling she had with Ross Chandler prior to her marriage to his father, Palmer. Palmer's jealousy and insecurity about being replaced by his son mount after he discovers Natalie and Ross in an embrace. Despite her ardent declarations of faithfulness, he disbelieves her claims of love, and walks out on her.

Natalie's role in her own abandonment illustrates to the viewer the woman's responsibility to maintain the family unit. The continuous monitoring of her own behavior and the demonstrable concern for the activity of the spouse and children both in and beyond the home may help the woman at home to deflect fears of distance, separation, and abandonment which are aggravated by the daily departure of spouse and children into the outside world. The maintenance of the family also provides the isolated daytime viewer with a sense of community in the family, just as the "community" she finds in the soap opera characters provides her with examples of abandonment and her moral imperative to prevent separation.

Separation
Subject: Natalie C...

Natalie Cortlandt ...
price for the fling...
Chandler prior to h...
father, Palmer. Pal...
insecurity about be...
on mount after...

Loss: Amnesia
Subject: Adam Garver (aka Cain)

Cain, a Vietnam veteran who was sexually abused and blackmailed by Elena while recuperating from a mental breakdown, now suffers from amnesia after Elena's attempt on his life. Although socially immobilized and isolated by loss of memory, the amnesiac suggests the possibility of an active imagination to the daytime viewer (who may also be socially "isolated" due to household responsibilities). As an amnesiac, Cain bears no responsibility for his past prior to the reconstruction of his memory, allowing him to freely imagine an alternative, meaningful life, and to live out this imaginary life in the masquerade as Cain.

Recovery brings about a confrontation between his masquerade as Cain, and the "real" character with a history, "Adam Garver." The portrayal of an amnesiac may seem liberating to daytime viewers overloaded with images of servile, dependent women, since it recognizes the value of imagination and fantasy. Unfortunately, the imaginary—the limitless possibilities available when one lacks a history—is cut short by the recovery of memory which displaces the amnesiac Cain.

Loss: Death
Subject: Elena Nikolas
(see also insanity, lost love object)

Her unusual death (presumably a suicide in which she hired a killer in order to frame Cruz, the object of her unrequited love) marks the end of a life confounded by unmourned losses. Abandoned by her natural father, Elena gradually loses her sanity and plots the destruction of her father's legitimated family. When threatened with exposure (the loss of the secret of her vengeful acts), she plans her own death and Cruz's demise.

Elena's death won't be mourned, but she will be missed. Since she never acceded to the symbolic order (as evidenced by her madness, ostensibly due to the lack of recognition by her father) she won't be mourned by her fictional Santa Barbara community, but she will be missed by soap audiences as the most exciting, if demented, character in the series. But in the soap opera's never ending narrative, viewers gain a whole new subplot—Cruz's probable loss of liberty and social standing when he's indicted for the murder of Elena.

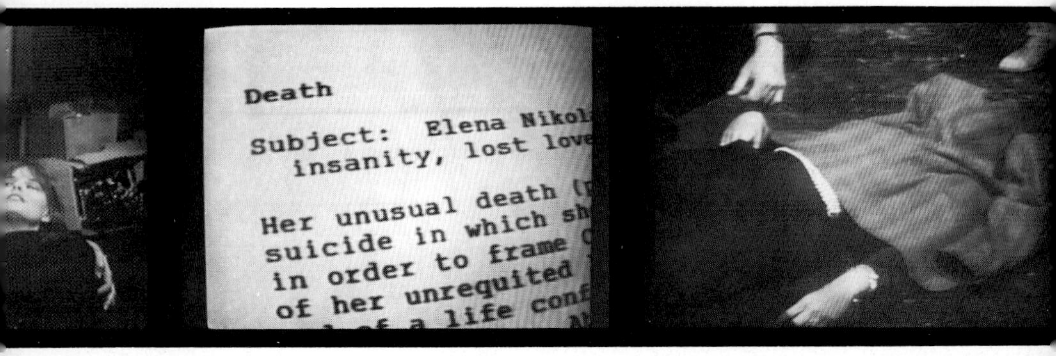

Death

Subject: Elena Nikol
insanity, lost love

Her unusual death (
suicide in which sh
in order to frame C
of her unrequited
of a life conf

Get Buf-Puf clean. Every day.

Bill Moyers and Timothy McSeed, from the CBS report, *The Vanishing Family: Crisis in Black America*, January 25, 1986.

Feminization of Poverty
and the Media

Maud Lavin

The "feminization of poverty" is a trend, the germ of a political movement, but also a poignant reminder that some problems generate attention only when white people are involved.[1]

T he "feminization of poverty" is a phrase coined in 1978 by sociologist Diana Pierce. It describes a situation that has become even more acute during the Reagan administration: increasing numbers of Americans are living in poverty, and, of these, the percentage of poor women and children, white and minority, is sharply increasing. In the United States today, two out of three adults living in poverty are female and over a third of all female-headed households are now classified as poor (based on an official designation of poverty as an annual income of $10,609 for a family of four). Of these impoverished families, the statistics are worst for black and Hispanic mothers: 51.7 percent of black female-headed households are poor as are 53.4 percent of Hispanic families headed by single women.[2] Because of such inequities, media coverage of poverty frequently focuses on women.

Almost all welfare coverage is marked by certain gender assumptions. For instance, female-headed households automatically tend to be described as problematic and even pathological. Specifically, moral indignation frequently leads commentators to assume that unmarried, underclass teenage mothers are to blame for their impoverished state because of their choice to bear out-of-wedlock children. This is based on the unspoken assumption that, without children, these teenagers could lift themselves out of poverty. Sweeping aside such considerations as unemployment, Nicholas Lemann, in the July 1986 *Atlantic,* echoes a typical blame-the-victim stance: "Out-of-wedlock childbearing . . . is today by far the greatest contributor to the perpetuation of the misery of ghetto life."

The poverty of women is inextricably intertwined with the poverty of men, but it is worth focusing specifically on the situation of the female subgroup as revelatory of the power structures which function in the U.S. Given contemporary ideologies of competitiveness and hyper-individualism, operations of power (although economically determined) are inscribed in the individual bodies of men and women who live in poverty. This means that although we can explain the existence of poverty with classical Marxist analysis in terms of the capitalist need for an available pool of desperate, cheap labor, the power in our society is deployed through a mythology of individualism and the *bodies* of individuals. In a late capitalism of national deindustrialization, service sector growth, and global monopolies, these hierarchies within hierarchies are ever further defined. Simply put, if your body is female, you are likely to earn less money, and if your skin is black, even less.

This essay focuses on the ways in which the mass media covers this feminization of poverty: how it displaces these large issues of white power onto the plight of black teenage mothers; how it concentrates on the individual instead of the state, thereby underlining our pervasive and unquestioned individualism; and how it addresses and constructs its media audience as passive. However, this essay also considers the media as a potential instrument of political change. Rather than assuming a distanced and judgmental view, I ask this pragmatic question: how do the everyday practices of mainstream newspapers and television shape the media's coverage of poverty, and how can these practices be changed? Thus my method weds radical critique with demands for practical activism. And it explores this coupling as an appropriate strategy within a dominant culture in a condition not of revolution but of continual crisis and oppressive action. Recently, for example, the 100th Congress passed a welfare bill, a reform effort seriously compromised by conservatives. In the face of today's poverty, pragmatism is too urgent to be left to the bandwagons of neoconservatives and neoliberals; it must be a strategy of radical intellectuals as well.

I. White Media, Black Mothers

Of the 7.3 million families in poverty in 1984, more than half had at least one worker and over 20 percent had two or more workers. But a person working 40 hours a week, every week of the year, at minimum wage ($3.35 an hour) will not earn enough to lift a family of three out of poverty.[3]

Since 1981 (a period of unemployment and rapidly increasing homelessness) the monthly caseload of families receiving AFDC [Aid to Families with Dependent Children, the most prevalent form of welfare in the U.S.] has been reduced by 440,000 while payments have been cut by a total of $3.6 billion per year. The Food Stamp Program has been cut back even more (by $6.8 billion since 1982) and has reduced benefits to 20 million families.[4]

In reviewing media coverage of American poverty, one finds many more stories on black teenage mothers than on the government's responsibility for their poverty (such as the Reagan administration's drastic welfare cuts or the inadequacy of the minimum wage). Not only is such press unsatisfactory, but further, it is open to misuse by the political right; it feeds too easily into the Reagan administration's public policy "debates" on the efficacy of welfare, and it ultimately contributes to justifying welfare reductions.

To examine the mechanisms of this deflection of focus away from the Reagan administration and onto black single mothers (the phenomenon frequently termed "blaming the victim"), I want to review a 1986 CBS television special, Bill Moyers's *The Vanishing Family: Crisis in Black America,* and the media response which this television event generated.

On Saturday, January 25, 1986, CBS aired this two-hour prime-time program (9-11 p.m. EST) decrying the disintegration of the black family. The film consists primarily of documentary footage shot in the Newark, New Jersey ghetto, with Bill Moyers interviewing young black men and women about their attitudes towards sexual mores, children, and family, and peripherally related issues of unemployment and violence.

Moyers's interview persona is one that only recently has been permitted to a white commentator visiting a black ghetto: a blend of the 1970s sympathetic, liberal, "reasoned," and "nonjudgmental" reporter, and the 1980s moralist holding himself back, with effort, from disdain and disapproval. The combination conveys concern laced with condescension.

Those interviewed are attractive and articulate, eminently telegenic. Two personalities emerge most strongly from among the interviewees: Alice Cassandra Jackson, unwed mother of three and welfare recipient, and the man who is her lover. Jackson worked until her first child was born and since then she has been at home (in one of Newark's roughest projects) caring for her children. Under Moyers's "guidance," she "admits" that she does not use birth control and that she might not have had her last two children if welfare did not exist. Jackson is prevented from functioning as the object of the viewer's moral disapproval by her portrayal as a caring mother and as a neglected victim—neglected by her lover, the father of her children, whose real name is Timothy McSeed. In this documentary, McSeed is presented as sin incarnate: too handsome and too self-satisfied. (Is one of his sins that he does not shuffle his feet and "act poor"?) McSeed brags to Moyers that he has fathered six children by three different women and that he supports none of them. He says that he loves Jackson, but he does not help, financially or otherwise, to raise their children.

The Moyers show was lauded in the mainstream press and given extensive coverage, primarily on the editorial pages of newspapers, even stimulating a six-part debate in the *Washington Post*. In magazines, it opened up a long-standing taboo subject—behavior in the ghettos. Praised as concerned and risk-taking journalism, it was nevertheless easily employed by neoconservative writers to further fuel that skeptical evaluation of welfare so widely pursued in the Reagan era: welfare benefits induce moral decay and dependency. Now neoliberals corroborate this view. Thus, at the end of Reagan's tenure, both neoliberals and neoconservatives are joining together to back federal welfare "reform" legislation that mandates demeaning workfare and threatens sanctions (cutting a recipient's benefits for a period of months) for those who do not comply. As background, the Moyers show exemplifies the kind of ideology that has encouraged neoliberals to support the conservative welfare agenda, even as they ignore the traditional liberal fights for raising welfare benefits (a national minimal level) and adequate federal funding for child care and job training. For neoliberals, the Moyers documentary seemed to vindicate the infamous Moynihan report of 1965, *The Negro Family*.[5] That report, prepared for President Johnson, was cited often in the discussion of the Moyers documentary.

In the Moyers show and in many of the media responses to it, there are two serious faults: an absence of an economic context for the familial issues discussed, and the commentators' failure to address their own biases towards the nuclear family structure. At the heart of this second issue is the white professional male's horror of illegitimacy among black poor and the resulting single-female-head-of-household families. Severe poverty *is* horrific, with its day-to-day existence of bad nutrition, constant violence, and limited health care; and much of this *does* often occur within single-parent families. However, any discussion of these problems cannot be separated from economic issues, even granting that ghetto (or any)

Bill Moyers and President Lyndon Johnson   Senator Daniel P. Moynihan

culture cannot be completely and reductively defined in economic terms. Central to the problem of a "culture of poverty" is the inequity of women's wages—the fact that the majority of families headed by a single mother have a significantly lower income than two-parent families or the relatively small number of families headed by a single father.

Most black mothers work. Why doesn't the media bemoan their low wages and their impossibility of finding affordable child care? Why this harping on the "sins" of black teenage mothers and fathers? To speculate on why such dissention is now so common in our media and so accepted by the consensus, this discourse must be related to a negative response to feminism and women working and also a displacement of attitudes towards the disintegration of traditional *white* families—all this inflected by the cult of nostalgia in the Reagan era. Barbara Omolade has argued:

These attacks on black single mothers occur in the context of tremendous changes in the white American family: a steady increase in female-headed households, a rise in the rate of out-of-wedlock births (5% in 1960 to 14% in 1975), more teenage pregnancy, more households where adults live alone or with one other person, more women who both work and rear children, and a general relaxation of sexual mores. Black single mothers have become convenient scapegoats for the backlash against these changes.[6]

Specifically, the media responses to the CBS documentary reveal a great deal about that profession's own identity. The reviews almost always expressed an admiration for the professional persona of Moyers and an attitude of condescension toward the interviewees:

. . . what we see is distressing. Men who take no responsibility for their children are not edifying. Even Mr. Moyers, reasoned, non-judgmental, once or twice seems ready to lose his temper.[7]

Listening to the bewildered young women who are "married to welfare" in order to support their children and the aimless young men whose idea of fatherhood ends with the sex act, Mr. Moyers was refreshingly judgmental, coming out frequently with such comments as: "Do you ever think that maybe you shouldn't do it unless you can be sure you don't have a kid?" (Wall Street Journal)

Illegitimacy and the ghetto problems which were glibly listed as its direct consequences were presented as a virtual disease that whites can catch from blacks. The *Wall Street Journal* story continues:

Now the rhetoric has cooled, and the grim statistics stare everyone in the face, white and black. As George Jackson, a Newark-based psychologist puts it: "What goes around comes around . . . It won't be long before this becomes a disease that infects the entire population . . . You [whites] can run but you can't hide." [8]

George Will used Timothy McSeed to justify a dismissal of the Civil Rights movement: "One reason they [men such as Timothy] feel little such guilt is that they have been taught by reflexive 'civil rights' rhetoric that they are mere passive victims, absolved by the all-purpose alibi of 'white racism' from all responsibility for their behavior." And Will concludes: ". . . the Timothys are more of a menace to black progress than the Bull Connors ever were."[9]

The documentary was praised in reviews in the *New York Times*, *People*, *Variety*, and *Newsweek*. The *Newsweek* article, in particular, excelled at the kind of rhetoric that predisposes this journalism so conveniently to a justification of Reagan's welfare policies: "In recent years television hasn't had much taste for the pathology of poverty. But Bill Moyers and CBS News look unflinchingly into the void: it's no longer only racism or an unsympathetic government that is destroying black America. The problem now lies in the black community itself, and in its failure to pass on moral values to the next generation."[10]

Such mainstream sentiments are uncomfortably close to those expressed by Michael Novak in William Buckley's right-wing *National Review*. Calling the Moyers show "one of the bravest TV documentaries ever made," Novak editorialized, "Behind the gruesome statistics lies a deeper story: the vanishing of male character. Only a tiny fraction of black children born in America has a father at home during all 16 years of childhood. Nearly 60% are born out of wedlock. Such matriarchy is proving colossally destructive."[11]

Not structural unemployment but lack of character is blamed for black male joblessness and homelessness; again it is not the state but the individual who is faulted. And matriarchy is feared.

In the same issue, Buckley himself claimed a centrist position for the blame-the-victim stance, saying, "It was a study of the black urban welfare culture that vividly bore out the much-denounced warnings of Daniel Patrick Moynihan and George Gilder: Rootless black males, displaced by welfare, would become a disruptive force . . . What makes the show especially significant is that Bill Moyers is the most certified of liberals. What's more, it has been enthusiastically hailed by important liberal commentators, including David Broder, Mary McGrory and William Raspberry, not to mention Jesse Jackson."[12]

In the face of such bigotry and welfare-bashing, the anger of black, nationally syndicated columnist Carl Rowan seemed particularly appropriate. He said: "I am really tired of seeing the black family analyzed, especially when the analysts do not inspire anyone to produce better schools or more jobs for blacks, but do provoke ill-informed people to unleash a new barrage of slander and venom at black people."[13]

What journalistic conventions and professional self-definitions were used and how did these influence the coverage of poverty? In examining Moyers's interview with Timothy McSeed, it is evident that a strongly negative portrait of a black man was created. However, in general, there is a reluctance on the part of the media to accept responsibility for the stereotypes it creates and for how these might function beyond the life of a public affairs report. The producer of the program, Ruth Streeter, claimed an apolitical stance: "You just tell the story that you see. If you're going to worry what the political implications are and mold the story to that, you're going to have a different type of story . . . My job is to get the issue on the front burner and let the public decide."[14] The *vérité*-myth of the documentary is embraced, even as Moyers is recognized as an influential presence in the interviews. Similarly, there is a contradiction in presenting Moyers as at once objective and moralizing. Such a tone incorporates elements of factographic presentation, first-person journalism of the 1960s, and the earlier moralizing tone of Edward R. Murrow. And Moyers's conclusion comes through, despite the careful language: it is morally wrong for poor teenagers to have babies.

In critiquing this persona, I am not advocating the pseudo-objective, seemingly apolitical stance of most American journalism. In some ways, even the willingness to create a negative picture of McSeed is a welcome deviation, presenting anger instead of a sugar-coated liberal tolerance—but anger with what focus and to what purpose? This is where the documentary is culpable. The Moyers persona can touch on moral issues but not on economic ones, personal concerns but not political problems. The repression of the economic and political is dangerous; among other points, it means that the documentary's negative portrayal of McSeed elicits an audience response of anger directed at McSeed and only at McSeed.

The posture of the CBS documentary is that Moyers is not intrusive in his interviewing, that he lets his subjects speak for themselves. It is an abdication of responsibility for the particular construction of the interviews and the lack of context provided for them. Statistics are stated throughout, but they are not connected in any thorough-going way to the lives of the interviewees. This practice evidences a naive belief that merely turning the camera on will produce a record of the truth. This truth-value is, in turn, "verified" by the presence of the media-personality journalist. The weight given to this presence directly influences the kind of questions that are asked. Moyers can ask moral questions because they reflect *his* "concern," such as when he asks McSeed, "Does it make you feel bad you can't support your kids?" But Moyers cannot delve into the economically disastrous context of McSeed's life because, after all, this is not an area in which Moyers's feelings pertain so directly—the lack of entry-level manufacturing jobs in Newark is less tangibly available for Moyers's reactions than is McSeed's sexuality.

The situation is this: statistically, McSeed as a young, black ghetto man has little chance of finding employment. As sociologist Ruth Sidel has explained, "Nationally, unemployment among blacks is officially twice the rate for whites, but [these] statistics tell only part of the story. Researchers at the Center for the Study of Social Policy claim that the true figure is that 4 million out of 9 million working-age black men—46 percent—are jobless."[15] So when Timothy comments on his children—"If you don't do nothing you can see something. . . . They might grow up to be doctors or actors and then you see you done something"—or on child support—"You can't give something you don't have"—then *his* words should be given weight; *these* points should receive follow-up questions. But, they do not, and these comments are lost among others which are more offensive and which reviewers pick up on with condemnation, such as statements about the government being able to provide child support when Timothy doesn't, or about girls not liking condoms. These are the quotable quotes used by almost all of the commentators on the Moyers show, and in these reviews, Timothy is almost universally despised.

W hat does it mean to broadcast such an extremely negative stereotype of a black man at this time? The Reagan administration has refused to deal with the chronic joblessness of ghetto men, and it has actually canceled the few stumbling, embryonic job-training programs which existed.[16] Furthermore, Reagan preaches self-help, urging the ghetto community to take care of its own so-called pathological problems. The *only* government assistance generally available to single, poor men is food stamps (maximum $80 per month per person).[17] This disgusting abdication of governmental responsibility for the poor and jobless ghetto male is actually "justified" by such a television program, which so negatively portrays the morals of Timothy McSeed (he is given more attention throughout the documentary than any other man interviewed). This type of interviewing highlights Timothy's lack of guilt rather than his lack of resources. Ironically, such documentaries allow middle-class America to feel an absence of guilt and to justify a government which systematically pushes more and more people beneath the poverty line.

Alice Jackson, although portrayed more sympathetically, is also interviewed in this "nonintrusive" style, which focuses on Moyers's moral sensibility and not on her economic plight. As previously mentioned, Jackson was employed before she had her first baby and she confessed that welfare made her feel lazy. Not surprisingly, this was the one quote repeated over and over in the media's coverage of the Moyers show. This admission by Jackson is explored by Moyers. However, what life is really like on her budget—$385 per month in AFDC, plus $112 in food stamps for herself and three children—is not examined. After rent, clothes, and utilities, how much money is available to her for food? And does this amount, as is often the case, mean a diet deficient in basic nutritional needs like fruits and vegetables? Why doesn't Moyers do the kind of interviewing found in Sidel's recent book, *Women and Children Last*? Sidel asked women whether they could afford to go to a movie, to get a babysitter and spend time with other adults, and what daily life is like when there is not enough to eat. Of course, Alice's statement that welfare makes her feel lazy could be used to justify the Reagan practice of reducing funds for Aid to Families with Dependent Children. Such quotes seem to verify Charles Murray's thesis in *Losing Ground* (which has been called the "Bible" of the Reagan administration) that welfare perpetuates poverty and therefore should be removed.[18] To take just one example of what such texts justify, consider that the administration has denied Medicaid and AFDC to women who work full time and who are, nevertheless, just above the poverty line.[19] Without government support for health care, for many that means no health care at all.

There is also a foreword and a coda to the Moyers program as a media event. The foreword concerns the internal history of the profession which produced the program and, as such, received much attention. The coda concerns one of the poor featured in the documentary, and, as such, got less play. It was often reported that Moyers had been LBJ's press secretary during the period when Senator Daniel P. Moynihan, then assistant secretary of labor, issued *The Negro Family* report. At that time, Moynihan's report was so heavily denounced as racist that it eliminated ghetto family patterns as a possible topic of discussion. Now, seemingly with greater sensitivity, Moyers was again raising the issue at a point when the disintegration of the family had been publicly acknowledged. Thus, Moynihan was often praised as farsighted by the 1986 reviewers.

However, these writers did not quote directly from or reexamine the Moynihan report, and the original report is worth reviewing. While the study did make certain valuable connections between shifts in family structure and economic conditions (for example, that black male unemployment correlated directly to the growing divorce rate), in other areas it was rendered useless by Moynihan's blatant misogyny. He blamed working black women for emasculating black men, speculating about the embarrassment of black men and resentment of black children when the woman of the family worked. He claimed that in single-female-headed households, mothers encouraged daughters more than sons. In a chapter entitled "The Tangle of Pathology," Moynihan stated:

In essence, the Negro community has been forced into a matriarchal structure which, because it is so out of line with the rest of American society, seriously retards the progress of the group as a whole, and imposes a crushing burden on the Negro male and, in consequence, on a great many Negro women as well.[20]

Lynwood Jackson, father of Alice Cassandra Jackson, Nora Jackson, her mother, and Antwan Jackson, her son, sit in the living room of their apartment in Stella Wright Homes, Newark, New Jersey, February 4, 1986.

Moynihan advocated a nuclear family structure dominated by a male head. The report can be considered reflective of Moynihan's desire to make over the black minority into his own image, to assimilate the black family into a model of Irish patriarchy, a desire which comes through blatantly in statements such as: "A number of immigrant groups were characterized by unusually strong family bonds; these groups have characteristically progressed more rapidly than others."[21] Despite these prejudices, most 1980s reviewers of the Moyers program directly or indirectly glorified Moynihan's report, raising the question of whether the contemporary writers had seriously considered the premises of *The Negro Family*.

Less coverage was given to an event which occurred after the taping of the Moyers show. On February 2, 1986, Alice Cassandra Jackson died after she accidentally fell down a flight of stairs. At her funeral, Jesse Jackson eulogized, exhorting Timothy McSeed to take care of the children. The children went to live with Alice's mother, Nora Jackson. Reported in the local *Newark Star Ledger* and, because of the presence of Jesse Jackson, on national television, Alice's death was portrayed as a martyrdom. Remarkably, the Newark community, including the Newark Municipal Council, sought to make CBS (that great preacher of responsibility) contribute to a trust fund for Alice Jackson's children. CBS refused.

II. Professional Practices, Alternatives, Audience

Human interest stories too often are separated from analysis of government policy in much the same ways that this now classic CBS documentary has done. Further, and also similar to Moyers, neoliberal critics—focusing on the culture of poverty as a self-perpetuating social phenomenon separate from national economic developments—exercise distortions which leave poverty and welfare reporting open to welfare-bashing by conservatives. Their omissions amount to inaccuracies.

The following kinds of crucial points are rarely seen in media analysis. As explained in William Julius Wilson's recent book, *The Truly Disadvantaged,* the poverty of many female-headed households is inextricably bound to: (1) the low pay our society affords women; (2) the unemployment of men, particularly black men, and its correlation to the dissolution of families; and (3) the continued existence in twenty-four states of the man-in-the-house rule which forbids AFDC money to mothers living with a man.

On December 17, 1987, the House passed a major welfare reform bill that proposes to replace Aid to Families with Dependent Children with a more in-depth Family Support Program emphasizing provisions for mandatory workfare and punitive sanctions and the possibility for improved job training and child care. The Democratic-sponsored Family Support Bill (floor manager, Rep. Thomas J. Downey, D-NY) is a more liberal version (it alone includes incentives to states to increase benefits and an earned-income disregard to aid the working poor) of a similar resolution sponsored in the Senate by Daniel P. Moynihan, D-NY. The Senate bill passed on June 16, 1988. A compromise was effected on September 27 in the House-Senate Conference Committee, and this was quickly passed into law by the Congress on September 30. The clear danger of compromises made in this conservative climate is that mandatory workfare and sanctions will stand on the federal level and job training and child care will be neglected by the states.

To date, media examination of welfare proposals has been dry and inadequate. Coverage of the passing of the House bill in the *New York Times, Washington Post,* and *Los Angeles Times* has failed to explain legislative proposals in terms of the economics of welfare recipients' lives. What's more, the political use of terms in the welfare debate often is not clarified. Job training, child care, and workfare mean different things to different Republicans, Democrats, and lobbyists. Yet these nuances have profound consequences for the more than 30 million people now receiving welfare.

Consider the *Los Angeles Times* article by Josh Getlin, "House Backs Billions to Tie Welfare to Jobs" (December 17, 1987). Getlin dutifully sketches the major proposals of the House Family Support Bill: mandatory workfare, child care, enforced child support, and incentives to states to increase benefits, but without explaining what these phrases mean. Getlin does not ask crucial questions about how these provisions contrast with existing programs and what specific improvements would be made in the lives of the recipients. For example, in discussing proposed increases in welfare benefits, Getlin neglects to point out that there have been no adjustments for inflation in welfare allowances for over a decade. Such omissions may lead an uninformed reader to conclude that the increases are unnecessary, rather than to see the grim reality that welfare benefits are now insufficient even to provide the most basic nutritional diet. Instead of specifics, the reader is given a vague and timeless description that could fit any welfare legislation: "Sponsors said the proposal would help end welfare dependency and put more poor people to work. But Republicans called it inappropriate to propose such legislation, given the nation's current financial difficulties."

What, then, are the alternatives to this type of bland glossing-over of the issues or to first-person journalism, like Moyers's, in which the observer is insulated and not accountable? I am advocating journalism that ignores neither economic determinants nor the socioeconomic position of the writer. Many structural factors discourage reporters from implicating or risking themselves or their class. For instance, journalistic career success often depends on obtaining human-interest stories that are front-page material, while reports on the intricacies of government and politics are often relegated to the back pages. Further, human-interest stories, as we have seen, are often written from the point of view of a white, male, upper-middle-class professional, with the potential to be heavily invested in existing power structures. American journalists are trained as fact collectors, not political essayists. The profession is classist and ostensibly racist: only 3.6 percent of journalists working for daily newspapers are black.[22]

Within these broad constraints, however, there are journalistic writers who have circumvented some of the more deadening professional traps. Brent Staples is one such writer, with his continued coverage of racism through political essays for the *New York Times*. Consider an article by

Staples in the *New York Times Magazine,* "The Dwindling Black Presence on Campus."[23] In this essay, Staples advocates college recruitment of poor blacks and is angry that such recruitment has been severely reduced. Staples makes it clear that his position emanates from his political beliefs and personal experience: he grew up in the Philadelphia ghetto, was recruited on a street corner, would probably not have gone to college otherwise, and is now, much later, after obtaining a doctorate in sociology from the University of Chicago, working as an editor at the *Times* and writing political journalism. He writes of feeling himself erased as he reads of the cuts in college recruitment from the ghettos. His own position and his background are as explicated as those of his "subjects." Most significantly, Staples does not write only about himself, rather he uses his experiences as a base from which to analyze and critique power structures, in this case, education in the U.S. and access to it.

Barbara Omolade also exemplifies first-person writing that uses the personal as a starting point from which to analyze the political, as in her *Village Voice* essay, "It's a Family Affair: The Real Lives of Black Single Mothers." Omolade, an instructor and counselor at the City College Center for Worker Education, is herself a black single mother. In the article, she combines movingly personal and incisively political analyses with a critique of past press coverage of black single mothers and how this reporting is open to conservative abuse:

The concept of a pathological underclass has become the rationale for continued racism and economic injustice; in attempting to separate racial from economic inequality and blaming family pathology for black people's condition, current ideology obscures the system's inability to provide jobs, decent wages, and adequate public services for the black poor.

Though social scientists choose to focus on black single mothers in crisis, they are not in the majority; if nearly half of all families headed by black women have incomes below the poverty line, as the Center for the Study of Social Policy reports, then over half do not. But housing, welfare and court systems that treat us like social lepers are constantly working to undo our struggle.[24]

Omolade then goes further, specifying the societal failures in child care and housing services, and how they impact on the daily lives of single mothers. She ends with two important points. First, she highlights the Brooklyn self-help organization, Sisterhood of Black Single Mothers, founded by Daphne Busby; thus, she addresses immediate practical

Bill Moyers talks with Rev. Jesse Jackson at the funeral service for Alice Cassandra Jackson at the Green Pastures Baptist Church, East Orange, New Jersey, February 6, 1986.

measures as well as the much needed long-term structural changes. Second, she concludes with a painful examination of those problems which she sees as currently important between black men and women. Omolade criticizes those who assert that black men must be allowed their "rightful" place of domination within the black family. (This is a position stated often in texts ranging from Senator Moynihan's 1965 report to the scripts of the current TV sitcom, *227*.) Omolade writes: "Yet dreams of patriarchal restoration have continued to permeate the black family debate. If this is to change, black women must speak truthfully, naming our own reality and vision of the black family."[25]

Another positive example of what the media can produce in poverty coverage is a *New York Times* article titled "Welfare Allowance Going Up But Homeless Worries Persist," by Michael deCourcy Hinds (December 28, 1987). In this front-page story, Hinds sought to examine the consequences of a single statewide governmental action: "New York State will increase the housing allowances of welfare families by an average of 13 percent on January 1." This information was considered not only in light of a general economic context—demonstrating that this allowance is still not enough to pay the rent and ward off homelessness for many in New York City—but was also poignantly illustrated with concrete examples of how this legislation would effect the lives of two single mothers on public assistance. Thus, Hinds was able to connect government policy, economic context, and human interest.

Unfortunately, reporting like that of Hinds, Staples, and Omolade is the exception and not the rule in daily newspaper journalism. Furthermore, coverage of welfare and poverty often involves negative stereotypes of minority women.

III. Conclusion

The Moyers show was typical of television programming in what it leaves out. It addressed poverty only in terms of blacks, not whites or other groups. Such unreflective reporting implicitly scapegoats black teenage mothers and fathers, and it deflects attention from critical and germane economic issues, such as how the current minimum-wage standard (still set at a federal level of only $3.35 an hour) keeps single working mothers in poverty. What Moyers did not explain was the economics of daily life in poverty—what life was really like for Jackson and her three children on a budget of $497 a month. Moyers did not tell us what it meant to face the limited job prospects in Newark, or about the difficulties of finding affordable child care. Statistics clearly show that most black single mothers do work, yet, in the Moyers documentary—as in most reporting on this issue—we heard very little about their daily lives and the impact of government policy on them.

At this juncture, when our welfare system is being restructured, journalists should cast aside their biases against female-headed households and start asking tough questions about the quality of compulsory workfare and government-supported child care that are being touted in Moynihan's bill in the U.S. Senate. Such questions were not asked in a *New York Times* editorial (January 29, 1988) which endorsed the bill and attacked welfare rights advocates (none were quoted) who believe the pending legislation does not provide adequate support for poor women. Activist organizations such as the Federation of Protestant Welfare Agencies and the National Puerto Rican Forum have argued that, while mandatory workfare and the accompanying punitive sanctions will be implemented on the state level if the current bills are passed, the lack of funding for job training and child care will insure that these programs are nothing but make-work situations that burden single head-of-households without assisting them in getting jobs. In addition, sanctions like the removal of welfare benefits for several months will increase homelessness. These arguments are rarely represented in the mainstream media.

Beyond this, welfare should not be the media's primary focus: the issue is not welfare but poverty and the socioeconomic structure which enforces it. Rather than let conservative welfare-bashers set the media agenda, radical media activism must continue to insist on and provide coverage of the deployment of capital and of government legislation that pushes people into poverty and sexist inequities that have created the feminization of poverty.

Notes

I would like to acknowledge the people interviewed for this article: Nick Lemann, Ruth Streeter, and Brent Staples. In addition, I would like to thank Carl Lavin, Douglas Lavin, Frank Lavin, Phil Mariani, Lou McDonald, Leslie Sharpe, Brian Wallis, and Phil Weiss for information and discussions which contributed to the development of this essay. An excerpted and revised version of this article appeared in *Extra! The Newsletter of FAIR (Fairness & Accuracy in Reporting)* (March-April 1988).

1. Julianne Malveaux, "The Economic Interests of Black and White Women: Are They Similar?" *The Review of Black Political Economy* (Summer 1985): 7.
2. Ruth Sidel, *Women and Children Last: The Plight of Poor Women in Affluent America* (New York: Viking Penguin, Inc., 1986), pp. 3-4.
3. William O'Hare, "The Eight Myths of Poverty," *American Demographics* 8, no. 5 (May 1986): 24.
4. National Coalition for the Homeless, *Safety Network,* Vol. 4-9 (May 1987).
5. Daniel Patrick Moynihan, *The Negro Family: The Case for National Action* (Washington, D.C.: U.S. Department of Labor, Office of Policy Research, 1965).
6. Barbara Omolade, "It's a Family Affair: The Real Lives of Black Single Mothers," *Village Voice,* July 15, 1986, p. 24.
7. John Corry, "'CBS Reports' Examines Black Families," *New York Times,* January 25, 1986, p. 49.
8. Martha Bayles, *Wall Street Journal,* January 27, 1986, p. 22.
9. *Washington Post,* February 13, 1986, p. A23.
10. *Newsweek,* January 27, 1986.
11. Michael Novak, "The Content of Their Character," *National Review,* February 28, 1986, p. 47.
12. William F. Buckley, *National Review,* February 28, 1986, editorial, ibid., p. 19.
13. *Washington Post,* February 1, 1986, p. A19.
14. Ruth Streeter, producer of *The Vanishing Black Family,* interviewed July 31, 1986.
15. Sidel, *Women and Children Last,* p. 108.
16. Sidel reports: "In the area of employment, the Reagan administration has eliminated all training and employment programs under the Comprehensive Employment and Training Act (CETA), reduced funding for the Youth Employment Projects Act by 80%, for the Summer Youth Employment Program by 20%." Sidel, *Women and Children Last,* p. 20.
17. Sylvia Nasar, "America's Poor: How Big a Problem," *Fortune,* May 26, 1986, p. 78.
18. Charles Murray, *Losing Ground: American Social Policy, 1950-1980* (New York: Basic Books, 1984).
19. Nicholas Lemann, "Washington: The Culture of Poverty," *The Atlantic,* September 1984, pp. 26-41.
20. Moynihan, *The Negro Family,* p. 29.
21. Ibid., p. 5.
22. 1986 Annual Survey, American Society of Newspaper Editors.
23. *New York Times Magazine,* April 27, 1986.
24. Omolade, "Family Affair," p. 26.
25. Ibid., p. 28.

Cultural Regulation and Censorship:
The Case of *Blacks Britannica*

David Goldberg

Central to the social definition of any modern state is its public representation of social data, events, and relations both to its own citizens and to foreign observers. Public representation involves not only communication through the media available to state bureaucracies (publications, films, and especially television), but also what is denied or excluded—in a word, censored—from public or private expression. "State truth and reality" are developed and deployed to propagate and protect the claim to social legitimacy. "Oppositional truth and reality" are constructed to challenge, undermine, and change relations of power and authority. "State truth and reality" are mandated in various forms: politically, legally, culturally. "Oppositional truth and reality" are allowed representation in each form, if at all, subject to severe though fluctuating constraints.

It seems, at a glance, that the cultural mandate differs not simply from one *sort* of society to another—liberal democracy and autocracy, say—but from any one society to the next. So, the form of cultural control appears to differ amongst those societies that laud themselves as liberal democracies. European countries *seem* to exercise far greater *direct* government regulation of culture than the United States. This appearance is manifested perhaps in the very active role some of these governments assume in *funding* cultural production—from commissioning individual artists to running community cultural centers and projects. The most obvious differences, of course, concern television. The countries of the European Economic Community tend mostly to manage television production and broadcasting directly, rather than simply to *regulate* them. An unconvincing reason often offered for this is economies of scale. A more compelling explanation—one that evades economic determinism of the right or the left—is ideological management. (The history of book printing in Europe provides a good precedent.) The liberal democratic rationalization for management as opposed to regulation, often heard in Britain, is that it takes government control to guarantee a forum for the free expression of ideas. Regulation may prevent unwarranted excesses; it would restrict expression by those who, for want of resources, might be denied a public voice. So the story goes.

By contrast, cultural regulation is the American way. Conservatives in this country are often criticized for inconsistency in this respect. It seems that the very principle of deregulation they laud in the marketplace of goods they chide in the marketplace of ideas. Principles of good economic management, conservatives fear, are principles of philistine ideological management. And while Adam Smith may be good for the wealth of the nation; his is bad medicine for the health of the nation's ideology. But this criticism of conservatives hides a deeper and more pervasive hegemony in the American way, both economic and cultural.

Industrial *deregulation* clearly does not mean the end of all regulation, though it is often represented in this way. An analogy with the "end of ideology" claim of the late fifties is apt. Those who argued for the "end of ideology" undertook to clear the field of a certain type of ideological posturing and to establish a space for the representation of special ideological interests, namely those of bourgeois democracy and expansion of the economic miracle. In a similar way, deregulation would substitute corporate interest for public interest. Deregulation, however, does not mean greater freedom of individual choice; it means greater corporate freedom. Let me, for the sake of space and provocation—since I am writing at the stroke of the Constitution's bicentennial anniversary and in the midst of the Bork confirmation circus—refer to this as the corporate equivalent of *constitutional libertarianism*. Corporate libertarianism is not simply the dominant economic sensibility; it has come to pervade all forms of ideological (and thus cultural) production and exhibition.

Corporate interests, according to this view, can be trusted with control of the mode of cultural representation. After all, politicians and executives of the same aesthetic are doing the trusting and being entrusted. Corporate power now determines what gets produced and exhibited culturally: books and broadcasting, music and movies, sports and soaps. Commercial interests have always influenced, if not controlled, art. Yet corporate raiding in the domain of art, as elsewhere, has now become more direct, more explicit, more brazen. Nowhere does corporate regulation and censorship have more effect than in television.

This point seems self-evident with regard to *commercial* television. Even the designation is self-congratulatory. The sign "Made in the U.S.A." fits no other good quite so snugly. But whose *good* is it? Television, we are told, is *a* free enterprise. Free enterprise it is, where viewing time belongs exclusively to commercial interests. This produces in television consumers a conceptual *tabula rasa* perfect for programming commercial values. Cultural imagination is wiped clean (if not out) so that the complex of social, political, and moral values may be programmed by those commerce and capital deem fit.

Two of many conceivable examples will serve to illustrate this. The first concerns the mode of commercial representation; the second concerns the manner of censorious exclusion. The first example involves the introduction by the ratings industry of new technology for determining the commercial success of programming—the so-called people meter. The aim is clearly to render advertising more cost effective. "*Representative television viewers*" (representative of whom, precisely?) are furnished with a dial that programs what they are watching in relation to their personal characteristics, such as age, sex, occupation, address—by extension ethnic group—and so forth. This new practice has been rationalized as more democratic, a way of increasing viewer determination of television programming. But it strikes me as a tyranny of the majority. More insidiously, the invasion by commercial interests of the living room—indirectly of *everyone's* living room—comes perilously close to obliterating any right to privacy. Of course, corporate constitutional libertarianism denies the constitutionality of privacy rights. But this simply highlights how self-serving its constitutional outlook is.

The second example concerns network news coverage. Mainstream media stereotyping of certain population groups has often been noted. Amongst the most interesting comments here are Edward Said's concerning the representation of Arabs in general, and of Palestinians in particular.[1] Yet it is not only *how* persons and population groups are portrayed, in news coverage as elsewhere, but whether events regarding certain groups are considered newsworthy and so covered at all. The Constitutional Bicentennial was staged with a flourish in Philadelphia. Events were scheduled not for the actual experience of the persons participating, but for the national television audience. Participants were mere players, acting out scripted roles. As with sports like football, baseball, and basketball (though ultimately less exciting), and unlike continuous sports like soccer or cycling, television dictated the structure of events. Major events could be attended by invitation only, and were celebrity-filled. An organizer revealed that the "public" parade had to be timed within three seconds to suit the requirements of television exhibition (read: "advertising time for sponsors"). Ralph Nader's Citizens' Watch was precluded by financial burden from participating in the street parade with a float representing two hundred years of civil protest and the struggle for constitutional rights. Float sponsorship, the group was advised, cost $150,000. Active determination of the content of the formal events in the constitutional celebration—and so also of passive consumption—was limited in the end to those who could afford to float a corporation on the stock exchange. A float representing the fight for civilian rights would be incongruent with the dominant ode to our military industrial complex.

(To digress, but marginally: the Congressional hearings of the Iran-contra collusion furnish further evidence of the staging of American politics. Witnesses first offered testimony—indeed twice, the second time only under oath—to the Committee in *closed* session. It was then determined what, in the interests of "national security," could conveniently be revealed in open, televised display "to the American people." Congressmen—they were all men, and very nearly all white—knew what they could ask, and what they could expect to hear. What was disclosed to the national audience was predetermined and rehearsed. There was a playing out, an acting, a propagation of a story line—in short, a censoring. For all the criticism of secrecy in politics, "sensitive issues"—sensitive for whom, exactly?—were conducted in secret, and interpretation was pre-imposed upon the information revealed. Good political drama, perhaps; but a politics of containment and deceit in the last analysis comes perilously close to no politics at all.)

The visitors mostly departed, the official celebrations in Philadelphia closed with a free five-hour concert hosted by and primarily for the black community. (The "back of the bus," a friend reminded me, assumes many forms.) The message conveyed across this "celebration," ironically, was clear: the history of the Constitution, in application as in its formation, has not been problem-free. Though it has served racist interests, it is clear that the Constitution could, with assertion of political power in voting, be part of a solution. Now Philadelphia is essentially a small city. Its population is nearly 60 percent black. This was the sole show in town that night; the audience was large, the participants notable—including Dick Gregory, Gil Scot-Heron, Oscar Brown, Jr., and the New Jersey Mass Choir. In short, it was a newsworthy event. None of the three

Police target resembling a black man: this entire sequence was censored from the broadcast version of *Blacks Britannica*.

networks had camera crews covering the show, though all have studios within shouting distance of the outdoor venue.[2] From the media point of view (including the *Philadelphia Inquirer)*, the show was a nonevent, the message safely to be ignored. Constitutional criticism, especially at this juncture, is not the goods for corporate sponsorship. The First Amendment guarantees only the right to express oneself. It does not—most problematically in the case of political speech it does not—guarantee the right to an audience. In one sense this is as it should be. In another sense, though, it fails to facilitate objective coverage, and in some cases this means no coverage at all. This continued denial of media coverage and audience adds credence to the view in politics that if one fails (self-)deceptively to identify (with) the solution, one remains part of the problem.

So, if it makes any sense to speak of "taking back the night," the proper object of critical attack is the likes of Michelob and corporate *possession* of our audiovisual lives. What deserves active opposition is the obscene presumption that our viewing time *belongs* to corporate manipulation and control.

What alternatives are available? It may be thought, indeed it is sometimes suggested in the promos, that we would be better off if we turned the dial (permanently?) to *public* TV. The very title implies that "we the people" exercise control here. The inference is that we can evade corporate control and improve the quality of our television lives by going public. Public control by definition excludes commercial constraint. Or so *this* story goes. The experience of *Blacks Britannica* reveals otherwise.

B oston's television station, WGBH, has consistently projected an image of commitment to politically provocative and liberal broadcasting. In keeping with this spirit, in 1978 WGBH instituted a new program entitled "World," proposing to present a "series of international documentaries" showing the world "as *others* see it" (my emphasis). With each airing the program declared itself to be "committed to the idea that we should include the views of those who normally do not get a chance to have their voices heard." Laudable liberal commitments, indeed. David Koff and Musindo Mwinyipembe were commissioned to produce *Blacks Britannica,* a one-hour film documenting blacks in Britain speaking about the socioeconomic and political conditions in which they live.

Shortly before the documentary was due to air, "World" executive producers demanded changes in it that reflected not the conditions of everyday life in black Britain, but the imperialism of public television's world. "World," it turned out, was being funded largely by the Corporation for Public Broadcasting (CPB) and by the Polaroid Corporation. Funding for the second year was at stake. The CPB was clearly concerned about its image with British cultural commissars, with an eye in particular to its dominant interest in obtaining rights to imperiously boring and soft-boiled BBC dramas (like *Jewel in the Crown,* or the "Mystery" series). Polaroid's history of concern for blacks elsewhere was less than exemplary. Despite a pronounced embargo, Polaroid products were being consistently used by the South African government to administer its pass system. In late 1977, the only copy of a WGBH program dealing with Polaroid's involvement in South Africa was "accidentally" erased, prior to its first airing, while assembling a Christmas show. WGBH executives initially refused to retape the program.[3]

Blacks Britannica hardly fit the picture-perfect Polaroid image. It documents, in the context of class analysis, the severe conditions under which most blacks live in Britain, a country both historically and contemporarily racist: economic exploitation, racist working and housing conditions, racist immigration legislation and social differentiation, a discriminatory legal system and tyrannical police repression, surveillance and violence. The changes required by WGBH officials sought to under-

Police target practice: this entire sequence was also censored from the broadcast version of *Blacks Britannica*.

mine the picture of police provocation and to muzzle the anti-imperialist Marxist message. They sought, that is, to contain—if not alter—the film's fundamental point. Koff and Mwinyipembe rightly refused to cooperate.

Claiming executive editorial prerogative, WGBH executives unilaterally edited the film to suit their purposes. The filmmakers, in response, took their case to the streets. Koff cried censorship; the public network claimed ownership. The TV airing of the cut version was preceded by this disclaimer: ". . . While the film does not include the views of those who disagree with it, we feel it is valuable to hear these voices. . . ." It was followed, even more pointedly, by an appearance of WGBH's president, David Ives, who commented that "The issue is not censorship but editorial control and integrity." A request by the filmmakers for an opportunity to respond on camera and for a live discussion of the issues was denied.

WGBH executives could not abandon the project altogether, for they would then be liable for misuse of the sponsors' resources. Nor did it behoove them to be seen as furnishing a forum for "a revolutionary message"—especially one with implications for American blacks. Yet, the constitutional right to free expression by commissioned filmmakers could not be violated. Hostage to the perceived interests of their sponsors, WGBH took action on three fronts. They cut the film to fit their needs;

they rationalized the cuts, both privately and publicly, as executive prerogative in ordinary journalistic practice; and they obtained a court injunction restricting the screening of the original version. Integrity wears the mask of its master. The layers of makeup must be peeled away to reveal the interests at issue.

WGBH claimed that the cuts left the film substantially unaltered. In total, close to five minutes was excised from the film. Of greater consequence, however, is the fact that sound and image were rearranged to produce a fundamentally altered representation of events originally portrayed. The language and logic of the film, that is, were deliberately changed. I will cite only the grosser examples.

The original version of the film included a sequence showing British police taking shooting practice. The target was a specially drawn poster stereotypically representing a black criminal type. WGBH previewed the uncut film for the director of the British Information Service in America. The director protested in print that "racism is not a significant factor in British life and politics," as evidenced by the lack of support enjoyed by the National Front. No racism here: Enoch Powell is a phantasm, not a member of Parliament; Maggie Thatcher—"Iron Lady, Victor of Inflation and the Falklands"[4]—welcomes immigrants comfortingly to her bosom. The television executives cut out the sequence entirely, claiming in public that "everyone knows the British police were not armed." The filmmakers had taken the footage from a BBC documentary on the British investigative police unit.

There were numerous additional cuts and reassemblage of sequences involving British police. The chanting by protestors of "The pigs, the pigs, we gotta get rid of the pigs" *in reaction to* a police assault upon a largely white demonstration was altered *to precede* the police assault. The police assault and accompanying violence was thus "legitimated" in the re-edit as *a response to* black protestor provocation rather than its *cause*. Further testament to police provocation and brutality was similarly altered or removed. A powerful reference to police beatings of blacks arrested under suspicion was omitted. Thus, a sequence that in the original is about police brutality became for WGBH an admission by blacks that they "know they get . . . in a few difficulties at times, a bit of problem with the law." This was, then, a racist affirmation of latent criminality.

Finally, in its original version the film ends with a youth asserting that *if* capitalism cannot deliver a better life for blacks, then ". . . capitalism has to go." This is followed in image and sound with street fighting. The

From the "bloody shirt" sequence: the community spokesman waves the bloody shirt as evidence, saying, "This was his jacket, covered in blood . . ."

assertion is erased from the re-cut version, and the film ends in freeze frames of protesting youths. Thus, a closing conditional statement about the social, economic, and political system of capitalism is replaced by one about human rights which executive producers considered more palatable to "the American people."

This is "editorial control and integrity" in the service of corporate power. Corporate libertarianism extends freedom of expression only to those voicing capital's interests. The identity of values of Polaroid and CPB in this instance might suggest that the interests of capital are too often The Capital's interests, though to establish this would require considerable elaboration. Nevertheless, it *is* clear that meaning may be moved around just like capital. This is underlined not only in the remaking of *Blacks Britannica,* but equally in the public rationalization by WGBH officials of the "necessity" to re-cut the film. For they claimed, on one hand, that *Blacks Britannica* was not "readily understandable to U.S. viewers"[5]; and on the other, that it was too readily digestible. American viewers, it seems, are too naive to comprehend these "garbled" voices of the Other; yet the Marxist message might strike a bell with those constituted in America as Other.

Now, the language in *Blacks Britannica* is other, the accent is other, the look is other. The language is that of class analysis; the accent

Caribbean; the look black and working class. A British audience could live with the language: they have had to, after all, ever since Marx appropriated their national library. What they find unacceptable is the cultural combination of look and accent—the cultural *difference* that the new British racism stresses to marginalize its people of color. For the innocent American public, by contrast, the accent of Caribbean immigrants is one amongst the many. What is found problematic is the combination of class-language and color-look. To the "trained" American eye and ear, color (black) and leftist language can only signify something like Cuba and Castro, Central America and Caribbean Communism.

Claiming that in its original version, *Blacks Britannica* endorses "a Marxist analysis," that "led to a call for revolutionary violence,"[6] WGBH executives obtained a court injunction restricting Koff from showing his cut to more than eighteen people at a time. There is a U.S. law that enables political censorship of films propagating the overthrow of the American political system. *Blacks Britannica* mentions the United States only to make the salient point that *its* racism was imported initially from Britain with the first settlers. Moreover, the constitutionality of the censorship notwithstanding, the numerical restriction on *Blacks Britannica* was altogether arbitrary. Restriction is a limitation both on the right to view and on the right to express without constraint. Artist and audience are muzzled.

The filmmakers clearly identify with the plight of persons whose views are expressed in *Blacks Britannica;* the conditions of existence after all are no different than their own. I know of no objections to such identification in *Yol,* say, or *Missing, Platoon,* or news coverage of Afghan rebels.[7] And I discern no "call to revolutionary violence" in the film. Indeed, the only mention of revolution is in the soundtrack appearances by Steel Pulse that begin and end the film.

What underlies any reading of this film as a revolutionary endorsement is an aesthetic I call *cultural realism.* This aesthetic pervades American cultural sensibility—film, television, and art in general represent the real—and has a direct causal effect upon consumers. Cultural realism denies that information is constructed, invented, and *re*-presented, that meaning is manipulated and history reconstituted. This attitude blinded WGBH executives to the central theme of *Blacks Britannica.* This is not a call to revolutionary violence—though a film that openly propagates revolution should not be met with censorship and ideological alteration, but with counteranalysis and counterargument. Rather, *Blacks Britannica* enfolds a prediction that, in the absence of deep-seated social and political changes, revolutionary violence in Britain is inevitable. From the vantage point of hindsight we can say that the prediction had the ring of truth to it. Public television should be more concerned, perhaps, with images of history in the making than with the making of history in its own corporate image.

Thus, in the case of both commercial and public television there is a privatizing of the modes of censorship. The media do not have to be curtailed; they censor themselves, either by active exclusion of material deemed unacceptable or by reconstructing and re-presenting events to fit corporate and state interests. Self-determination demands that we actively oppose the merger of corporate and state control, just as we resist each form of control. Resistance to all forms of censorship must involve not only the identification of what is blatantly denied expression. We must also refuse the rewriting of history, the forgetting—through alteration—of our own recent past, and the sensibility of cultural realism that imputes natural causation to the social construction of visual narratives. Resistance, in short, should assume as many modes as there are modes of censorship, constraint, and control.

Notes

I take this opportunity to thank David Koff for the extensive documentation he furnished me in putting together the second part of this article, and for the accompanying text and image from *Blacks Britannica*. I thank also Alena Luter for her valuable comments.

1. See especially Edward Said, "An Ideology of Difference," *Critical Inquiry* 12, no. 1 (Fall 1985): 38-58; David Goldberg, ed., *Anatomy of Racism* (Minneapolis: University of Minnesota Press, forthcoming 1988).
2. CBS ran sixteen straight hours of commercially interrupted coverage of the celebratory events in Philadelphia on Constitution Day.
3. See "Erased Tape Causes Flap," *Boston Globe,* January 16, 1978.
4. On contemporary British racism, see M. Barker, *The New Racism* (London: Junction Books, 1981); Centre for Contemporary Culture, *The Empire Strikes Back* (London: Longwood, 1984); Frank Reeves, *British Racial Discourses* (Cambridge: Cambridge University Press, 1984); and Paul Gilroy, *There Ain't No Black in the Union Jack* (London: Hutchinson, 1987).
5. Cf. letter from David Ives, president of WGBH, to the *New York Times* (Sunday edition), August 3, 1978.
6. *New York Times,* August 9, 1979, and April 22, 1980.
7. Godard and Gorin's *Letter to Jane* raises pertinent questions, precisely in a political context, about the notion of "identification." A partial translation of the script appears in *wedge*, no. 7/8 (Winter/Spring 1985).

Blacks Britannica

Directed by David Koff
Produced by David Koff and Musindo Mwinyipembe
in association with Colin Prescod

Colin Prescod: If one weren't wary of talking about conspiracy, one would say that there was clearly a conspiracy against blacks in this country, because in all parts of this country that you look—whether you're looking at Ladbroke Grove in London, or Brixton in London, or Moss Side in Manchester, or Handsworth in Birmingham—in all the parts that you look at, it's clear that the state, at top national level, and certainly at local level, the state has moved to manipulate blacks in any way that it's wanted to. In this area—this used to be called in those days, "Brown Town," because a lot of black people had settled in this area—most of those people, a large number of them, have moved out of this area. They've been moved out by rehousing, and however else institutionalized racism works to mobilize black people into places where they want them. In places like Moss Side, it's more devastating, it's clearer that they've just moved through areas where black people, for a longer period now—Moss Side clearly has a much longer history of black presence than Ladbroke Grove. I mean, Ladbroke Grove begins to have a black presence in the mid-fifties, and thereon; Moss Side has one that goes way, way back, certainly into the Second World War period. In 1945, as most people now know, there was actually a Pan-African Congress which was held there because there was a strong black community there. Now, that community, in this more recent period of heavy racism in this society, has just been mown down, destroyed, completely destroyed, in a way, viciously.

Ron Phillips: The excuse was that Manchester was developing a ghetto. Ghettos, as had been seen from the American experience, were bad things, because out of ghettos came riots and so on, and they were determined not to let it happen here. So that it now became necessary, during the late sixties, to find a way of containing this very threatening presence. And the way that was found was the destruction of the black community.

All along here there used to be black people's houses: Carter Street and Monton Street, and so on.

Anonymous Woman: I mean, I was born 'round here, and it gets you very angry that you face it and see that you've got to go wherever they've got places for you. This is before they even consider anything else. It's not an ideal community, but it is a community where people know one another, and you don't want to move out. We've got a lot of old people, we've got a lot of black people in the area that feel very, very strongly about this.

Ron Phillips: We, as a community, fought a long campaign to persuade the city council to refurbish these houses, to bring them up to an acceptable living standard. What happened was that they chose to bulldoze the lot.

Many of the people who owned these sorts of houses were ripped off in a peculiarly brutal way, because after paying for a mortgage for perhaps ten years, people received as little as fifty pounds in what was called "bricks and mortar value" for their homes. Now, fifty pounds was just enough to pay about two weeks rent for the new flats that the council offered as an alternative to homes.

What you have here in Hulme is interesting, at least, because it is the area in which Engels did much of his work for the book, *The Conditions of the English Working Class*. It's interesting because the black people have now become the new underclass, that structures British society by being maintained at the bottom. So what they meant was, by integrating black people at the very bottom of society, with the worst families, who had the major kind of problems and had fallen to the bottom of white society. This in fact satisfied the city, and they felt that their policy was successful; they advertised it widely throughout Europe as an answer to the problem of black people.

There are two entrances, only, and this means that in a situation of social control—if, for instance, one of the famous British black riots develop, or whatever, because they make these things when they decide to—it is perfectly feasible and easy to control these buildings because there are only two points of access. And a relatively small force of army or police can control all the people within these buildings.

I think the whole point is that the British school does in fact negate the personality of black children and it doesn't do so accidentally, that it actually sets out to remove any feature that might threaten the society. And since the society has defined blackness as a threatening feature, what happens is a kind of deliberate attempt at inducing a psychosis in the child's mind, so that whatever it is, it isn't black. And I think that one of the things that the Saturday school does is motivate children and engender the demand, in the community, for our children to have that right to be black, to understand and be proud of what they are.

Jessica Huntley: We are a community bookshop. Each year, since we've been here, we have had sessions, where we talk about culture, art, music, history, and we have had quite a lot of people coming from the black community, writers and journalists and artists and musicians, coming here and giving the kids that which is lacking in the present school system at the moment.

Anti-immigration rally, early 1960s

"There are two entrances only . . ."

Selwyn (Steel Pulse): Well, after drifting through school . . . [laughter]. When you're in the system, a careers officer comes and says, "You, too, can become a doctor." And there's a finger pointing at you on the wall, saying, you can become a teacher, you can go in the army, and all that kind of thing. So, my mind was completely lost. All those people coming to you and saying, you can do this and you can do that. So, alright, I did a few O-levels and I left and . . . [laughter]

Michael (Steel Pulse): I mean, it's something that was sort of generated from school. They were saying, "You're gonna want a car, you're gonna want a house, and you gotta do this and you gotta do that, and you wanna earn a wage above a certain amount." It's all drummed into you, you know, time after time. "You're gonna need this, and you're gonna want that, and so on—you're gonna need a holiday at least once a year, and all them things; and you gotta study, you know." And what they didn't tell you was that "You're black, and we're going to stop you doing all this, we're going to do our best to stop you getting all this."

Tony Sealy: If we are simply here, saying, "Okay, we understand all the problems and we're crying about it," then the man will come along and shift us. He'll shift us from here, he'll shift us from wherever we are, because we are on his land, we are on his premises. I'm saying that what we have to do is to hold land, create institutions, places that young people can move around.

Embodied in this short space is a restaurant, a supermarket, a combination of a record shop and a bookshop, and a center for West Indian handicraft. The reason for this development is mainly to provide jobs, to establish some form of independence in this area, and to project in the area generally that young black people—because it will be young black people involved in this project here—can actually move in their community and do constructive work. We envisage that in the region of thirty jobs will come out of this particular scheme, and that is a fair amount in an area where, as you probably already know, the unemployment is very high.

Young Man #1: When you go for a job, when you go for an interview, you talk pretty on the phone to the guy, then when you come through the door and he sort of sees your face, seeing that you're black, he's trying to hide his shock, "ahh, such and such," and then, you're gone, you got no chance. Job centers and all that, they all try, but there's nothing really, you don't get naught. Lucky ones, say, like you have to be better than them to get the same privileges as them.

Young Man #2: In the past two weeks, I've been down there everyday, everyday I just go in and look at the same board, and I see the same jobs, and it just makes me sick. I feel bad when I see them.

Young Man #1: Then, when you're fed up, without finding a job, and you come out at night, the police are pressuring you, every little thing you do, can't even walk the streets, they're picking you up, beat you up or something like that, and then you're up at court for something stupid.

Colin Prescod: We began to arrive in Britain, in large numbers, in the mid-1950s. The places we came from were stagnating economically after years of colonial exploitation: the Caribbean, India, Pakistan. We were waiting there, in a sense, like a massive pool of labor, with a history of having to move in order to work.

Pathe Newsreel Commentary: In 1954, about ten thousand West Indians came to Britain. In 1955, it is believed another fifty thousand will make the long journey. Already, their coming has caused a national controversy. But one point must always be borne in mind: whatever our feelings, we cannot deny them entry, for all are British citizens and, as such, are entitled to the identical rights of any member of the Empire.

Colin Prescod: In fact, we were invited to Britain to do certain jobs: on the buses, and the underground; in the sweatshops; in the foundries; in the hospitals. We did the dirty jobs, the uncomfortable jobs, for low pay. And, we met racism. The riots in Notting Hill Gate were evidence of this. But more than that, the economy was going into deeper and deeper recession. Unemployment was rising, the working people were getting restive. Among other things, the state reached for the weapon of racism, and by 1962, the first in a series of immigration acts was passed. Now, from that point on, a new pattern was set in British politics.

Claudia Jones (1963): Again, here the ill-feeling of course was spawned as a result of this Act, in which West Indians felt that they had now become second-class citizens, the Open Door policy had been reversed. What is important to recognize now, it's not so much their feeling directed against the Act as such, because they're responsible, the Act is law, they're fighting to repeal it—but the consequences of the Act, namely, the fact that the population at large, because of the whole propaganda against the West Indians, regard them as second-class citizens, and they themselves, on the job, in virtually every sphere of life, find this difficulty, since the Immigration Act, in terms of discrimination, color bar housing, etc.

Colin Prescod: The issue of "immigration" and "immigrants" came to be used quite deliberately by the state, whipping up racism and confusing the working class. So that, despite the fact that immigration has been effectively stopped, and despite the fact that we've proven our worth to the economy, we are still the target of a very mischievous, and hypocritical debate, about our presence here, our right to be here.

Enoch Powell (Independent): The picture is not that of a province, or corner of a country, occupied by a distinct and growing population—though that would be perilous enough—the picture is of the occupation, more and more intense, of key areas, and it may be added, of key functions, in the heartlands of the kingdom.

Margaret Thatcher (Conservative Party): And I think it means that people are really rather afraid that this country might be rather swamped by people with a different culture. And, you know, the British character has done so much for democracy, for law, and done so much throughout the world, that if there's any fear that it might be swamped, people are going to react and be rather hostile to those coming in.

John Kingsley Read (National Party): We will fight you back, and we'll fight you with every bone, every nerve, every feeling, every ounce of blood we've got. We will have our country back!

Harold Wilson (Labour Party): There can't be any doubt that in many areas, we have reached the ab-sorptive capacity in respect of new immigrants. The load on our educational system, to say nothing of housing, health, and welfare, is such that the strictest control is now necessary, and this is true irrespective of where the immigrants might come from. This would be true if they were coming from . . .

A. Sivanandan: Looked at in terms of the history of race and immigration in this country, it says one thing to me. It says that, what Enoch Powell says today, the Conservative Party says tomorrow, and the Labour Party legislates on the day after. With slight modifications.

Darcus Howe: I don't believe there is any person in this room who could be sincere that the Labour Party will be a vehicle for our freedom. I have observed one thing about politics in Britain with regard to blacks. The Labour Party, because it says it's working class, and we are working class, can't do certain things. They get the Tories to do it and then follow them afterward.

Colin Prescod: The political parties in Britain today are closing ranks not only against blacks, but against the entire working class. They have to, because they face a working class that's refusing, more and more, to pay for their mistakes, in the form of chronic unemployment, rising prices, cutbacks in social services. In other words, a working class that is suffering a real decline in its living standards.

At one level, the state has moved to control all forms of resistance. There's been state control of wages, limitations on the right to strike. At another level, we've seen politicians stepping up the use of racism to break up that resistance. Now, the crudest extension of this policy is seen in the rise of the fascist policy, the National Front, which spreads racist ideas, suggesting that the two million Asians and Afro-Caribbeans, who've worked here and are now settled here, are responsible for the deepening crisis of the economy. In fact, blacks are under attack not only as a part of the very bottom layer of the working class—because that's still where we are massively represented after twenty to twenty-five years in this country—but we're also attacked in our communities. So it's not surprising, out of this dual oppression of class and race, that blacks are among the leading elements mobilizing in the working class against the government, against the state itself.

National Front Youth Rally Chant: We're gonna send the blacks back, we're gonna send the blacks back, la la . . . We're gonna shoot the reds dead, we're gonna shoot the reds dead, la la la. The reds, the reds, we're gonna get rid of the reds.

John La Rose: In the last year, the most serious of the attacks has been the firebombing and destruction of a bookshop on August 10th. The bookshops obviously mean something to the National Front, the National Party, and the various fascist terrorists who are operating in the country at the present moment. And they're seeking to terrorize us out of existence. And we are saying they won't terrorize us out of existence. But we recognize that the

state has a certain responsibility and we must bring it to their attention. Because if we were to arrange self-defense groups here, you can rest assured that the police would be attacking us, and not the fascists, who would be attacking our bookshops.

Colin Prescod: The National Front today throws bombs at black people's premises, they beat up black people, black young ladies on the street, and so on. So they are harmful. But in a sense, they're not the major, major threat to black people. Any black youth on the street will tell you that the major threat for them, for all their lives in this country, has been represented by the police, the blues, the men in uniform, on the beat, who humiliate them every day, who pick them up on "sus," who take them down to the station, who beat them. They all have—one out of four black youths has a story to tell.

Ron Phillips: David Oluwale was a young Nigerian, who came to this country with the intention of studying to become an engineer. He was kept out for some years of institutions of learning, he just couldn't get admission to an engineering college, partly because he was poor and couldn't pay. And, therefore, refusing to go into a factory, which was difficult enough, he was unable to find work, and slowly deteriorated to a tramp, a bum. During the course of his last five years, in a famous trial of Sergeant Kitching and Sergeant Ellerker, it was revealed that an entire police force in the city of Leeds had picked David Oluwale for the most terrible persecution. They picked him up at night, they

From the "bloody shirt" sequence

Police cadets on parade at graduation

beat him, they urinated on him, finally they killed him, and they threw his body in the river Ayre.

Man at Investigating Commission Meeting: Why, when a Jamaican or a West Indian be picked up, why should he be beaten in the police station? Why should he be beaten? Ladies and gentlemen, we all know, we get ourselves in a few difficulties at times, a bit of problem with the law. If we do something, we be picked up at the police station, charged, but why should we be beaten up? Ladies and gentlemen, will you please quiet. Now, we've got proof here. Two weeks ago, one of our brothers was assaulted by a number of men in Wolverhampton. So, he decided to defend himself, protect himself, by carrying an offensive weapon. The Bible tells you harm no man and let no man harm you. He walked with the chopper. He was picked up by the police, his brother was there, while his brother was there, his brother said to him, get in the police car, come up the station. Another set of officers came, and they grabbed him by the neck, punched him in the face, broke his nose in the car, and he was beaten up. Ladies and

gentlemen, will you please look. This was his jacket, covered in blood. The police decided to take his clothes to wash them before he came to court. Mr. Buck, here it is, here it is. This is proof. And he's still in jail, was remanded in custody, but when he came up in court he could hardly speak. Here it is, Mr. Buck, here it is, ladies and gentlemen. Now we come back on the tee-shirt. Here it is. So we took it here, for each and every one of you to see this. Why should they be beaten up when they're taken to the police station?

Two Young Men Walking: Myself and my friend met, and we came down Oxford Street, primarily to see about a job I'd applied for in Boots, and to see a girl who worked in Selfridges. We reached down here about half past four, something like that, and went into Selfridges. We never met the girl because they had too many people. So we decided for me to go and see about the job. But before we went to see about the job, we went into C & A's to see about a coat, for my friend to buy. When we came out of C & A's, I went to Boots to see about the job, and my friend went in Virgin

Records 'round the corner to wait for me. After I'd seen about the job and came out and met him in Virgin Records, we came out of Virgin Records and turned the corner onto Edgeware Road, where we saw my friend across the road at the bus stop. The traffic was too much so we couldn't cross, so we just waved, said hello from across the road. We carried on walking down to Mr. International, where a man came in between us and put us against the window. He said he was a police officer and that we'd been followed from when we came out of C & A. He said we was under arrest, and said anything we said would be taken down and used in evidence against us. A police car pulled up in the center of the road and a uniformed officer came across and escorted us to the car. We was taken down to the police station, searched, questioned, and charged. The charge was: "suspected person of loitering with intent to commit an arrestable offense." After that we was put in a cell, where we stayed for about three to four hours, until my father came and collected us.

Ian MacDonald: One of the most potent weapons that the police use against black youth is the charge of "sus," that is, being a "suspected person loitering with intent to commit a crime." And that's an offense which the police can pick someone up for if they think they're about to—not that they have—but are about to commit a crime. And the standard pieces of evidence used in practically all the cases I've ever heard of are, "I saw the defendant wandering down bus queues dip-ping in ladies' handbags" or "I saw the defendant trying car doors." And it's something which tends to be used against youth, either because the police think that they ought to be at school and are not, or ought to be at work and are not.

Police Spokesman: It is imperative, from a general preventive point of view, that any offender who is seen in such circumstances that he is a suspected person loitering with intent to commit this type of crime, should be arrested, before he does it, rather than afterwards. And, if you have got, on occasions, a number of arrests for suspicious persons, it is because they are there in abundance at that particular time.

Young Man: They heard the case, and whilst the case was going on, it's then when I knew what the police were really like, I never thought that they could lie so much. All the time the case was going on, the magistrate, he just didn't seem interested. It looked like he's just reading something on his desk in front of him. And that's how it went. And when it came to giving us the sentence, or finding us guilty or innocent, all he said was, "I don't believe a police officer would come to court and commit perjury." Which just shows that he was intending to find us guilty all the time, because anything the police say, he would just take it as law.

Gus John: Now, it seems to me, what the police have been doing, particularly in a whole series of incidents over the last few years, is launching an assault, predominantly on black young people. Black

Police target resembling a black man

Police target practice

young people whom the schools, and the careers service, youth employment service within the schools, have not persuaded to accept jobs which employers view as being the particular claim of black people. In other words, the situation in which a number of black jobs, and continued to be largely at that level within the economy—that situation is not repeating itself, because the children of those black people are refusing to accept those kind of jobs. Now it is at that level that they are in confrontation with the state, and with the police as agents of the state.

Scotland Yard Pistol Range: I want you to go! As if you were pointing a Patchett. Got it? Right. Up to the firing line, and adjust your earmuffs. You are loaded in the holsters, remember. Draw weapons! Right. That's it. Now stop looking at the gun, look at the target. That's the one who wants to kill you. Are you ready on the firing line? The line is ready. Stand by! Now!

Young Man In Car: Well, if the police don't need any provocation or reason to arrest you, as it is, if they see my face doing an interview like this, that is just asking for trouble. Because they'll say, we don't want people like him, who'll tell the truth. 'Cause there's hardly been any programs that I've seen where the truth has been really told, they don't want anyone telling the truth about the happenings that's going on now. So, they'd just . . . it'd just be worse for me. I doubt if I'd be able to walk the streets.

Sir Robert Mark (former Commissioner of Police): Two very important elements in the police function in this country are, firstly, that we must never in any circumstances appear to be the tool of government or the tool of any political party, and secondly, I believe that in all disputes, whether they arise from politics or industry, I think we also must be clearly seen to be impartial. And as a policeman, I don't think that what we call crimes of violence, though they naturally give rise to a great deal of heartsearching and regret, I don't think that they are anything like as severe a threat to the maintenance of tranquility in this country as the tendency of people to use violence to achieve political or industrial ends. Now, as far as I'm concerned, as a policeman of many, many years of experience, that's the worst crime in the book. I think it's even worse than murder.

Demonstration outside West Yorkshire Police Headquarters, Bradford: The pigs, the pigs, we gotta get rid of the pigs! The pigs, the pigs, we gotta get rid of the pigs!

Ron Phillips: At one point, Britain was making four times as much profit out of one Caribbean island, that is sugar production, as it did out of all its trade with the rest of the world. So that was the level of profits that black people were generating into Britain. And it was only at this level of superprofit that allowed the period that's called the period of primitive accumulation—that is, there's so much money being made out of black people, that the factory system could be paid for, the new kinds of machinery could be paid for, the new sort of production, that brought into the world factory production, the new line system, that expanded the world's economy to a degree that was unimaginable.

Colin Prescod: One of the things we have to remember about Britain today is that it's not so "great" anymore. Its empire has been taken away, and the economy is technically bankrupt. All that wealth that was accumulated here is basically gone, consumed, dispersed. The predicament of blacks highlights the inability of British capitalism to deliver the goods. In some of Britain's major cities, places like Manchester, Birmingham, and London, official government statistics show that up to 80 percent of black youths be-

tween the age of sixteen and nineteen are unable to find work, and have no visible prospect of finding full-time employment. Now, significant numbers of these youths have turned to what is called "street crime." They take what they're not given; they "capture," in their own terms, in order to survive. In some cases, their resistance has led them to take on the monopoly might of the state itself, as for example in the case of the Notting Hill Gate carnival, in London, in 1976 and 1977, when there were pitched battles for the streets between the police and black youths. Now it is impossible to pretend that this response of black youth is simply criminal activity. It becomes increasingly politi-black youths. Now it is impossible to pretend that this response of black youth is simply criminal activity. It becomes increasingly political.

A. Sivanandan: The Spaghetti House siege of 1975, when three West Indian youths held up the Spaghetti House with guns, was the first time that there had been such a siege in this country. It was very, very significant, because one of them, Wesley Dick, used to be a voluntary worker here, in the Institute of Race Relations. He used to help on the telephone and with *Race Today.* And the second person, Tony Monroe, was on the eve of going to Nigeria, I believe, on a medical scholarship.

Sir Robert Mark: Today's events confirm our original belief, that this was an ordinary armed robbery, with no racial or political connotations.

The "police assault" on the Grunwick strikers and supporters (shot 159).

Police at end of the assault, strutting around and "mopping up" (shot 159).

A. Sivanandan: The press had tried to make out that this was part of the lumpen, "spontaneous combustion" element in the black community. Not so. And they were not irresponsible people in the sense that society understands it. They were responsive. I remember Wesley coming into the Institute one day. He had been to a dance the previous night. And he was absolutely het up, it was like an incubus on his brain. He said that a policeman had kicked a pregnant sister! And there was murder in his eyes. So, however mistaken the siege might have been, however mistaken it was to be able to, you know, what they said was they want to get monies to service the struggles of the black community, that is why they held up the Spaghetti House. They didn't want to "thieve" Spaghetti House to line their own pockets. What motivated them was the impossibility of living in this society with any sort of dignity, with any sort of family life, and be marked out as a section of the community which was totally undesirable, unwanted, rejected. That is the significance of the Spaghetti House siege. And that is only a part and parcel of the things that black youth have been saying. They have been saying in effect—they may not articulate it in these terms—they have been saying in effect, Look, you want to reproduce the subproletariat that you imported into this country in our father's time. You now want to reproduce that same subproletariat, and make us do the shitwork that our parents did. And all that we can say to you is, get stuffed, fuck you, we're not going to do that.

Colin Prescod: In the months before October 1977, two young girls, black girls, had been apprehended by security guards and police officers and maltreated, on suspicion of shoplifting. In particular, in October a young girl went into the Boots chemist's shop in the precinct and was apprehended by the security guards and police, and was seen by the public to be punched, hair pulled, and so on, maltreated, and was accused of having shoplifted inside of Boots the chemist. One day later, a large group of youths, perhaps twenty to thirty youths, turned up in the Moss Side precinct, at the Boots chemist, they posted a guard, and they went into the Boots chemist, and they wrecked the joint completely. They attacked the security guard and the cashier, and they split. It was what one local black newspaper, *Bradford Black* newspaper, called a "military operation."

Courtney Hay: If a man rob 1500 pounds, I say power to him, and if the police grab him, I move to defend. Right? To me, it not a case of guilty or not guilty, yeah? It's whether we win or whether we don't. Right? On this the police made a cockup. They ain't got no friggin' evidence. No evidence whatsoever. So we gonna fight on that level. But in our hearts, we ain't fighting because, well, Tony or Geoffrey innocent, huh? We fighting it because they're black, and they're black youths, and we know we're engaged in a war. Tony, Geoffrey, Franklin, and Mark, when he gets sentenced, are prisoners of war. Because we have to take. We're unemployed, we ain't got. A lot of rich people got. And when we take, then they send down the law and the police and say, you shouldn't take and so forth. Well, we have to get them out. It ain't for—anybody in this room thinking about whether they're guilty or whether they're not guilty, I say they go somewhere else and think about it. That isn't the question. The question is they got three black youths, three of you, that means you're three short, yeah? And the question is, we get them out. And it's also the question of mounting some pressure on the ass of the police, because they're taking a whole heap of friggin' liberties with you. Like Mrs. Ramsey say, they don't come pick up she, they come pick up you. And why they

pick up you? Why? One, 'cause you're black. Two, 'cause you ain't conformin', you ain't behaving how they like you to behave. You ain't running after a job. Yeah? I see a whole heap of you wearin' your tams. They don't like it, 'cause you're trying to make out like you're different, right, and they don't like difference. And when a policeman step on one of your foot, you step back. They say you're too uppity, you won't sit down and take it like they want you to take it, you won't stay in your place. Yeah? That's why they're gunnin' for you. And Mrs. Ramsey, and Desna— well, Mrs. Ramsey's unique—no, wrong, she's not unique, but she's one of an older generation, and I would have liked more parents to be here tonight. Because they care, they care. They show it in a different way, but they care. And the question, huh, if more and more of you are not going to end up inside, is whether we can get some power, yeah, to get the pigs off our backs.

Ron Phillips: The question of race has always been, right throughout the history of the last four hundred years of the United Kingdom, a central political issue. Because either they were dealing with outside, you know, how to conquer Africa, how to control black people in the Caribbean or elsewhere, or how to control black people here. So that when we look through the history of Britain, we see major deportations starting as long ago as 1596 and 1601, when Queen Elizabeth signed orders deporting black people. This was before the establishment of the United States of America, which has gained the reputation of being the leader in racism in the modern world. No, I think the argument is clear, that racism, and the problem of race, actually was imported from Britain to the United States with the pilgrim fathers. And that is a continuing strand of British history. So that the political battles around race represent an important and crucial part, a central issue, of British life throughout the centuries.

Darcus Howe: If you believe that it began with this lot, you know what you are likely to say? Margaret Thatcher is evil, so is Jim Callaghan, so is Steele in the Liberal Party and Kingsley Read and John Tyndell and those, and if we get some nice people, everything is going to be alright. I don't want you to believe that. That if we get some blacks, and put them in the exact positions where those are, everything is going to be alright. I don't want you to believe that. And the only way you could go beyond that is if you understand that what we're dealing with is a system of exploitation of which those are only the political organizers. And if you go back to recall your own history, you will have met them before. I am addressing this meeting in English. I never knew any other language. It means I have been around these people all my life. This is not the first time that we're in confrontation with them; this is not the first time that they are focusing on us.

Courtney Hay: If I could add to that. I learned my politics in my mother's kitchen. The same woman who was telling me to walk safely on the streets at night, not to go to "those kind of places" and mix with "those kind of people," was the same woman who, in her inspired moments, was telling me how she was burning canefields in the 1940s, against them!

Colin Prescod: Britain, "mother of the empire," has had to welcome in her children, and to allow them to settle. Because of racism, they have not been allowed to settle in a dignified manner. And because the blacks have refused to accept indignity and victimage, Britain is stuck with a rebellious black presence in its centers. And there is no way that Britain can get out of this situation. And what the blacks who've been born here are saying is that they intend to obtain their rights, as dignified citizens, here.

Courtney Hay: Our struggle, the struggle for what we want, we cannot get what we totally want in a capitalist Britain. I am not one for saying that because we can't get it in a capitalist Britain, we go somewhere where we believe there is some socialism or something. Anywhere, any place, any time, we can't get it under capitalism, well then capitalism have to go.

Notes

Blacks Britannica is available on film and video. Write to David Koff, 23603 Park Sorrento, Suite 104, Calabasas, CA 91302-1321.

Bodies and Anti-Bodies: A Crisis in Representation

Timothy Landers

Aids is not only a medical crisis on an unparalleled scale, it involves a crisis of representation itself, a crisis over the entire framing of knowledge about the human body and its capacities for sexual pleasure.

—Simon Watney

Commercial television introduces its AIDS specials by emphasizing the mass media's responsibility for public health and its concern for the welfare of each individual viewer. Presented with the humble intention of "saving your life," these programs promote a contradictory agenda that encourages the consumption of information (and products) through the creation of fear. Tom Brokaw demonstrated this when, on *NBC News National Forum: Life, Death and AIDS* (January 21, 1986), he called AIDS "the plague" while promising to put an end to confusion. Over and over, with dramatic urgency, straight-talking newscasters warn us, "AIDS will kill you if you get it." This earnest approach promises the viewer that this is one story that won't be sugarcoated but, inevitably, it is. Such incitements to panic are followed by soothing reassurances that AIDS is largely confined to others. The *raison d'être* of the AIDS special is to keep it that way.

One of the shortcomings of commercial television's AIDS coverage lies in its insistence on speaking to one audience—the *you* addressed is presumed to be white, middle-class, heterosexual, and healthy, grouped in cozy, stable families. Those responsible for these television programs completely ignore the possibility that many of those watching may be struggling with AIDS on a more immediate level. In his *CBS New Special*, titled, appropriately enough, *AIDS Hits Home* (October 22, 1986), Dan Rather unwittingly spoke this premise when he blurted out, "The scary reality is that gays are no longer the only ones getting it." Rather and others' skewed notion of "reality" is under attack, and the "home" must be rigorously defended. More ominously, these programs suggest that gays exist outside and against this "reality," their deaths having little consequence.

The prevailing representations about AIDS indicate that it threatens not only physical bodies and institutional bodies, in particular law and health-care systems, but that it is attacking the immune system of the social order itself. When Science fails—by not developing a cure for AIDS—the scientific explanations of disease and sexuality, similarly constructed and frequently intersecting, are revealed as the precarious fictions that they are. Models of sexuality and disease—and their sites, the mind and the body—are postulated as "normal" or "abnormal" through a series of binary oppositions: masculine/feminine, heterosexual/homosexual, and healthy/ill.

Commercial media representations in general are informed by a variation on the normal/abnormal paradigm—one better suited to a visual medium: that of Bodies/Anti-Bodies. The Body—white, middle-class, and heterosexual—is constructed in contrast to the Other, the Anti-Body (frequently *absent* from representation)—blacks, gay men, lesbians, workers, foreigners, in short, the whole range of groups that threaten straight, white, middle-class values. It is important to note the complex, often paradoxical nature of this model, bisected by class, gender, sexual preference, and other qualifications. For instance, advertisements are structured around a subdivision within the primary category of Body—the "beautiful" (thin) Body vs. the "ugly" (fat) Anti-Body. Applied to the subject of AIDS, oppositions revolve around the nexus of health. The body is, above all, healthy. The Anti-Body becomes, specifically, gay, black, Latino, the IV drug user, the prostitute—in other words, *sick.* Tinged with the stigma of illness that dramatically destroys the body, what was usually absent from representation becomes spectacularly and consistently *visible.*

Mass media images of people with AIDS show isolated, emaciated, hospital-bound, bed-ridden individuals. The message is clear—*AIDS is fatal.* The Anti-Body is consumed, while in advertisements during the commercial breaks the Body consumes. The camera dwells on healthy bodies in these documentaries, with images of people with AIDS acting as punctuation. Healthy, but anxious, Bodies discuss how to avoid AIDS: singles boogie in discos, work-out in mirrored health clubs, and exchange AIDS-era dating tips: "I never sleep with anyone unless I know them first," says one blonde model-type. Another says, "Sex is like playing Russian roulette," a metaphor that has found favor with newscasters in search of the no-nonsense catch-phrase.

Another common element is stock footage of laboratory science at work—microscopes, test tubes, hardware, etc. An anchorperson often narrates a segment standing in a lab, while a white-coated technician tinkers with test-tubes and impressive machines churn blood in the background, suggesting that Science is perfecting a cure even as we speak. In these sequences, media and science are also wed in dazzling displays of technology, where photographic magnification reveals the HIV virus and electronic manipulation colorizes and animates it.

In addition to the standard lab shot, the conventional intro-to-AIDS documentary contains one or more of the following: an in-studio panel and "experts" from around the world communicating via satellite; interviews with people living with AIDS (PWAs); an IV drug user and gay man vs. a hemophiliac or unsuspecting partner of a bisexual man; a scene of drug users shooting up, usually in a Lower East Side vacant lot; shots of a streetwalker soliciting business (this shot always has a voyeuristic, "hidden camera" look, with the "hooker" often bathed in red light while she saunters up to a car); shots of blood being drawn, illustrating "testing"; shots of two men, often wearing jeans and flannel shirts, walking arm-in-arm down Castro Street to illustrate "homosexual liberation," which, we're told, resulted in the "promiscuity" of the seventies that is the source of AIDS; distressed parents picketing schools; and the obligatory singles aerobicizing, dancing, socializing.

The documentary claim to objectivity in these programs—and the structure imposed on this kind of illustrative footage—is founded, once again, in the point/counterpoint treatment of the "issues" that have become synonymous with AIDS: condom advertising, safe-sex education, schooling for children with AIDS, people with AIDS in the workplace, mandatory testing, and quarantine. Given what is known about how AIDS is transmitted, that certain positions should be treated as "controversial," implying that they exist within a rational, moral arena and are, therefore, worthy of debate, legitimates morally and medically questionable solutions under the guise of objectivity and in the name of democracy. In this regard, we're asked to consider the pros and cons of clearly barbarous measures like William F. Buckley's proposal to tattoo people who test positive for HIV, or quarantine laws, now on the books in Louisiana and other states.

ABC Nightline's AIDS: A National Town Meeting (June 5, 1987) deserves special notice, not only because it was broadcast live but because it was the baroque version of the AIDS special—four hours long, with a studio panel of nineteen "experts" (more than comparable shows combined), numerous satellite hook-ups, studio audience participation, phone-in questions from around the nation, and vignettes on topics from "epidemics" to "euthanasia." The title indicates one of mass media's central mythologies: the United States is one big, democratic town, and television provides the democratic forum, a Town Hall where tough issues are grappled with and resolved and where a show of hands is replaced by the results of a nationwide poll. Because of its excesses, and the fact that it was live, and thus open to unpredictability, the program periodically threatened to erupt into chaos. The studio audience repeatedly heckled when Senator Dannemeyer—homophobe extraordinaire—spoke, and some articulate panel members were able to forcefully argue positions more radical than those on Ted Koppel's moderate agenda. For instance, much to Koppel's chagrin, playwright Harvey Fierstein stressed that it is risky *behavior,* not "risk groups" or promiscuity, that exposes one to the HIV virus.

The compulsion to give AIDS a "face," to externalize the HIV antibodies characteristic of AIDS by identifying Anti-Bodies, provides the impetus for many mass-media representations of PWAs as well proposals for mandatory testing. The attempt to "humanize" AIDS by presenting the "face of AIDS" offers a justification for this approach that anthropomorphizes the virus and dehumanizes the PWA. The "face" inscribed with the state of its internal fluids becomes a cipher through which a dreaded disease speaks its ugly truth. *AIDS: A Public Inquiry* (March 25, 1987), an hour-long documentary produced by WGBH-Boston and aired on the Public Broadcasting Service's *Frontline* series, is obsessed with identifying the enemy and demonstrates the insidious underside of the "face of AIDS" mentality. The program starts out fairly typically: Judy Woodruff gives the "facts" about AIDS, backed up with statistics made easy-to-understand by playful computer graphics. The panel of experts is introduced, carefully balanced with doctors, representatives from gay organizations, and right-wing ideologues. The stage is set for one of the most irresponsible representations of AIDS aired in this country.

"This is a portrait," Woodruff announces, "of a man with AIDS who continued to have unsafe sex." In this way she introduces the centerpiece of the show, Fabian Bridges. Bridges is "not typical" we are told, in an

On June 5, 1987, *ABC Nightline* convened a four-hour marathon Town Meeting to discuss AIDS, employing about every clichéd emblem of AIDS now in the mass-media lexicon.

attempt at reassurance. He is gay, black, poor, and not particularly alert or articulate. The characteristics of AIDS—lethargy, confusion, and incoherence—become his personal attributes and not the result of the HIV virus, although, as some critics have pointed out, it's likely that Bridges was in the early stages of dementia, a physical result of the HIV virus' attack on the brain. The camera crew, Woodruff then explains, follows him on "his tragic journey across the U.S.A."

Bridges is encountered in *medias res*, having been diagnosed, hospitalized, and released. Rejected by his family, without insurance or a job, he begins to wander. Since the filmmakers discovered Bridges through a newspaper item, they must first track him down. So the story begins with his absence—we see an empty hospital bed, a vacant phone booth indicates calls for help made to his family. And his absence indicates the threat his presence represents to "the nation": if he is not on camera, he must be out there, somewhere, spreading the HIV virus. Television, then, becomes the vortex of the storm, and its inability to contain the agent of destruction foretells the chaos that lies just outside the screen's perimeters. By casting the central character in this way, the documentary leads to an inevitable conclusion: quarantine, the only way to solve the acute anxiety that Bridges represents.

While Bridges is found, then lost, then found again by the crew, the situation grows more urgent. As an example of impartial reporting, the *Frontline* crew is a model of disaster, giving Bridges money, doing his laundry, and ultimately reporting him to health officials. Thus public officials are made aware of the threat, the walking AIDS virus, a modern-day Typhoid Mary. Along with shots of Bridges wandering aimlessly and confessing to the camera that he has, as we are led to suspect, had unsafe sex because he "just doesn't care," is footage of police and government officials who voice their frustration with Bridges's right to be assumed innocent before proven guilty. There is no doubt in *AIDS: A Public Inquiry* that Bridges is guilty. Legal and ethical problems posed by his situation are trivialized and individual rights and democratic processes are depicted as a paralyzed and ineffective bureaucratic circus that leaves the public vulnerable to a deadly threat.

The Body/Anti-Body split prevalent in the conceptualization of AIDS operates on a series of already formulated definitions. In the first volume of his *History of Sexuality* (New York: Random House, 1978), Michel Foucault discusses the ideological mechanisms that allow an act capable of being committed by any body—sodomy—to become firmly anchored to a specific Body—the "homosexual." And, in *AIDS in the Mind of America: The Social, Political and Psychological Impact of an Epidemic* (New York: Anchor Press/Doubleday, 1986), Dennis Altman notes, "The fact that the first reported cases [of AIDS] were among gay men was to effect the entire future conceptualization of AIDS." Other have also pointed out that the extant discourse on homosexuality provides the shape, the invisible framework, the explanation-by-association for AIDS.[1] It is the reigning idea of "homosexuality" that is never represented but upon which many representations of AIDS rely.

Because the gay man has been established as the icon for AIDS, it is important to see how this conflation of disease and desire informs conceptualizations and descriptions of AIDS, particularly through the panic-inducing theory of casual transmission. A chapter in Simon Watney's *Policing Desire: Pornography, AIDS, and the Media* (Minneapolis: University of Minnesota Press, 1987), entitled "Infectious Desire," illustrates some of the contradictions that the figure of "the homosexual" embodies. He cites a school textbook from the 1960s that provides a revealing "contagion/seduction" model of homosexuality:

Dr. Anthony Fauci of the National Institutes of Health on *Nightline,* June 5, 1987.

The greatest danger in homosexuality lies in the introduction of normal people to it. An act which will produce nothing but disgust in a normal individual may quite easily become more acceptable until the time arrives when the normal person by full acceptance of the abnormal act becomes a pervert too.

Homosexuality, this statement implies, is a contagious "disease," transmitted casually and capable of breaking down individual will power, resulting in its spread through the "normal" population. This suggests that will power must unrelentingly police the boundaries of desire, locating homosexuality within, as well as outside, the individual.[2]

As anyone who pays even minimal attention to mass media knows, this model structures AIDS as well as "homosexuality." At work, then, is an analogy of the immune system with will power: both become barriers against "abnormality." When AIDS is thus conflated with homosexuality, some of the imagined properties of "homosexuality" are grafted onto AIDS, despite all evidence to the contrary. The logical outcome of this conceptual system is an innocent/guilty dichotomy of "victims"—both the "victims" who succumb to homosexuality and the "victims" of AIDS. The "normal" person who, through a combination of seduction (breakdown of will power) and contagion becomes abnormal, is both "innocent victim" (previously "normal") and "guilty victim" (who allowed him- or herself to catch it). In the case of AIDS, there are sharp divisions conforming to these innocent/guilty categories, with children, hemophiliacs, female partners of bisexual men occupying the former, and gay men, IV drug users, prostitutes, Haitians occupying the latter. However, it is important to note that all are guilty of being "victims," a stigma which, according to the prevailing interrelated mythologies of strength of will and rugged individualism, could be prevented.

In *Illness as Metaphor* (New York: Vintage Books, 1977), Susan Sontag quotes Karl Menninger in her discussion of how illness is blamed on the victim and how certain illnesses (in this case, cancer and tuberculosis) are formulated:

Illness is in part what the world has done to a victim, but in a larger part it is what the victim has done with his world, and with himself. . . . Illness is interpreted as, basically, a psychological event, and people are encouraged to believe that they get sick because they (unconsciously) want to, and that they can cure themselves by the mobilization of will; that they can choose not to die of the disease.

Similarly, homosexuality can not only be prevented but "cured" through self-discipline, a mobilization of the will. In their 1987 pamphlet *What Homosexuals Do (It's More Than Merely Disgusting)*, the right-wing Family Research Institute echoes a sentiment common to more respectable institutions like the Catholic Church:

Those who would recognize homosexuality as a legitimate lifestyle are being manifestly unkind because they refuse hope and motivation to those homosexually involved and are adding to the sexual difficulties of our civilization. Homosexuals should be encouraged to abandon their unfortunate habit as millions have before them.

Just as safe-sex education is seen as encouraging homosexuality (or sexuality in general), so, too, dispensing clean needles to IV drug users is seen as encouraging drug use. Both homosexuality and drug use, threatening in the potential pleasures they represent, are defined as unhealthy, counter to the "natural" state of the body. In recent years, this threat has been countered with the strident campaigns to "Just say no"—to drugs and sex. When AIDS became worthy of presidential attention (i.e., when it became acknowledged that white, middle-class heterosexuals were susceptible), "Just say no" to sex was added to the "Just say no" to drugs slogan in an effort to mobilize, once again, the all-American virtue of individual initiative. The frightfully similar policies devised in conjunction with both

IV drug user as shown on *Nightline*, June 5, 1987.

campaigns—the testing of bodily fluids—marks the contradiction at the heart of New Right thinking: the rhetoric of a meritocratic social and economic system that stresses individualism while concealing an agenda of state intervention, control, and surveillance of morality.

AIDS: Just Say No (1987) is, appropriately enough, the title for an educational videotape produced for the New York City public schools and distributed across the country. As the most innocent victims in a cruel world, the children's bodies have been the frequent sites for media exploitation—on subjects like drug abuse, incest, kiddie porn, child molestation, alcohol, drugs, sex, and so on. Community decisions to educate children and teenagers about AIDS are accompanied by much hand-wringing and eulogizing of lost innocence. Commissioned by the New York City Board of Education to produce an educational film on AIDS, ODN Productions, a nonprofit educational media-production company, became aware of this as they watched their first effort, *Sex, Drugs, and AIDS* (1986), sit on the shelf for six months. At the request of the Board of Education, ODN revised the tape to emphasize abstinence rather than safer sex. The result, *AIDS: Just Say No,* was subsequently approved and put in circulation. The difference between the two tapes is minimal. *Sex, Drugs, and AIDS* features three white teenage girls stretching in a ballet studio and chatting about birth control, sexually transmitted diseases, and AIDS, reaching the conclusion that condoms are a preferred method of prevention. *AIDS: Just Say No* substitutes a school staircase for the ballet barre. In this version, only one of the girls has had sex, the other two state that they're waiting, but the girl who is having sex doesn't apologize and has a mature, responsible attitude as well as an impressive understanding of birth control, AIDS, and STDs.

Both ODN videos start off with an MTV-like bang, with a disco beat pacing the montage of images that illustrate ways you *cannot* get AIDS (door knobs, swimming pools, shared glasses, etc.) that effectively eases most fears about casual transmission. However, both videotapes run into problems in the discussion of the ways you *can* get AIDS. The "host," Rae Dawn Chong, fidgets noticeably when she has to say the words "anal sex." One wonders why a retake wasn't ordered, or if her body language is meant to be a signifier of disapproval, permissible even within a climate of tolerance. Not surprisingly, the video never acknowledges or addresses gay or lesbian kids. Instead, "homosexuality" is mediated through a straight man. "I still dunno why guys wanna sleep wit oda guys," says the big lug with a heart of gold who has just told the story of how he hated "fags" until he realized his brother, who died of AIDS, was one. This featured character utters a meek cry for tolerance and a thunderous roar for maintaining gender roles and rigid sexual identities, all the while congratulating himself for his "sensitivity."

Whether stretching in ballet class or just rapping in the hallways of USA High, the kids in *Sex, Drugs, and AIDS/AIDS: Just Say No* are considerably hipper than the squares, who sit docilely behind their desks, hands folded, faces scrubbed, and embarrassingly overdressed for what appears to be just another biology class in *The AIDS Movie* (1986), another educational video designed for high school students. This tape has the look of *Sixty Minutes* but comes across like one of those outdated hygiene films that evoke so much eyeball rolling and giggles among today's image-sophisticated kids. A lecture on AIDS provides the structure, interspersed with the testimony from PWAs who describe their illnesses and make "don't end up like me" pleas. In contrast, the *vérité* look used by ODN cleverly presents information in a nonauthoritarian manner, and Chong's rap appeals to kids, who will trust an admired peer—and celebrity—more than a stodgy biology teacher. Still, *AIDS: Just Say No*'s appeal, its savvy use of commercial television's language, also presents its essential problem: the conventional representation of black and Latino teenagers and reinforcement of homophobia. In addition, the kids talk to

Two teenagers debate the pros and cons of sex in ODN Productions' *AIDS: Just Say No.*

one another with all the friendly, spontaneous intimacy of TV sit-coms and tampon commercials, employing the mass media's style that claims to reflect real life. Praised widely for speaking to kids "in their own language," *AIDS: Just Say No* does no such thing. Rather, by speaking to the commercially defined notion of "kids," this tape denies participation of actual children and teenagers in the representation of their sexualities.

Though it is, in fact, educational, the Gay Men's Health Crisis' *Chance of a Lifetime* (1986) would never be approved by the Board of Education—or, probably, by any governmental agency. An enthusiastic "yes" to (gay men's) sex, this videotape is a curious blend of instruction, pornography, and romantic fantasy, all marshalled to eroticize and encourage safer sex practices. Structured like conventional porn, *Chance of a Lifetime* inserts safe-sex talk into scenes of pre-sex chit-chat and safe-sex demonstrations into the sex scenes, blurring these categories and stressing fantasy and foreplay over the exchange of body fluids. Couples romantically involved get it on and so do strangers, with an emphasis on eliminating risk behavior, not dictating moral standards, and the tape wisely avoids confusing safer sex with monogamy. While suggestive of post-AIDS pleasures, *Chance of a Lifetime* seems a little confused about exactly what these are, but, then, the list of "safe," "possibly safe," and "unsafe" activities has only recently been generally agreed upon.

The tape is most successful when it acknowledges the difficulty of adapting to safe sex and to what videomaker John Greyson has wittily named "ADS: The Acquired Dread of Sex."[3] In one section, a man repeatedly interrupts his dinner with a hot date to telephone a friend who allays his escalating fears. The friend, who appears superimposed on the screen in a little box, outlines safe-sex practices and tells him there is no reason he can't have sex. *Chance of a Lifetime* should also be commended for refusing to address only the worried well. In the third vignette, a man who has tested positive for the HIV virus has safer sex with his lover in a radical representation and refusal of Anti-Body status. One of the only education videotapes on AIDS interested in salvaging sex, *Chance of a Lifetime* is, however, too ambiguous to be a lesson-plan and at the same time unable to generate the raw heat of a good porno flick. Nonetheless, it suggests the areas that need exploration and the pleasures that need redefinition.

When Michael Lumpkin, director of the tenth San Francisco International Lesbian and Gay Film Festival, was asked about the festival's films on AIDS, he replied that they were "a pleasure," adding, "Many of them show ways the crisis is changing people for the better." Along the same lines, the *San Francisco Chronicle,* in a review of *The AIDS Show,* said, "In the end it poses the only 'solution' [to AIDS] available: to persevere and endure through our own best resources of humanity and humaneness." A welcome antidote to the homophobic products of network television, including *Frontline's AIDS: A Public Inquiry,* the response of independent film- and videomakers has not exactly been to paste a happy face over the AIDS crisis, but much of what has been produced so far does tend to depoliticize it by concentrating on the death and suffering that often accompanies AIDS.

The AIDS Show: Artists Involved with Death and Survival (1986), by Peter Adair and Robert Epstein; *Living With AIDS* (1986), produced and directed by Tina DiFeliciantonio; *Hero of My Own Life* (1986), produced by Tom Brook; and Mark Heustis and Wendy Dallas's *Chuck Solomon: Coming of Age* (1986), are, in various degrees, informed by an appealing but still problematic "humaneness." The latter three view AIDS through the prism of individual experience by focusing on individuals with AIDS: Todd Coleman, David Summers, and Chuck Solomon respectively. Scenes of daily life are intercut with the reminiscences and testimonies of friends, lovers, and health care workers. Each provides a mini-bio: coming

Anticipating a sexual encounter, a nervous man calls a friend for advice in the Gay Men's Health Crisis' *Chance of a Lifetime*.

out as a gay man, family rejection and/or acceptance, and insights gained from being close to death. In *Living With AIDS,* Coleman's poor health is evident, and his daily routine centers on the prosaic efforts of staying alive. Summers and Solomon are shown as active men in reasonably good health, although both discuss the ongoing battle with various illnesses that they have experienced as a result of their weakened immune systems. Each of the three men is depicted surrounded by lovers, friends, family, and elaborate networks of volunteers from gay and lesbian community organizations.

Living With AIDS, however, presents the most sensitive relationship between the individual and his community, perhaps because the twenty-two-year-old Coleman is not as financially well-off or socially established as Solomon and Summers and, therefore, more dependent on community services. In one eloquent scene, a volunteer masseur pays a call, and the viewer realizes that many PWAs are often denied human touch. Coleman is also shown attending the Gay and Lesbian Freedom March with his lover, and this, along with footage of an AIDS candlelight vigil, somewhat diffuses the emphasis on personal heroism. In *Hero of My Own Life,* Summers also stresses his reliance on a network of support groups, but his story is told in a more autobiographical fashion, as is Solomon's. Solomon's personal history as a playwright in the sixties *(Crimes Against*

Nature) and a participant in the struggles for gay and lesbian rights is inextricably bound to that of the gay and lesbian rights movement. He links events in his own life to community events, such as the Stonewall rebellion in 1969. A number of sequences in the film take place at his fortieth birthday party, where friends and family gather to say farewell and celebrate a life well lived, rendering a powerful representation of individual and collective strength and courage dramatically counter to those of commercial media.

Unfortunately, because these documentaries are so relentlessly biographical, they can only be as informative and engaging as the people they spotlight. Treating AIDS as a personal crisis still situates the struggle against it in the individual. And the reinvestment of the Anti-Body with subjectivity—individuality, emotions, a biography—tends to participate in cultural mythologies of individual heroism that also sustain the "Just say no" campaigns, locating complex social and political issues within the self. The flip-side of blaming the individual is to celebrate him/her for "battling" the particular problem. I don't mean to say that there aren't heroes or to diminish the psychological factors of illness, and I especially do not mean to trivialize the personal struggles of people with AIDS and those lovers, friends, family, and volunteers that struggle with them. These videotapes and films are effective in eliciting a sympathetic identification with the main character, an admiration for the courage, humor, and determination exhibited, and a sense of inspiration. But, by using AIDS as a dramatic catalyst in a familiar format of heightened emotion saturated with the rhetoric of personal heroism, these videotapes tend to overlook the specifics of AIDS. A narration in *The AIDS Show* reinforces this: "Whenever a catastrophe hits, be it a flood, an earthquake, a plague, the initial reaction is to ask, Why here? Why us? Often we blame ourselves for a loss that is arbitrary."

Steven Winn, writing in the *San Francisco Chronicle,* began his review of *The AIDS Show* by calling it a "funny, tender, at times angry—and ultimately human—documentary." Although *The AIDS Show* doesn't center on one individual, the tape does, however, concentrate on individual responses through a series of skits from the San Francisco Theater Rhinoceros company's production of the same name, along with commentaries by the cast and crew of the show. Well-written and skillfully presented, the skits are effective in easing feelings of isolation and despair through humor and knowledge. Because the original show was presented in 1984, the tape is most informative when it contrasts some of the earlier

Members of the Theater Rhinoceros cast of *The AIDS Show* and the documentary of the same title.

skits with those from an updated, 1985 version, *Unfinished Business: The New AIDS Show*. In the 1984 edition, four men at a pajama party discuss safe sex while playing Trivial Pursuit. One man announces he's had hot sex in a jeep the night before. His friend teases, "I thought you were Sally Safe-Sex!" "We had the emergency brake on" is his friend's campy reply. *Unfinished Business* has a different tone: the same group holds a pajama party reunion, but now one of them has AIDS. Safe sex is no longer a joke but *de rigeur*. "You can still have a good time without exchanging bodily fluids," announces one character as a segue into safe-sex information. The campy humor is still there but AIDS has become a long-term concern.

Like the first segment of *Chance of a Lifetime, The AIDS Show* adroitly mixes safe-sex information with entertainment, using humor to diffuse the uncertainty, frustration, and anxiety that accompany sex in the age of AIDS. Since part of the project, director Leland Moss explains, was to leave audiences "more knowledgeable and less frightened about AIDS," many of the pieces are similarly didactic, although a number concentrate on emotional education rather than health information. Two of the most moving sequences are monologues about personal loss. One man speaks to his deceased lover, who died of AIDS: "In this land of free speech the dying are supposed to go quietly for the sake of the living. Well, Jeffery shattered the myth of the dignified death. He was pissed off and he didn't care who knew. He said, 'Fuck *Death Be Not Proud* and *Love Story* and *Brian's Song* and *Marcus Welby* and *Bang the Drum Slowly. . . .*' He had this voracious self-pity that's usually reserved for home owners who've lost their belongings in mudslides." While *The AIDS Show* is too smart to fall into crass sentimentality, it does bear certain resemblances to the litany of heroic death films that this monologue parodies.

The immediate response to AIDS has been fear, anger, despair, and self-blame. To put AIDS in the same category as natural disasters, however, ignores the specific way in which AIDS has developed and been conceptualized, the way gay men have been blamed for it, the way it has been cast as a "gay disease," the ways that the government has not responded while stalling drug testing and refusing to restructure an inadequate health care system. AIDS does indeed highlight the peculiar ways in which our culture chooses to pretend death doesn't exist, leaving us without a framework for understanding and accepting loss. *The AIDS Show* provides a community for mourning and articulates a stubborn refusal to retreat into the closet. What it does not provide is a community for organized response to the ways in which AIDS is an eminently *preventable* cause of death and the ways in which people *living* with AIDS are not being cured or cared for.

Bright Eyes (1984), produced in Great Britain by Moral Panic Productions and directed by Stuart Marshall, acknowledges the importance of individual activism while refusing to participate in the cult of the individual hero. Its last sequence consists of interviews with individuals working with a variety of gay and lesbian organizations who speak about a number of interrelated topics—AIDS, police harassment and entrapment of gay men for "soliciting," and censorship. The interviews have a staged quality, as if they had been rehearsed or scripted. Previously, in diverse dramatic scenes, an ensemble of actors recite their lines in deadpan fashion. This blurring of the "real" and the "acted" not only blocks emotional identification but resituates struggle outside the individual in political-historical terrain. Furthermore, this method and structure alert the viewer to the problems of representation within documentary formats—a carefully constructed, acted out, acted upon narrative with questionable claims to "objectivity."

The first part of the tape examines the construction of Anti-Bodies by nineteenth-century science, aided by a newly discovered tool—the camera. In the opening scene, a doctor explains to a colleague, "Sometimes a symptom is invisible, and we need to hunt it out quite aggressively.

Network news presenting the "face of AIDS."

Sometimes a symptom is visible, and we just don't see it. I imagine that is what is meant by the expression, 'It was right before my eyes.' " The need to see symptoms, to categorize and label people "normal" or "abnormal," characterizes the project of science in the latter half of the nineteenth century. The camera, thought to have "no preconceived notions" and presenting things to us "as they are," became an accomplice in this project which was, according to Marshall, to "identify and isolate social groups and describe them as being inherently ill." Photographs that might appear innocuous become powerful condemnations when accompanied by the captions "Hysteric," "Intermediate Type," "Moral Imbecile," "Homosexual."

The need for systems of visual identification led to theories that posited an anatomical relation between violent criminals, sexual offenders, and skeletal structures. Sexual offenders, in addition to "swollen eyelids and lips," usually had "bright eyes," according to one theory of physiognomy. Using photographs from contemporary British tabloids, Marshall reveals how such representations of disease and deviance have informed the AIDS crisis. One headline, "Pictures That Reveal Disturbing Truths About AIDS Sickness," contrasts a picture of a handsome, smiling gay man "before" with one taken of his face swollen and disfigured "after" AIDS. *Bright Eyes'* second part details some of the methods used by the Nazis to persecute gay men. In one dramatic scene a young man is accused of homosexuality on the basis of a single piece of "evidence," a snapshot of him and a school chum. The processes of identifying and isolating Anti-Bodies, so crucial to the Nazi project of racial purity, are revealed to be remarkably similar to those proposed today by U.S. government officials, public health officials, and presidential candidates as a "solution" to AIDS.

Another video documentary, *Testing the Limits* (1987), like *Bright Eyes*, realizes that the battle against AIDS occurs in a political arena. Unlike *Bright Eyes*, though, this tape stirs emotions, although not by eliciting the emotional catharses of *The AIDS Show* or *Coming of Age* but by effecting emotional identification in shared outrage. Produced by Testing the Limits Collective members Gregg Bordowitz, Sandra Elgear, Robyn Hutt, Hilery Kipnis, and David Meieran in New York City in order "to document emerging forms of activism that are arising out of people's responses to government inaction regarding the global epidemic of AIDS," the program consists of interviews with people working in various AIDS organizations—the Hispanic AIDS Forum, the National AIDS network, the Minority Task Force on AIDS, the Institute for the Protection of Gay and Lesbian Youth, among others—edited together with scenes from various AIDS Coalition to Unleash Power (ACT UP) protests, excerpts from lectures delivered at the June 1987 *Village Voice* AIDS Teach-In, and a few safe-sex tips.

Testing the Limits uses the style of commercial media—skillful camera-work and editing, a catchy soundtrack—without becoming reductive or reinforcing the ideological assumptions that this style can mask. Covering the period from March to August 1987 and located specifically in New York City, the tape not only gives voice to all those generally silenced by commercial media—minority groups, gays, lesbians, PWAs, drug users—but also *addresses* them. Ruth Rodriguez of the Hispanic AIDS Forum speaks to the Latino community in Spanish, while Barry Gingell, a doctor and a PWA, provides information on potentially useful drugs. Community Health Project nurse Denise Ribble's safe-sex tips are the most imaginative and direct I've seen so far. Throughout, analysis meets activism, as when Mitchell Karp of the New York City Commission on Human Rights observes, "Testing deflects from the real issues which are a modification of behavior and protection of civil rights," followed by protesters shouting, "Test drugs, not people."

Years after AIDS began striking gay men, AIDS is a hot topic. From daily stories in newspapers and magazines to after-school specials, movies of the week, nightly news bulletins, scores of new works by independent film- and videomakers, and educational videos targeted at every conceivable audience, there has been a proliferation of information and disinformation on AIDS. It is important to recognize the ways in which commercial media and its spin-offs refuse to recognize AIDS as anything other than a medical crisis threatening the heterosexual, white, middle class or a drama of personal struggle in the face of death, not only providing limited information but limiting the potential for the social changes that this crisis so dramatically calls for. As Phil Reed, from the Minority Task Force on AIDS, said at a protest in *Testing the Limits,* AIDS will "either kill us or politicize us."

Notes

The author thanks Jean Carlomusto for assistance in researching this article, Carlos Espinoza for the loan of his VCR, and especially Martha Gever and Lee Quinby for their input, editing, and encouragement.

1. See, in addition to the sources cited, Alan Brandt, "AIDS: From Social History to Social Policy," in *Law, Medicine and Health Care* 14, no. 15-16 (December 1986): 231-241.
2. The recent amendment to the Labor, Health and Human Services and Education Appropriation Bill (which provides close to a billion dollars for AIDS research and funding), sponsored by Senator Jesse Helms, prohibits use of federal funds for any AIDS education or information materials that "promote or encourage, directly or indirectly, homosexual activities." Despite the proven success of safe-sex education materials among gay men, the Senate voted ninety-four to two in favor of this amendment, indicating the degree to which the "casual transmission" concept of homosexuality operates among liberals as well as conservatives and that they are more concerned with preventing the "spread" of homosexuality than the HIV virus.
3. In his humorous five-minute videotape, *The ADS Epidemic,* Greyson produces a condensed parody of *Death in Venice* and a send-up of the kinds of public service announcements about AIDS that encourage sexual abstinence.

Michael Jackson,
Black Modernisms, and
"The Ecstasy of Communication"

Michele Wallace

According to a recent quantifying study of MTV, videos featuring white males take up 83 percent of the 24-hour flow. Only 11 percent of MTV videos have central figures who are female (incidentally, the figure is even lower for blacks), and women are typically, like blacks, rarely important enough to be part of the foreground.

—E. Ann Kaplan

We must therefore begin to think of cultural politics in terms of space and the struggle for space. Then we are no longer thinking in old categories of critical distance but in some new way where the disinherited and essentially modernist language of subversion and negation is conceived differently.

—Fredric Jameson

Any evaluative interpretation of Michael Jackson's recent contribution to the music video scene must constantly struggle for space alongside considerations of consumerism and televisual postmodernism. But perhaps it is precisely these conditions that provide the ground for a different conception of "the disinherited and essentially modernist language of subversion and negation." Music videos are a prime example of how consumer society or late capitalism has co-opted the alternative and/or the oppositional in a once avant-garde rock 'n' roll/rhythm 'n' blues aesthetic. A hybrid of music performance documentaries and television ads, music videos not only sell us that which we expect to be free, namely our own private and unfulfillable desires, but they also make it increasingly impossible to distinguish between the genuine mass appeal of an artist and the music industry's simulation of that appeal.

Further, the encroaching "postmodernism," or nonsensical redundancy and fragmentation of the televisual medium, particularly in its music-video format, implies a lack of "interpretative depth," which Marxist critic Fredric Jameson describes as "the idea that the object [is] fascinating because of the density of its secrets and that these [are] then to be uncovered by interpretation. All that vanishes."[1] Here Jameson refers to a postmodern aesthetics marked by its rejection of historical sequence and individual subjectivity as supreme organizational principles. In other words, music videos are irreversibly implicated in what Jean Baudrillard would call "the ecstasy of communication," in which "all secrets, spaces and scenes" are "abolished in a single dimension of information."[2] So we might reasonably conclude that there's nothing to say.

Yet despite music-video consumerism and televisual postmodernism's powerful deterrences to interpretation—especially the kind of interpretation that bestows value—there are extenuating circumstances which indicate that Jackson's videos may be capable of playing a key role to evolving public discourses of race, sex, and class. First, Jackson is a black performer. Given his race, he has achieved an entirely unprecedented and gargantuan fame in a previously white supremacist music industry, which routinely objectifies and colonizes the Third World and people of color. He may, in fact, be, as his own media hype never tires of suggesting, the new Elvis Presley or the new Beatles. Or perhaps he might have been—as Jesse Jackson might have been president—if not for racism.

In any case, not only does Michael Jackson's extraordinary fame and wealth mean that he may be able to supersede previous (dispersed and inarticulate) standards of industry control, Jackson's videos are also first rehearsed in a special format, independent of the unrelenting twenty-four-hour flow of videos, music news, and DJ chatter on VH1 and MTV. These peculiar shows constitute a curious new form of television program as unnameable as it is unspeakable. None of this means that Jackson escapes the corrupting influence of the commercial. Rather, I am suggesting that Jackson, both because of his race and his extraordinary success (even if it is equal parts hype and reality), has reached the stage at which we can usually expect an artist, consciously or unconsciously, to show signs of public resistance to his own formulaic social construction.

As for postmodernism, Jackson's status as a black male is even more important in understanding his case as an exception to the rule. I would like to suggest that the past for Afro-American culture, particularly that oral "tradition" (which includes jokes, stories, toasts, black music from spirituals to funk, and black english[3]) pursued by the black masses, has been precisely a postmodern one inevitably inscribing (and inscribed by) our absence from history, the dead-end meaninglessness of the signifiers

Michael Jackson dancing in the music video *Bad*, 1987.

"equality," "freedom," and "justice," and our chronic invisibility to the drama of Western civilization and European high culture. Therefore, it should come as no surprise when the telltale "schizophrenia" and "pastiche" of postmodernism are considered by some black artists to be characteristic of the enemy within, or racism internalized. In contrast, the most enlightened trends in contemporary Afro-American culture are in consistent pursuit of meaning, history, continuity, and the power of subjectivity. I am calling these various, heterogeneous, and sometimes conflicting efforts, Black Modernisms, of which Jackson's recent performance is perhaps a new type.

There aren't too many people in the media who agree with me. In fact, it is precisely the breadth of the Michael Jackson controversy that has drawn me to this topic. Where does this controversy focus its attention? Is it on his videos, his music, his wealth, his fame, his sexuality, his race, his lifestyle, his aesthetics, his unwillingness to be interviewed, his family, his plastic surgery, his skin lightening and hair straightening, or is it some ineffable combination of any or all of the above? Why, at this moment, at the peak of his career, is he being attacked and criticized on all sides? Why not attack Bob Dylan, who is also more wealthy than political; Prince, who also exhibits signs of ambiguous sexuality and white fever; Elizabeth Taylor or Lena Horne who also appear to have had plastic surgery? Is it because Jackson's album announces that he's "Bad"? Why was his sister, Janet Jackson, not attacked when she announced that she was in "Control" on her album, in the process utilizing many of her brother's stylistic trademarks? What is the criticism really about? Where does it come from? Could it have to do with Jackson's participation in what E. Ann Kaplan describes as a "second, softer androgynous group" of rock performers (that includes Annie Lennox, David Bowie, and Boy George), which is "not so concerned to stress the masculine that lies beneath the feminized veneer" and is "less obviously (and manipulatively) erotic"?[4] Could it be that we find it intolerable to hear a black male speak from this position, especially now that his recent videos substantiate that he thinks of himself as speaking for/to the black male?

More than once in the supermarket check-out line, I've noticed covers of *The Star* and *The Enquirer* that exhibited an intense preoccupation with the question of whether or not Jackson has ever had sex with a "girl." These headlines offer one sign of how Jackson has lately been marked "other" in the entertainment industry. Another kind of sign has been the way the *Village Voice*—or young hip left-liberal opinion, in general—has turned against him: "There's no longer any question that Michael Jackson is America's pre-eminent geek," Guy Trebay wrote recently. In the same issue of the *Voice,* black cultural critic Greg Tate described Jackson's plastic surgery as the "savaging of his African physiognomy" in an article entitled " 'I'm White!' What's Wrong With Michael Jackson."[5] But all this criticism seems to circle around the same problematic of racial and sexual difference, the inauthenticity and un- trustworthiness that are implied when such issues are invoked by a black male (instead of, say, Diahann Carroll) because "Michael just looked too much like a woman to strut around like a homeboy in chains," as one of Trebay's respondents said of Jackson in the video *Bad.*

Whereas, a recent *New York Times* article, written by Jon Pareles and entitled "A Political Song That Casts its Vote for the Money," attacks Jackson's work directly, apparently ignoring his persona. Pareles charac- terized Jackson's *Man in the Mirror* as "the most offensive music video clip ever" because "its particular sales pitch is that buying the song equals concern over issues. . . ." Part of Pareles's complaint is that the video wouldn't arouse would-be censors: "there's not a whiff of sex, no blood and little violence." And, "Mr. Jackson doesn't show up either."[6] In a consummate gesture of objectivity, Pareles pretends to be color blind, but in the process he only renders invisible (i.e., irrelevant) Jackson's race, the races of people who suffer "the homelessness and poverty" (that he

Michael Jackson looking androgynous in the music video *Thriller*, 1983.

says the video only "glances at"), and the video's unmistakeable preoccupation with racism and white-supremacist values. Perhaps this is why Pareles thinks the video, like the song, "points no fingers, reveals no underlying causes, assigns no blame, suggests no action." Perhaps this is also why Pareles didn't see Jackson in the video, for he is certainly there in one of the final frames, laughing, a small figure in red in a sea of Japanese children, who appear to be tickling him. Jackson, as was explained in *The Making of Thriller* video, is very ticklish.

The refrain of "Man in the Mirror" is "I'm starting with the man in the mirror. I'm asking him to make a change. No message could have been any clearer. If you wanna make the world a better place, take a look at yourself and make a change, change, change, change." Certainly not a revolutionary lyric (what is a revolutionary lyric?), but, significantly, it comes from an artist who has been transfixed by the hands-on mutability of his own face (as his extensive plastic surgery demonstrates) and his own image (as he demonstrated also in the video *Thriller*, in which he turns into a werewolf). We have in these lyrics, no doubt, an objectification of the self, in that he is addressing himself, along with other men, in the third person. But while we might reasonably expect the video to elaborate on this potentially narcissistic text, instead, for the first time, Jackson is the smallest image in his own video, the least imposing figure, so much so that Pareles missed him entirely. For the mirror is the television screen itself.

The video, directed by Don Wilson, is, as Pareles says, "a smoothly edited, slightly tricked-up montage of news footage." But it does not, as he also says, "demonstrate remarkable—I'd say monumental—gall, insensitivity and megalomania." Or is that finally racism speaking? The images are, in sequence, white police beating black South Africans in a riot, two successive images of mostly black and nonwhite homeless people, four successive images of starving brown children in Ethiopia, a swarming mass of mostly black people in a Civil Rights march. Up until now, all the images have been in color except the first image of South African violence, which was in black and white. The next image, which is important, combines, for the first time, color and black-and-white film. It features a solitary figure of a black boy dancing in what appears to be an urban riot. On either side of him there is fire. The fire is colorized.

Pareles also apparently missed this image, or considered it unimportant (probably because he's never been a little black boy, never expects to become one, and never will have to worry what may happen to one). Yet it is the first to combine colorization and black-and-white film. Like Michael Jackson, the boy dances, and the dance intersects ambiguous emotions of joy and despair, recalling to me children caught up in political/religious violence from Soweto to the West Bank. Moreover, that this child dances alone amidst fire makes this frame crucial to the video's self-understanding. This frame is followed by a headshot of Bishop Tutu crying into clasped hands, two more shots of the homeless, then a headshot of Lech Walesa—the first facial shot of a white male—which dissolves into a shot of a Solidarity rally. This is followed by a shot of an unidentified black male yelling something in the context of what appears to be Civil Rights violence, a Ku Klux Klansman in full attire, then a side view of a bus in black and white, which has written on the side of it, "We Hate Race Mixing." Then the back of the bus is shown, with "Hate Bus" written in colorized red, then a black-and-white Hitler with a colorized armband, which Pareles describes as "red, like a soda-pop commercial."

Pareles is right enough in pointing out that, as we listen to and watch the video *Man in the Mirror,* we are snapping our fingers and tapping our feet to world hunger, violence, man's inhumanity to man and woman. But isn't that what we're doing anyway when we rock 'n' roll? Or when we engage in any cultural activity, which inevitably masks the seriousness and gloom of our global plight? Moreover, would it be

Young black boy dancing in the music video *Bad*, 1987.

considered such monumental bad taste if *Man in the Mirror* were made by David Bowie or Mick Jagger or even Stevie Wonder? Pareles's flight from the letter of racism and the way it intersects with sexism (or, in this case, homophobia) allows the importance of a little black boy dancing his way to global multi-racial and androgynous interpretations to escape him.

Perhaps this is the time to emphasize that the critical refrain of the lyrics is couched in the past tense: "No message could have been any clearer" the words of the song say. Is this megalomania or history? After pointing the finger at racial bigotry and economic marginalization as epitomizing the administration of men (class distinctions become ethical and moral ones), *Man in the Mirror* focuses upon children (who dance) as the hope of the world. Perhaps the suggestion is somewhat lame in a first world in which black discourses are consigned to an awkward, unwanted, and self-reflexive postmodernism (which exists in autistic relationship to Western modernism). But this is new speech from a position once silent. That position speaks for a multi-racial, androgynous (non-patriarchal) future in which children no longer dance to the tune of class and/or religious (the same thing?) violence. The important thing to notice here is not the inevitable closure, but rather the very existence of the discourse in a first world in which blacks still fail to occupy positions of power in the media or academia, still fail to shape the interpretation of events, or the interpretation of interpretation. Is Jackson—or Don Wilson in Jackson's name—attempting an historical understanding of racial hatred? Who is this Don Wilson? Is he black? Is his mother black? Who is speaking here? And from where?

All functions abolished in a single dimension, that of communication. That's the ecstasy of communication. All secrets, spaces and scenes abolished in a single dimension of information.

—Jean Baudrillard

Despite Baudrillard's "ecstasy of communication," American television still keeps one unfathomable secret: this country's Afro-American presence. Almost everyone on television has blonde hair. But watching this year's Grammy Award ceremonies—which promised to emphasize Jackson's participation—you got an entirely different impression. Precisely because of the record industry's history of apartheid and the crucial role that Afro-American music has played in the genesis of all American forms of music, blackness is an ongoing crisis in the discourse of this annual program. Here the order of spectacle (or "entertainment") is substituted for the politics and/or history of heterogeneity.

The host was the white comedian Billy Crystal, an excellent choice (since he is known for his impression of Sammy Davis, Jr.). In his comedy monologue, he told us about his father's intensive involvement with (black) jazz greats. Then he launched into an impression of an old-time (black) jazz-musician, which sounded vaguely like Louis Armstrong. Thus, Crystal consolidated his mediational role in this drama of racial difference. This racial sketch inaugurated an endless stream of musical categories—Latin Pop, Latin Traditional, Traditional Gospel, Pop, R&B, Reggae, Rock, Contemporary Gospel, Country and Western, Folk, Classical, etc.—each featuring presenters carefully chosen for racial, sexual, age, and aesthetic balance. It seemed as though even the decisions about whether presentations of particular awards should be made on or off the air were weighed in terms of creating impressions of fairness and equality (but then this is probably the paranoia of invisibility speaking). Overall, dare I say that the process was tense in its misrepresentation of an egalitarian televisual practice? Like one would imagine a one-day special-session United Nations of Music, there were repeated standing ovations from the industry audience.

Anti-integration sign in the music video *Bad*, 1987.

The location was Radio City Music Hall in New York City. The racially insensitive Mayor Koch occupied a prominent seat. Blacks did much of the entertaining for the Awards Ceremony, which is kind of interesting since blacks actually received very few awards. Whitney Houston sang "I Just Wanna Dance With Somebody," backed up by a veritable rainbow coalition. George Benson sang "On Broadway." Cab Calloway sang "Minnie, the Moocher." Latin drummer Tito Puentes accompanied a black Celia Cruz, who sang in Spanish. The white performers—Lou Reed, who was backed up by one black and one white female; David Sanborn, who was accompanied by two black guitarists; and Billy Joel—all sounded black. Billy Joel's Ray Charles-like piano playing and singing "A New York State of Mind" was particularly striking in this regard. When Run DMC descended upon this spectacle from the audience—three slightly overweight black boys rapping, signifying, making a music of the unmusic of political marginality, and looking very much as though they knew they were assaulting the sensibilities of the Grammy audience—the exorcism of New York City racial tension seemed complete.

Then a very strange thing happened, which either threatened or confirmed the provisionality of the peace, the falseness of the synthesis. Jackie Mason, an elderly Jewish comedian, came out and did the only other comedy monologue in the show. It was supposed to have been an excerpt from his album, which was nominated in the comedy category, but some of its improvisatory elements revealed an "entertaining" banter that came dangerously close to piercing the unknowing of the "political unconscious" and revealing all. Mason began by lamenting his never having won any kind of award. Then he said he would take an award from anybody, even the Ku Klux Klan. He said this was a joke.

And perhaps Mason thought it was simply a joke (funny to whom?) and not racism, as if the two weren't binary oppositional faces of the same systemic dilemma. What do North Americans joke about, anyway? Hasn't the joke always been the outhouse of the racial/sexual, or what Julia Kristeva calls "the abject"?[7] In his comedy routine, Mason's shtick is that he plays a bigot—a Jewish version of an Archie Bunker—with a particular focus on Jewish/Gentile animosities. Ordinarily, in moments of ideological tension in cultural spaces (remember the early Telethons?), sex is the ice-breaker. But at the Grammies, already racially coded, Mason was almost irresistibly drawn to the off-color humor of race. Characteristically, he chose to focus on somebody in the audience.

That person, as the camera quickly revealed, was Quincy Jones, perhaps the most powerful black male in the music industry, the single figure who has most clearly transcended all the barriers and made good the promise of the Civil Rights Revolution. In recent years, he has not only produced and scored the movie *The Color Purple,* but he has also produced a succession of commercial hits for Michael Jackson. Perhaps Mason was trying to "roast" the industry's most successful producer or perhaps he really didn't recognize him, but he proceeded to heckle him in the following way:

Mister, are you a black person or just a Jew with a tan? It's not nice. I don't pick on black people. I have the highest respect for black people. You know the reason I have the highest respect for black people, Mister? Because the black people are finally making progress, the progress they deserve all these years in this country. And this is a show that proves it, this is where it's happening. This is where it's at. Thank God for them. I'm not like these fake Civil Rights crusaders, who tell you "Black People are as good as anybody else!" They sit in the back of their cars and when they see a black person walking towards the car they tell you to lock the door, "Lock the door! Lock the door! Click it! Click it! They're as good as anybody else. Are they coming back? Click it! Click it!" Why do you think black people dance so good? Wherever they go, they hear clicking and clicking.

Then Mason did a little dance to demonstrate Afro-American dance ability, derived, as he said, from their keeping pace with the incessant clicking of exclusion and social death. "I was in favor of black people when they started making fires twenty years ago," Mason went on to say. "They were 100 percent right for making fires because they never had true equality in America." Which made me think of the young boy dancing amidst fire in *Man in the Mirror*. But, as Mason felt compelled to remind us, "they only succeeded in burning their own houses down." On the other hand, Mason continued, Jews set smaller fires, "and every fire shows a profit."

What was Mason doing? I don't know; televisual "fact" melts before the eyes. I only know that Mason seemed somehow responsible for everything important that subsequently happened that night. First, Crystal parodied Jimmy the Greek's racial wisdom as Mason left the stage: "Jackie was bred to be a comic," Crystal said. "In the old days, they would get a comedy writer to breed with the funny man . . ." But the apparent inscription here of "racism" as just another "harmless" item on the menu of American comedy only continued the practice of mythologizing history and "nature."[8]

Much later, during the presentation of an award, Little Richard playfully declared himself the unacknowledged originator and architect of rock 'n' roll. Then during another awards presentation, Joe Williams sang "Everyday I have the Blues" to the accompaniment of Bobby McFerrin's basslike scat singing. These gestures seemed to be poised between old strategies of black postmodernism—in which the critique of racism is effaced by the autism of aesthetic demonstration—and old strategies of black modernism, which propose to reconstitute the critique as an aggressive dialectic.

On the other hand, Jackson's performance at the Grammies, which I count among the black responses to Mason's inscription of racism, seemed to announce a new black modernism in that it is critical of racism, even as it formally challenges conventional hierarchies of class, race, sexuality, and aesthetic mastery. Jackson began by lip-synching to a recording of *Man in the Mirror*, accompanied by black gospel star Andre Crouch and his largely black female choir. But then Jackson didn't stop. The tape of the music ran out, the microphone was off, and Jackson was left singing soundlessly in one of those moments of televisual aporia that the medium/industry abhors. Then the microphone was switched on: Jackson's singing and the background singing was live now. He whooped, he jumped in the air, he shook his hands frenetically, and, showing most of the classical signs of "getting happy," as it is referred to in the black church, he fell on his knees. Crouch left his position on the stage and walked over to Jackson, evidently to help him to his feet, and then stopped. What did he see? That Jackson didn't need any help? That it was all an act? Or that it was a deliberate spectacle in which Jackson was now having his say, just as Mason had had his? Crouch danced away lightly. Jackson began to shout and exhort the people to "stand up," which this standing-ovation-loving audience seemed suddenly disinclined to do. But Jackson wouldn't stop until they stood up. The black female choir moved forward, clapped harder, sang louder. "White man's gotta make a change," Jackson cried almost inaudibly. "Black man's gotta make a change." Needless to say, Jackson won no Grammies this year.

The one by whom the abject exists is thus a deject *who places (himself), separates (himself), situates (himself), and therefore* strays *instead of getting his bearings, desiring, belonging, or refusing. Situationist in a sense, and not without laughter—since laughing is a way of placing or displacing abjection. Necessarily dichotomous, somewhat Manichaean, he divides, excludes, and without, properly speaking, wishing to know his abjections is not at all unaware of them. Often, moreover, he includes himself among them, thus casting within himself the scalpel that carries out his separations.*

—Julia Kristeva

Have you ever wondered about Michael Jackson's education? Have you ever had a problem understanding the words he sings, or the words in black rock 'n' roll in general? My mother, who is a total fan of Jackson's, says he makes up words. But isn't that what black singers have always done? Ella Fitzgerald and Louis Armstrong simply made "scatting" official. Henry Louis Gates calls this aspect of black culture "critical signification."[9] It is a process in which black culture "signifies" on white culture through imitating and then reversing its formal strategies and preconditions, thus formulating a masked and surreptitious critique. The perfect example is the relationship of "jazz" to white mainstream music. But what I'm beginning to wonder is: how "critical" is it?

Bad, on the other hand, is deliberately and forthrightly critical of the world we live in. Very elaborate for a video, it attempts to address problems of class and race, and diminish or marginalize problems of sexuality and gender. First, the camera fixes on Jackson's face in a shot

Michael Jackson looking like Dracula in *Thriller,* 1983.

that reminds me of Dracula. I half expect him to reveal fangs, as in *Thriller,* but he doesn't. Filmed in black and white, the video continues by suturing together, in classic filmic mode, an alienated Jackson at a white, all-boys prep school called Duxton, somewhere within commuting distance of urban New York. His train ride home illustrates the unspeakable psychological distance he feels from his white classmates, who are playing with him one moment and literally dissolve the next. Then a subway ride—in which the camera pans a row of subway riders, mostly black and all female, except for one elderly white male—slowly eases him back into the ghetto.

When he gets home—a small, poorly furnished ghetto apartment—he is greeted by a note from his mother, which is read aloud by a female voice who tells him that she's at work and there is food in the refrigerator (there are no women in this video except the women we see briefly on the subway). The camera pans the walls, which are covered with photographs of adult black men (many recognizable R&B performers), perhaps one of whom is his father.

In short order, Jackson's character joins his black male friends in the street only to have elaborate communication problems, as though he hasn't seen them in a long time. They make fun of his speech. They also think he's making fun of their speech. That Jackson's character occupies a position outside the power of language to describe is thus established. Then his friends expect him to join them in their usual pastime, which appears to be robbing people. First, they try to rob a drug pusher, but the drug pusher has a gun. The image that conveys this information involves the only full shot of an adult black male character in the video as he pulls his coat back to reveal a gun which is stuck in his pants.

Then Jackson's character—identified only by the nicknames "Home Boy" and "Joe College"—and his black friends go into a subway station to rob people on their way home from work. Jackson's character dissents. There is a break in the action and Jackson, who had been dressed in a drab sweatshirt with a hood and a jacket, now reappears in color, fully made-up, hair elaborately done and gleaming, and in a black outfit that features multiple metallic fixtures, which I think of as industrial nipples. He is joined by a collection of male dancers of various races—he is flanked by an Asian male and a white male. Together they dance a very athletic dance which attempts to substitute discernibly masculine gestures for the feminine gestures of an old-fashioned chorus line. Beside the refrain, which says "You know I'm bad, I'm bad, you know it, you know it," Jackson also sings, "The word is out. You're doing wrong. Gone lock you up before too long. Your lying lies don't make you right. So listen up, don't make a fight. Your talk is cheap. You're not a man. You're throwing stones out your hand." Once the dance concludes, his ghetto friends are quiet, yet impressed. They show mute indications of making peace with him. As they leave, the color images vanish and we pan to Jackson standing alone in a sweatshirt again.

First, the obvious: the video seems to be grappling with Jackson's problematic professional identity in relationship to a world of white, established wealth or cultural hegemony, and a world of black homelessness and poverty. In the process, it constructs a third racial view. Beside the white and the black, there's Jackson's new (fantasy) race, exemplified by his dancing and singing "I'm bad" with a team of multi-racial male dancers. Meanwhile, the video revels in the full splendor of his plastic surgery, his processed hair, his skin peelings to lighten his complexion, all of which can be seen as Jackson's attempts to alter his racial characteristics towards this "third race."

Less obvious: the video also struggles with Jackson's problematic personal identity in relationship to a world that insists upon distinct and meaningful sexual difference. The absence of women in this video signals that the inscription of sexual difference will occur among men. But it also means that Jackson's subjectivity is doubly split in a perfect illustration

Dance scene in the subways in the music video *Bad*, 1987.

of Jackson's proposal in *Man in the Mirror*. The first split is: "Home Boy" (black), who goes to private school (white) in order to learn to speak, vs. the rich black boy (Jackson), whose roots are in a black oral tradition, which doesn't speak, but who performs in the context of a white postmodern culture, which speaks only to deny his history. The second split is: Home Boy's fantasy of a utopian revolutionary consciousness (boys dancing) that would transcend the real (material) conflict between himself and his friends vs. the real Jackson in an actual performance. It is appropriate to speak of such doublings precisely because videos are hybrids of music performance documentaries and television ads, and also because Jackson probably has more control over his own videos than he knows what to do with. Not only is the *Bad* video selling the consumer the album, it is also selling the commodified Jackson to the generic Jackson (black males collectively) as a utopian vision which challenges the diverse appropriations of black and white postmodernisms.

In *Rocking Around the Clock*, E. Ann Kaplan identifies five basic categories of videos: romantic, socially conscious, nihilist, classical, and postmodern. *Bad* shows indications of all these categories (that Martin Scorsese was its director suggests this video's complexity). But it also seems to cross two kinds in particular: the socially conscious and the classical. The "socially conscious" video, Kaplan says, is characterized thematically by a love interest which is problematic with sex as a struggle for autonomy, by parents and public figures as forms of authority, and by the presence of a cultural critique. The "classical" video is characterized thematically by love in the form of the male gaze with sex as voyeuristic and fetishistic.

Both parents and public figures were present as vicarious authority in the scene that shows "Home Boy" in his apartment—these are his mother's voice and the photos of the black male R&B stars. Of course, the visualization of ghetto conditions shapes the cultural critique, and presumably the fact that he stops his ghetto friends from robbing a Puerto Rican male signals redeeming socialization. The fantasy dance in the subway I see as an articulation of a problematic love interest and sex as a struggle for autonomy. It is clearly defiant, ostentatiously unrequited, and obviously a struggle for aesthetic, professional, sexual, and racial independence, or autonomy, in the most profound sense. At the same time, "love in the form of the male gaze" is present in the illicit voyeurism of the camera when it surveys Jackson in his performance outfit or as we watch Home Boy's friends watching the sexually ambiguous Jackson and his team of multi-racial boy dancers in full color. Moreover, "male as subject, female as object," which Kaplan identifies as the form of authority in a "classical" video, undeniably points the finger at Jackson, in the fictional performer mode of the video, as the female (white?) locked inside the subjectivity of Home Boy (black male), who is locked inside the subjectivity of the real Jackson (androgynous and multi-racial), the producer of this and all his texts.

Sexual difference, racial difference, and class difference, especially in tandem, are not subjects which the televisual medium can deal with forthrightly (who can?). Nevertheless, *Bad,* in an anachronistic and dialogical attempt at concealment, reveals the grounds for a new interpretive space, and the possibility of a new "modernist language of subversion and negation," which subverts postmodernism from inside its last secret.

In conclusion, I would like to historicize my interest in Jackson. My mother, Faith Ringgold, was asked to donate a work of art to a benefit auction for Bishop Desmond Tutu being sponsored by Jackson. As her contribution to the benefit, Faith chose to do a mural/quilt presentation of *Bad* with Jackson in the foreground. Still living in Harlem, in an apartment fourteen flights directly above the subway station where *Bad* was filmed, Faith is convinced that Jackson has made a worthwhile critique of the

Faith Ringgold, *Who's Bad? Painted Quilt,* 1988. Acrylic on canvas with pieced fabrics, 70 × 92½".
Courtesy Bernice Steinbaum Gallery, New York.

values of black boys in the streets. In her video, which documents the making of her "Bad" quilt, we have a provocative intersection of the power of performance and the performance of interpretation.

On the one hand, the image shows the "Bad" dancers led by Jackson no longer in the subway station but upstairs in the streets of the ghetto dancing. On the other hand, these could be generic black male youths engaged in frantic physical activity of unclear intent. They could be fighting, or are they throwing off the mantle of drug addiction, under-education, and repression, shirking the rage that blocks their progress in school, and multiplies the precarious homes of their numerous offspring, exorcising the inarticulate and unspeakable that paves their way to the prisons? Or are they dancing at the end of racism's strings?

In her video, Faith talks about badness as part of that "struggle for space" that Jameson considers essential to the reconceptualization of cultural politics. She describes her images by saying,

I could use these so-called bad guys and play them against Martin Luther King, Bishop Desmond Tutu, Zora Neale Hurston, people like Nelson Mandela, Winnie Mandela, Rosa Parks (whose names are written in the borders of the quilt), and Michael Jackson himself, because these are the people who are really bad in that they are able to defy very destructive forces in order to help not only themselves but other people. That is what is really bad.

Perhaps in a related gesture, Martin Scorsese, the director of the *Bad* video, includes himself, briefly (almost an invisible mega-second), in frontal and side photos on a "Wanted for Sacrilege" poster also marked "Bad" in bold letters.

For me, the key thing is that the perception of Jackson (and of every other aspect of black culture) is shaped by a world process of information gathering, dissemination, and interpretation (spanning mass media and academia) which notoriously marginalizes the significance of people of color. Jackson appears to be groping for an individual solution to a global problem as he attempts to generate somewhat primitive or naive historical readings from a position (that of black male pop star/black male in the street/black male of ambiguous sexuality) in cultural discourse ordinarily experienced by mainstream (white) culture as profoundly silent, nonexistent, and unspoken for. That he should have the energy to engage in such a process—despite the Pepsi commercials, despite the sexual anxieties he seems to arouse in a fairly large proportion of the heterosexual male audience over thirteen—strikes me as good, which is to say bad.

Notes

1. Anders Stephanson, "Regarding Postmodernism: A Conversation with Fredric Jameson," *Social Text* 17 (Fall 1987): 30.
2. Jean Baudrillard, "The Ecstasy of Communication," in *The Anti-Aesthetic: Essays on Postmodern Culture,* ed. Hal Foster (Port Townsend, Wash.: Bay Press, 1983), pp. 126-134.
3. Lawrence W. Levine, *Black Culture and Black Consciousness: Afro-American Folk Thought from Slavery to Freedom* (New York: Oxford University Press, 1977).
4. E. Ann Kaplan, *Rocking Around the Clock* (New York: Methuen, Inc., 1987), p. 102.
5. *Village Voice,* September 22, 1987, pp. 15-17.
6. *New York Times,* March 6, 1988, p. 32.
7. Julia Kristeva, *Powers of Horror: An Essay in Abjection* (New York: Columbia University Press, 1982).
8. Mason has since said in a *New York Times* interview that the lights prevented him from seeing who Quincy Jones was. His target was supposed to have been "anonymous."
9. Henry Louis Gates, Jr., *Figures in Black: Words, Signs, and the "Racial" Self* (New York: Oxford University Press, 1986).

Contributors

Ien Ang is a Lecturer in the Department of Political Science at the University of Amsterdam. She is the author of *Watching Dallas: Soap Opera and the Melodramatic Imagination*.

Chris Bratton is a writer and video producer. He teaches video production in the New York City school system for Rise and Shine.

Julianne Burton teaches Latin American literature and film at the University of California at Santa Cruz. She is the editor of *Cinema and Social Change* and *Documentary Strategies: Focusing on Latin America*.

Lisa Cohen is a graduate student in the Department of Comparative Literature at Yale University.

Richard Collins is Head of the Communications Faculty at Boston University's London Program. An editor of *Media, Culture, and Society*, his books include *The Economics of Television: The UK Case*, and *Television News*.

Jonathan Crary teaches art history at Barnard College. He is a founding editor of *Zone* and his book on the observer in the nineteenth century is forthcoming from MIT Press.

Xavier Delcourt is a co-author, with Armand Mattelart and Michèle Mattelart, of *International Image Markets* (Comedia, 1984).

Thomas Elsaesser is Senior Lecturer in English and American Studies at the University of East Anglia in Norwich, England. His book, *The New German Cinema*, is forthcoming from BFI.

Peter Fend is an artist and president of Ocean Earth.

Jill Forbes, Head of the Department of Modern Languages at the Polytechnic of the South Bank, London, has written a study of French television, *INA: French for Innovation*.

Coco Fusco is a New York-based writer and curator. She is the editor of *Reviewing Histories: Selections from New Latin American Cinema*, and *Young, British, and Black*.

David Goldberg teaches at the College of Humanities and Philosophy at Drexel University. He edited *Philosophical Forum*'s issue on apartheid, and the book *Anatomy of Racism*.

Annie Goldson is a writer and video producer. She teaches video at Brown University.

David Koff is a filmmaker whose work includes *Black Man's Land,* a trilogy on colonialism in Africa, and *Occupied Palestine,* a documentary on the Palestinian resistance.

Timothy Landers is a freelance writer who lives in New York City.

Ernest Larsen's novel, *Not a Through Street* (1984) was recently reprinted by Grove Press. He is working on a second novel.

Maud Lavin is Visiting Assistant Professor at SUNY, Binghamton, and is writing a book on the representation of women in German mass-media and avant-garde photography of the 1920s.

Julia LeSage is the co-editor and co-founder of *Jump Cut*, and has made a number of videotapes in Nicaragua, including *Las Nicas, Home Life,* and *El Crucero.*

Armand Mattelart is Professor of Information Sciences and Communications at the University of Upper Brittany (Rennes II). He is the author of numerous books, including (with Ariel Dorfman) *How to Read Donald Duck,* and *Communications and Information Technologies.*

Michèle Mattelart is the author of *La cultura de la opresion feminina, Women and the Cultural Industries,* and many articles on the mass media in Latin America.

Micki McGee is an artist and writer whose work has been published in *Afterimage, Top Stories,* and *Heresies.* She is Visiting Lecturer in Video at Rutgers University.

Patricia Mellencamp is Associate Professor of Art History at the University of Wisconsin, Milwaukee. She co-edited *Cinema and Language* with Stephen Heath.

Sherry Millner works in video, film, and photomontage, and is an Assistant Professor at Rutgers University. Her videotapes are distrib-

uted by Women Make Movies.

Musindo Mwinyipembe is a nationally syndicated radio commentator on African affairs for "In the Public Interest."

Karen Ranucci is a community video producer who has worked for Downtown Community T.V. Center and NBC television.

Cynthia Schneider is a student at CUNY Law School and co-wrote/co-produced *Superstar: The Karen Carpenter Story.*

Leslie Sharpe is an artist who lives in New York. Her current project concerns women, design, and labor in the garment industry.

Carol Squiers is Associate Editor at *American Photographer.* She writes a regular column for *Artforum* and is editing an anthology of essays on photography.

Tapio Varis teaches at the University for Peace in Costa Rica. He is the co-author of *Peace and Communications* and *International Flow of Television Programmes.*

Paul Virilio is the author of *Speed and Politics, Popular Defense and Ecological Struggles,* and *Pure War* (with Sylvère Lotringer).

Michele Wallace, cultural critic and short story writer, is the author of *Black Macho and the Myth of the Superwoman.* She is currently Assistant Professor of Women's Studies at SUNY, Buffalo.

Brian Wallis is Senior Editor at *Art in America* and the editor of *Art After Modernism: Rethinking Representation* and *Blasted Allegories.*